FAST JETS
TO SPITFIRES

To Anne, Sarah and Emma

FAST JETS
TO SPITFIRES

A COLD WAR FIGHTER PILOT'S STORY

RON LLOYD

AIR WORLD

AIR WORLD

FAST JETS TO SPITFIRES
A Cold War Fighter Pilot's Story

First published in Great Britain in 2020 by
Air World
An imprint of
Pen & Sword Books Ltd
Yorkshire – Philadelphia

ISBN 978 1 52675 906 1

Printed and bound in India by Replika Press Pvt. Ltd.
Typeset in Ehrhardt MT Std 11.5/14 by
Aura Technology and Software Services, India.

Pen & Sword Books Ltd includes the Imprints of Atlas, Archaeology, Aviation,
Discovery, Family History, Fiction, History, Maritime, Military, Military Classics, Politics,
Select, Airworld, Frontline Publishing, Leo Cooper, Remember When, Seaforth Publishing,
The Praetorian Press, Wharncliffe Local History, Wharncliffe Transport, Wharncliffe
True Crime and White Owl.

For a complete list of Pen & Sword titles please contact

PEN & SWORD BOOKS LIMITED
47 Church Street, Barnsley, South Yorkshire, S70 2AS, England
E-mail: enquiries@pen-and-sword.co.uk
Website: www.pen-and-sword.co.uk

Or
PEN AND SWORD BOOKS
1950 Lawrence Rd, Havertown, PA 19083, USA
E-mail: Uspen-and-sword@casematepublishers.com
Website: www.penandswordbooks.com

Contents

Introduction

The Royal Air Force has played its part in defending the nation for one hundred years as the design of aircraft and the training of crews to fly them has followed the lead of technology. When single-seat jet aircraft were first developed, pilots were required to interpret large amounts of information presented to them in the cockpit and integrate this with the operation of flying controls and systems to achieve the task. Computers were barely involved, and it was the aptitudes, skills and training of pilots that made success possible. Selection for pilot training was fiercely competitive and many suffered bitter disappointment at not being selected or not completing the course. Today, the skills required are very different.

Advances in avionics and flight-control systems have meant that pilots are relieved of many cockpit tasks, allowing concentration on systems management and tactical thinking, so essential in modern warfare. Has something been lost as a consequence? The sense of independence and self-reliance with direct responsibility for the success of the mission, for handling the aircraft, getting best performance, navigating accurately with map and stopwatch and landing in bad weather with minimal landing aids was more than satisfying. The physical and mental agility to achieve this was engaging and intoxicating for a new pilot. Yet young pilots of today no doubt find just as much excitement in the glass-cockpit environment with the prospect of space flight a gleam in the eye for some. Venturing into the atmosphere and beyond in a man-made machine still confronts a hostile environment where readiness for the unexpected, be that hazard or discovery, is a must. Nostalgia can prompt wistful thoughts in the minds of retired pilots that 'It was better in my day … '. I prefer 'things were different in my day,' but it would be dishonest to deny that *different* can be seen as more connected, more tactile, more demanding in earlier aircraft. Think of driving a vintage sports car along a narrow country road with no power steering, agricultural suspension, crash gear-box and drum brakes and you will get the idea, but it might just be indulgence in fond memories, even exaggeration – you decide.

I served in the RAF at the height of the Cold War, when the fast jet pilot had his hands full in the cockpit controlling the aircraft and manipulating its systems together with a crewman if he had one. The stimulation of the job is relived in this book, together with adventures and stories that go with life in the RAF. Some detail of what it means to fly a single pilot aircraft, from initial training to squadron operations, will be the foundation for a virtual cockpit experience, especially for those unfamiliar with flying. When you next watch that evocative vintage machine, memorable Second World War fighter, or gleaming fast jet as it roars, gyrates and rushes past in a cacophony of engine and airframe noise, you may feel more at one with the pilot in the cockpit. For those who have flown professionally it might bring back pleasant, perhaps humorous memories of those earlier years and no doubt prompt reflections on technique.

Pilots, like anyone else, must be ready for surprises. Being invited to fly Spitfires in the filming of *The Battle of Britain* in 1968 was more than a surprise; it was astonishing, and a privilege I still savour. Flying these famous aircraft to relive the battles of 1940 was a unique experience that I am always pleased to talk about.

A few tales of instructing at flying clubs will resonate with those who have enjoyed that experience. Teaching people to fly is immensely satisfying as they grow in self-confidence and come to share feelings of achievement and adventure. Despite the electronic assistance available to pilots flying modern and expensive types, the basic skills taught at clubs still predominate during initial training. All professional pilots, military or civil, must reach a high standard in the same hands-on flying skills as earlier generations before they can be let loose to fly complex machines with advanced avionics and automated flight control systems. After all, they might fail … !

Since the Royal Air Force was formed, developments in aircraft have accelerated rapidly. The early years of discovery and excitement, launching a man into the skies astride a powered machine that he could, more or less, control, must have been breathtaking. Only the wealthy, the reckless or the entrepreneur could indulge in flying those flimsy, unreliable machines, albeit with the glamour and distinction of showing the world something novel to inspire the imaginative to wonder how it could transform travel, sport and spectacle. But after a very few years it became clear that air power would be a significant factor for success in military conflict. Young men from all walks of life, intoxicated by the thrill of flying, were pitched into the horrors of war to find that the machines that gave them such freedom became death traps. The courage, the fears, the fatalism of wartime pilots and their crews have been the themes of films, books and history lessons ever since.

As artificial intelligence and automation change the way we work, drive our cars, fight our wars and fly our aircraft it might be expected that interest in the role of the pilot would diminish. Perhaps it will one day, but for now the elegant designs and awesome performance of modern aircraft, military and civil, continue to inspire boys and girls, men and women to connect with the world of aviation as flight crew, designers, engineers, air traffic controllers or just to enjoy an air display. Some will harbour the dream of flying as a pilot. This was my ambition from an early age.

I was born in 1940 in London. Had I been born twenty years earlier my chances of living beyond 1940 as an RAF pilot would have been poor, as the war in the air took its toll. I joined the RAF In 1957 as the arms race between the Soviet Union and the West brought the fear of an even more devastating war that could start by accident or default and end catastrophically in a few days. The UK defence posture, as a member of NATO, was changing from graduated responses to any Soviet attacks using manned aircraft to a heavier reliance on nuclear deterrence. ICBMs (Intercontinental Ballistic Missiles), medium-range missiles that could reach the UK from Eastern Germany, Soviet bombers with stand-off capability and submarine-launched weapons all required a rapid response in kind. Manned aircraft were becoming too slow and NATO policy shifted towards missiles for attack and defence to deal with the new threats. But changes in defence procurement are not implemented quickly and cancellation of programmes that are well advanced is very expensive, sometimes impractical. It took ten years of design and development before the English Electric Lightning interceptor even began to equip squadrons in 1959 and it was in service until the 1980s, fulfilling roles for which it was not ideal. Its astonishing rate of climb and speed produced by its swept wing form and twin Avon engines was specifically designed to reduce the success rate of Soviet bomber attacks on RAF V-bomber bases, allowing them to get at least some aircraft airborne with a nuclear capability. This was the essence of the UK's contribution to deterrence but the margin of success over failure was perilously thin. The Polaris submarine-launched weapon announced in 1962 was to provide the mobility and subterfuge to restore the UK's confidence in deterrence to address the latest threats to the UK and NATO as a whole.

But neither Lightning nor Polaris was available in 1957. The RAF was equipped according to the Flexible Response strategy that required readiness and strength in every role to counter attacks across Western Europe, the Near and Middle East, and to fulfil bilateral and treaty commitments elsewhere. Gloster Javelins backed by surface-to-air missiles and a comprehensive radar network provided air defence to protect V-bomber airfields in the UK and bases in RAFG (RAF Germany) and the NEAF (Near East Air Force). Strike, attack, maritime, transport and air-sea rescue were covered by fleets of Canberras, Hunters, Shackletons, Hastings and Whirlwind helicopters. I was joining a sizeable air force with a constant throughput of new pilots in all roles, together with other aircrew for multi-crew types. The selection process needed to ensure that increasingly complex and expensive aircraft were operated safely but to maximum effect. It was thought by the MoD (Ministry of Defence) that minimum standards of education, especially in the sciences, together with greater emphasis on tactical decision-making and leadership, would require that the use of non-commissioned pilots, who had served so effectively and with such distinction in the Second World War, be gradually phased out. Tests for 'officer qualities' were added to the range of aptitudes and abilities needed to be selected for pilot training. The search was on for well-educated boys with a sense of adventure and other attributes to make them attractive to the RAF including, critically, an interest in military flying. Girls were not yet trained as pilots despite having proved their capabilities during the Second World War in the shape of the Air Transport Auxiliary ferrying new aircraft from factories to operating bases. This reluctance to train female pilots and combatants was to change. Today there are female airline captains, fighter pilots and front-line combat troops. If you train as a pilot you could just as well be taught by a woman as a man. But this was an evolutionary process and with this acknowledgement I refer in my story of earlier times to 'he', when today it could easily be 'she'.

I flew as an RAF pilot from 1957 to 1979 and at clubs thereafter. I've written about joining the service, the job of a pilot, the aircraft I flew, and stories that might interest you more than a biography which perhaps wouldn't. It is also an attempt to contribute to a historical record of flying the early jets. There is a chronology, but this is merely a framework for you to vicariously experience what it is like to fly, and gain some impressions of RAF life, where the serious business of flying jet fighters had a necessary counter in the zest for fun, humour, repartee and the outrageous that most people in aviation enjoy to this day. Before we look at what it's like in a jet fighter cockpit I'll tell you a story of how a schoolboy dream turned into a reality.

Chapter 1

The Dream

*Flying is more than a sport and more than a job; flying is pure
passion and desire, which fill a lifetime.*

General Adolf Galland,
Luftwaffe, *The First and the Last*, 1954

It was routine morning assembly at Wandsworth Grammar School in south-west London in 1955. A time for raising the sights of boys to higher things, higher than feigning a cold to avoid the afternoon's cross-country run, being picked as third reserve for the second fifteen rugby team or jostling to join sister school Mayfield Girls' 5th form for Biology. A feeling of community, a time to celebrate achievements, a parade to re-affirm a sense of purpose (postwar hangover from a war not long finished) were all good for the boys, engendering high morale and development of character so the headmaster thought. Five hundred fidgeting 'investments in our future' braced themselves for the headmaster's booming announcements, biblical readings by bored masters, and ritual hymn singing with no obvious purpose. But today there was a *visitor*, announced as a Schools Liaison Officer (SLO) from the RAF, whom the more intelligent boys identified as a government agent, poorly disguised as an RAF officer, set on press-ganging boys into joining the military. He extolled the virtues of RAF life, majoring on the juicy initial salary, even during training, and many other goodies. Only by implication did he allude to the irresistible attractions of a uniform to the opposite sex, the spotted scarf streaming in the breeze as you collected your beloved in the green sports car, with steely gaze, grudgingly acknowledging hero status. The boys didn't buy it. Only two responded to the 'come up and have a word if you're interested' invitation – me and a likeminded fourth-form friend with whom I had been at school from five years old, playing child war hero games in the playground. It was the beginning of a journey for a very ordinary schoolboy to find exhilaration, challenge and diversity that he could never have dreamed of. The interest derived from a number of things that had happened in my earlier years.

My father died in the war just before I was born. As the bombing of London intensified in 1940 I was evacuated as a baby with my mother from London to Wales, separated from two elder brothers until we returned to London as a decidedly poor family living on welfare and free school meals. My two brothers left school early to find work, and it was my good fortune to be allowed by a hardworking mother to take up the offer of a place at Wandsworth Grammar School in London, only to face a hostile new stepfather who thought I should give up education to earn money for the family. My eldest brother, eight years older than me, left to join the RAF as a pilot and flew Vampires and Venoms for eight years, leading to a lifetime as an airline pilot with many tales to tell, from flying Dakota twin-engine transports out of dirt strips in Africa to long haul DC-10 flights out of Zurich with Swissair. He was followed by my other brother, six years older than me, who also joined the RAF in his teens to fly Canberras and Shackletons. He subsequently attained a Master's degree and worked as a secondary school teacher of history and religious studies before ultimately becoming ordained as a priest in the Church of England. So I did have role models to cover the exhilaration I could expect from flying and an evident commitment to the spiritual and social wellbeing of our fellow men, which was a harder act to follow. With such inspiration from two brothers, discomfort at home and school reports that showed good academic results but a need for a sense of direction, you can perhaps see why I fell for the pitch from the SLO.

Boys growing up just after the Second World War could not help but be influenced by stories of the heroism and suffering of military campaigns, and the ravaging of civilian life in Britain, in Germany and so many other countries. A career in the armed forces was still highly regarded, with the offer of world-wide travel, a life of action and adventure and an escape from the humdrum as the recruitment advertisements would have it. Of course, the more conventional professions offered their own attractions and many war-weary parents might well have steered their offspring towards more secure and rewarding futures. But for me the prospect of escaping from home, flying as a pilot and joining the RAF was irresistible. My mother, having endured a war and many years of hardship, would at last have domestic contentment with her new husband who would probably not miss me.

Grammar schools today are the subject of much political argument and controversy regarding their status, indeed their very existence. The controversy was there in 1951 when I began studying at Wandsworth Grammar, dressed in a maroon school uniform, carrying satchel and rugby boots, apprehensively eyeing other joiners who displayed a confidence I lacked. Grammar schools were part of a divided system that separated those showing aptitude for academic studies from those thought to have better prospects by studying at a secondary modern school, supposedly offering a more technical and job-focused education. It all turned on the examination at eleven years old – the '11 plus' – which determined which children were eligible to attend a grammar school for the next six years or more. While the arguments raged about the merits of the system amongst the adult public, at eleven years old the debate was invisible to me. I found the experience of studying at Wandsworth Grammar elevating and have regarded it ever since as the epitome of meritocratic education and development. I was a beneficiary and too young to consider the justice or fairness of such a system in the context of contemporary social structures. Let's just say that it was my good fortune to have the developmental horsepower of a reputable institution to lift me out of a blinkered home life to reach my potential, something which any education system should aim for.

It was a well-run school delivering good results in academics and sport in fierce competition with other local state-funded grammars, of which there were many at that time. When I arrived the school was populated largely by boys from middle-class backgrounds and was known for its discipline, school spirit and results, academically and on the rugby field. Masters were inspiring in their flowing black gowns, engaging in witty dialogue with boys who, in those days, were respectful of authority and complied with the strict discipline but took every opportunity to show spirited appreciation of anything remotely amusing. Shaped to some extent by Wolf Cubs and Boy Scouting I revelled in this structured system, only later appreciating just how important was the active encouragement and support from schools and schoolmasters for future success.

So it was that a relieved SLO briefed the two of us on the next steps. He no doubt had a quota to achieve of 'boys hooked' by his pitch, both to justify his job and deliver a performance that would mean a posting to something more interesting, so he was keen not to lose us. And there was another motive. I discovered later that the structured career for those officers destined for the top jobs meant that staff postings were interspersed amongst flying tours. This meant no flying unless the job required it or volunteering to spend your spare time flying air cadets for air experience, hoping they might rush to the recruiting office on landing. If the SLO found boys genuinely interested he could offer to take them flying to give them a taste of being airborne and enhance their interest in a flying career. He would receive a gold star for salesmanship plus more hours in his flying logbook.

A few weeks later on a bright summer's day two 15-year-old boys turned up at RAF Kenley which, together with Biggin Hill and Croydon, was among a clutch of airfields that were the mainstay of defence against air attacks on London during the Second World War. We were excited but mildly apprehensive at what flying might do to us. The de Havilland Chipmunk gleamed in the sunlight as I was helped up over the wing, fearful that I would puncture the fabric with a misplaced boot, cancelling the whole day.

I was strapped into the rear seat, plugged into the intercom and immediately briefed on how to jump out of the machine and parachute to earth should the engine stop over rough terrain or catch fire, which was not the start I had anticipated. Neither was I expecting to sit deep down in the tandem rear seat cockpit, with limited forward visibility from an aircraft that sat nose high and rear cockpit low, as it taxied to the take-off point. Once airborne things improved as the aircraft levelled out and I was able to take in the scenery through the side windows, the instrument panel still blocking the forward view but this became quickly irrelevant.

After some pretence of asking me how I felt about aerobatics, which I couldn't even spell, having never flown, he launched into a sequence of astonishingly vigorous

De Havilland Chipmunk trainer. (*Rod Brown Collection*)

In flight visibility was good. (*Rod Brown Collection*)

manoeuvres designed, it seemed, to break up our flimsy craft and me with it. Once he had vented his frustration at having the misfortune to work at a desk in the Ministry he levelled out and cheerfully asked whether I had enjoyed it. Not wishing to appear a wimp, and fearing that anything short of ecstatic enthusiasm would be the end of my ambitions, I expressed due wonderment at the thrill and his skill, hoping he would stay level while my stomach sank back to where it started and he wasn't tempted to repeat the treatment.

But he had clearly found release in subjecting me to this 'treat' and we landed with no further gyrations. While this initial experience gave me pause for thought, I assumed (rightly) that a little passing discomfort in an environment entirely new to me would not affect my prospects of a future in flying. Mild air sickness is not unusual in the initial stages of learning to fly and usually subsides. The cure I found as a flying instructor is to give control to the student who then anticipates each force exerted on him, since it is he who is applying it, the unexpected movements being the source of motion sickness. Pity my SLO friend didn't know that. What he did know was that we were both keen to go to the next stage, whatever that was. He duly briefed us on ways of applying to join the RAF and on a more immediate method of confirming suitability and potential acceptance by applying for an RAF Scholarship (as opposed to an RAF Flying Scholarship which is available to this day). This was effectively a pre-acceptance for a place at the RAF College, subject to medical and aptitude tests, a weekend selection board at Daedalus House, Cranwell, in competition with many others, and achieving A-level GCE passes in two scientific subjects. The clincher in selling this to my mother who, bless her, had had no significant education

A classic, dainty, aerobatic tail-dragger. (*Rod Brown Collection*)

and very little understanding or interest in the machinations of military recruitment, was that the scholarship included financial support for the remainder of the time needed at school to attain the requisite A levels.

There followed medical and aptitude tests at RAF Hornchurch. The aptitude tests were mostly about hand to eye co-ordination, steering dots on screens and doing several things at once – a bit like juggling. But one of the tests was entitled 'matrices' and meant selecting logical matches from a book of patterns or the next in the sequence from several options. I found these challenging for some reason and did not feel I had done that well. I was gently taken aside by the supervising officer and made aware that I had passed every other test with flying colours and was there something in the instructions for the matrices tests that I didn't understand? Somewhat desperately I answered 'no, can I have another go?', not knowing if this was a trap to reveal my inability to read instructions. 'Of course you can,' he beamed and I sat down alone to grapple with another book of matrices finding them just as puzzling, spirits declining as my life threatened to fall apart. Curiously I heard no more about matrices and was awarded a sound 'pass'. I guess they must have wanted pilots pretty badly. Next was an arduous weekend at Daedalus House where we were subjected to interviews, intelligence tests and leadership exercises, which typically meant getting your eerily compliant team across an imaginary crocodile-infested swamp equipped with a puzzling collection of poles, ropes, and lumps of wood that were supposed to help. My only consolation as I tried to get everyone across was that in saving the many you're bound to lose a few. The grim-faced examining officer showed no sense of humour at this practical approach and I had to think up another. Inevitably an extra complication was fed in if the testing officer thought you were performing too well. The successful crossing of the swamp was on an escape route following a commando raid which required peak fitness since you and your team had to negotiate high mountains, raging rapids, a four-mile swim and one team member had got dengue fever and allowed tropical insects to eat his foot. What do you do? Do you carry him and get shot, leave him to get shot, or just shoot him to avoid secrets being tortured out of him? The example is over-egged, but it is typical of the extremes to which testing officers could resort in relieving the boredom as they dreamt of returning to a proper job in flying, engineering – or anything really. Most terrifying for me was giving a one-minute speech at short (or long) notice on a subject of my choice, surrounded by swaggering, confident and articulate public schoolboys who had been groomed for this moment and delivered outrageously funny lectures on the sex life of the green iguana.

Against the odds I was successful, duly awarded the scholarship and sent back to school to study for A levels. Having seen how passionately the wealthy, well-educated boys jostled to get into Cranwell I worked even harder to shake off any doubts about upbringing and compete with the best. My friend also passed the selection and after a careful two-minute evaluation we decided to devote our time at school to mathematics and drop all extra-curricular activities, aiming to take the exams at the first opportunity. This was less well received by the school with regard to my friend, a brilliant first fifteen three-quarter and top sprinter for the school, than it was for me, a second fifteen forward with plenty of energy but little flair on the rugby field, albeit hot on academics provided it wasn't history or chemistry. Nevertheless, our French master who intimidated any hapless boy who didn't come up to his standards by spraying saliva into their faces using a theatrical 'contrived temper' teaching technique accompanied by shouting and threats, did quietly tell me I should study French at university and forget the RAF. I politely rejected this offer. It might reveal a mentality that prompted masters to write in many early school reports 'If Lloyd were more co-operative socially to complement his evident abilities, he could go far.' Put bluntly I was *bolshie*, concentrating on what I liked more than what was expected by the school. This hint of arrogance morphed into an apparent self-confidence that was to see me through many challenges. We both passed in Pure Maths and Applied Maths at A level in one year and duly joined 77 Entry at the RAF College in September 1957. Cranwell was the Air Force's answer to Sandhurst and Dartmouth *plus* learning to fly, so no contest there, but many similarities. It was a three-year course to train as an officer and fulfil the dream of learning to fly.

Chapter 2

Cranwell

In the afternoon heat, white cotton wool clouds grow quickly into towering pillars of brilliant white and shaded valleys that change, writhe and bubble up into wisps of white mist tugged by updrafts to dissipate and reform against the intense, dazzling blue. Race between the summits, turning and climbing, dive into the dark valleys, shoot out into sunlight in a rush of speed and exhilaration, alive to the beauty of natural things, and excited by the sheer power and response to the controls at your fingertips.

This was the intensity of feeling when I was first let loose in an RAF Percival Piston Provost trainer aircraft on a summer's day over Lincolnshire in 1958. It was the culmination of everything I had grown up to pursue – the challenge, the achievement, the privilege, the attainment in a competitive world of something regarded by most boys as the ultimate adventure. In today's jargon it was really cool.

Flying is a challenge many aspire to without necessarily having an ambition to enter the professional world. The first solo flight for any student pilot at a flying club or on a professional course is a very personal and memorable event that is the pinnacle of achievement for some and just the beginning for others, but the memories of those early years of training are vivid for every pilot I have met. Pilot training follows a well-established pattern of lessons that bring challenges and successes for some, disappointments and failures for others. There is an intense desire to succeed and prove something to yourself as much as others while facing the risk of failure and hurt pride. For the romantic, solo flying can inspire a sense of freedom and wonder that is unforgettable. But I hadn't reached that point yet as I headed for Cranwell in September 1957.

The first thing I saw on arrival was a truly stunning white stone college building set back from an expansive and immaculate oval lawn, forever called The Orange. More engaging, however, were the jet aircraft flying over the airfield to the south of the College. The de Havilland Vampire was the second British production jet aircraft to enter service after the Gloster Meteor and the first to be powered by a single jet engine. The Meteor was used at Cranwell for pilots with a height or leg-length that exceeded Vampire cockpit limits to ensure legs were retained in the event of ejection and the canopy could be closed for flight. Following the design concept of its only operational predecessor, the Messerschmitt Me-262, the Meteor's two engines were

RAF College Cranwell in 1954 known as College Hall. (*MoD Crown Copyright via RAF College*)

located out on the wings and contributed to the distinctive noise of an approaching Meteor at speed known as the 'Blue Note'. The Vampire design, however, originating from as early as 1942, buried its single engine within a central nacelle in the fuselage with a twin 'boom' structure mounting a tailplane and twin fin and rudder assemblies. Maximum speed at sea level was 355 knots (kts) rising to 455 knots above 10,000 feet. It cruised at some 280 knots depending on height and glided beautifully at around 175 knots. As I watched them flying at around 170 knots in the Cranwell circuit, emitting a distinctive whistle from the Goblin 3 engine with its centrifugal compressor, I was entranced, hardly daring to believe that, if I could get through the basic course in the Percival Provost and whatever else was in store, I could be flying them in two years' time.

For the first year, cadets were not considered ready for the comforts of the College building with its single rooms that came with a batman to bring morning tea, press clothes and clean shoes to make life bearable. Instead we were treated not as officers but as raw recruits to suffer the indignities that military trainees of all ranks have endured throughout time. We were crammed into wooden huts located on the main RAF station to the south of a main road which separated it from hallowed College grounds. Huts were organised in squadrons, imaginatively labelled A, B, and C, and we had our very own parade ground.

Similarities with Sandhurst, the Army's Officer Cadet College, took the form of 'd, b and p' *(drill, bull, parades)*, then more **d**, more **b** and more **p**, laced with 'crowing'. There was a longstanding tradition, perhaps derived from mild sadism endemic at public schools at the time, whereby some senior cadets, having achieved notional seniority and endured the indignities and tedium of **d, b** and **p** without so far failing the course ('chopped' in the jargon of the day), found it somehow cathartic to taunt, bully and torture the Junior Entry as an initiation ritual they would later appreciate – mainly when it stopped. The targets tended to be those who showed some characteristic that Senior Entry advocates of this practice didn't like, or saw as vulnerable – being small, artistic, different, singing in a high voice etc. I did not qualify against any of these criteria and I was never bothered by the practice; neither did I indulge in it. Cruel though it might sound, it is not so different from any number of initiation rites that young men joining groups of other young men are put through to confirm that they are 'tough'. However, any inclination to thrust junior cadets into cold showers naked in December had little bearing on success or failure in pilot training, as many of the bullies would find out to their cost. The practice of crowing was known to the College staff but a blind eye was turned, putting it down to tradition and sorting out men from boys, a rationale that has, as far as I know, become rather dated.

More open than clandestine crowing was the institutional belief that punishment was good for development and that resistance to regimentation that brought obedience and discipline to any military force was, metaphorically, to be beaten out of recruits early on. Whilst questionable as a preparation for leadership and decisiveness, it created a curious motivational bond amongst cadets in each entry and each squadron group living together in one hut, with its hard beds, cold ablutions and rules on everything, including arranging socks in a top drawer folded identically and dressed off in rows, ready for inspection. I am sure this preoccupation with order created the cavalier attitude towards domestic tidiness I have exhibited ever since. Loyalty in each squadron group within each Entry continued to develop when, at the end of the first year, we moved into discrete wings of the College allocated by Squadron where we suffered, celebrated and socialised together in tight-knit groups.

Every morning, before normal humans would get out of bed, it was drill – marching, manoeuvring, dressing (not the sartorial kind) and a forensic inspection of 'kit' to search for blanco on brasses, smudges on boots, dust in or on rifles – all clearly essential to flying with the RAF. For the psychological grooming of future officers, non-commissioned drill instructors worked hard to exploit weaknesses such as wearing boots that had been incompetently 'bulled'. I learned how to iron the dimples out of the leather to produce a more mirror-like shine when they were spat and polished for an hour or two, usually late the previous evening. Like any authority figures to be (anonymously) challenged, drill instructors attracted nicknames. The most famous was a solidly built red-headed Flight Sergeant Holt, who sported a bristly moustache, neatly trimmed to match his immaculate turnout, complete with pace stick. Successive Cranwell entries knew him fearfully, respectfully and ultimately fondly as Bogbrush. He was both famous and infamous in bringing spirit, commitment and wicked humour to tedious drill practices and parades and was to be awarded the MBE for his services to successive generations of young officer cadets, encouraging them to face military life with a fortitude and tenacity that he displayed by example. His tall, thin sergeant colleague was known as 'Pullthrough', alluding to the long thin rod used to pull a cord and cloth through a rifle barrel to clean it. He, too, was aware of his nickname and I think secretly relished the celebrity status bestowed on him by these potentially great leaders – well, some.

Pilot training did not start until the second year. The focus seemed to be on testing and developing cadets as officers on the assumption that they would rise to positions of enormous power and deliver incisive judgements in defence of the nation mainly based on a good grounding in **d, b** and **p**. The degree-level academic programme seemed to plausibly support this hope, comprising scientific, military and leadership studies and exercises. In retrospect, climbing in the Cairngorms in winter and evading the Seaforth Highlanders whilst negotiating each island of the Hebrides chain on foot must surely have helped us prepare for a nuclear exchange of missiles with the Soviet Union in some way – if only to help us to endure cold waits on platforms during later years of rail strikes that prevented us getting to our Ministry of Defence desks in Whitehall by 0900.

And of course the **d, b** and **p** did take up a great deal of time as we tried to match the standards of the Grenadier Guards, fixing bayonets to charge for England. But the ceremonial was stirring and sufficiently memorable that today I regularly attend Trooping the Colour for a dose of patriotism, spine-tingling military bands and nostalgia. Memories fade of the fear of retribution from Bogbrush if our turnout was less than immaculate, we put a foot wrong in the parade or, worst of all, collapsed in a clattering heap during a hot summer parade with the ignominy and embarrassment that goes with it. Luckily I didn't die that particular death.

We did get airborne. Varsities and Valettas, affectionately known as 'Pigs' due to their appearance, provided regular opportunities to feel airsick, as grinning, ageing pilots flew at 2,000 feet for maximum turbulence to test the strongest of stomachs, already nauseous from the odour of cadets having lost their lunch on the previous sortie.

To take our minds off the lurching we were tasked to peer into various 'scopes' at each navigation training position and track our position. The Air Position Indicator was an ingenious electro-mechanical forerunner of computer-based navigation, taking inputs from airspeed sensors and gyro-magnetic compasses to give a continuous readout of latitude and longitude which might, with considerable luck, be confirmed by looking out of the window. If in doubt we could also look into the GEE equipment scope. This was a radio transmission-system comparing time differences for a signal

Vickers Varsity used for navigation training. (*BAE SYSTEMS*)

to arrive from two transmitting stations, each positioning the receiving aircraft on a specific line on a GEE chart colour coded for each station, then adding a third transmitting location to achieve a triangulation and ground position with what proved to be reasonable accuracy. It was in service during the Second World War and until as late as 1970. It required us to see signals in oscilloscopes drop into boxes on the screen and transcribe the readings to large ungainly charts covering different areas of the UK. It made me even more admiring of wartime navigators plotting courses on desks as the aircraft bucked and shuddered their way through weather and flak. More relevant to our forthcoming training was low-level map reading from a 1:500,000 ('half-mil') aeronautical chart that was made almost unreadable by the multiplicity of controlled airspace designations such as control areas and zones, airways, danger areas, bird sanctuaries, Military Air Traffic Zones etc. that took up so much of the UK, especially England. Ominously, I did not find map reading easy and this was to focus my mind later when it came to pilot navigation. I was more comfortable when it was my turn to go up to the cockpit to handle the controls and play with the levers.

Vickers Valetta also used for navigation training – a taildragger. (*BAE SYSTEMS*)

There were 'jollies' presented as educational trips designed to prevent us becoming drill junkies. Visits to West Point, the American equivalent of Sandhurst and to the USAF (US Air Force) Academy at Colorado Springs revealed curious cultural differences from Cranwell. These were characterised by the 'Honour Code' under which you not only tried to uphold high moral standards personally but you had to snitch on your mates if they (inevitably) fell short. It was an interesting 'take' on loyalty and it would be fascinating to research its impact on operations in Vietnam and beyond where a moral code to hang on to when up against such a fanatical enemy might, or might not, have proved the code's value. We Brits were accustomed to putting on pained facial expressions to indicate what was 'not on', or resort to denouncing somebody's misjudgements with 'It's just not cricket, old chap', which was a puzzle to most foreigners and evidence of being a 'toff' to most Brits. It also meant unifying against 'them' – anybody in authority who 'had a go' at a friend.

Transport was a Bristol Britannia turboprop which whispered its way across the Atlantic and attracted sympathetic glances from Americans as they raced ahead with the Boeing 707 which overtook the pioneering but ill-fated de Havilland Comet, designed and built in Britain, to lead the field in jet-powered air transport.

We drove the Army's tanks on Salisbury Plain, went to sea with the Navy and discovered that the submarine force spent surprising amounts of time in dock drinking 'Horse's Necks' (brandy and ginger) with anyone who was prepared to join them, even the RAF. Perhaps it was a cure for claustrophobia. All these visits and activities together with thermodynamics, aerodynamics, electro-mechanics, sport and **b**, **d** and **p** clearly left little time for flying, even in Pigs. From the classroom, I could only hear the Vampires roaring and whistling overhead as senior cadets left behind their student's image and turned into jet pilots commanding respect from instructors who were only recently out of training themselves. The prospect of flying the Vampire seemed as far away as ever. Then we started flying the Percival Provost.

The Percival Provost T.1
The Provost was a two-seat aircraft that replaced the Percival Prentice as the RAF's primary trainer. Introduced in 1950 it was all metal with a 550hp radial engine and came with a tail wheel, so a tail-dragger in modern jargon. It was fully aerobatic, had a good rate of climb and a roll rate similar to contemporary operational fighters, preparing students for the higher performance types coming into service. It had a

Percival Piston Provost. (*BAE SYSTEMS*)

'stick', derived from 'joystick', a term used in the very early days of aviation for the primary flight control in many light aircraft of the time and sport aircraft today. In early jet fighters it was called a 'control column', confined largely to single-pilot aircraft, while larger aircraft originally had a control wheel, then a 'yoke', with two grips akin to a scooter or upright bicycle. More recently, fly-by-wire sidesticks mounted on the side panel have become common, although in fighters some designers prefer to retain the centrally-positioned control column seen as easier to operate under high 'g' forces. The Provost had a roomy cockpit with side-by-side seating, thought to be more effective for early training, with the added visibility of the instructor's hand movements, body language and facial expressions. This was very useful if you were doing well, but were you to be thrown by expressions of frustration, sadness or fear, then the tandem arrangement might be better for you, where only the instructor's controlled, if tense, voice would convey his assessment of your handling skills until the stick snatched out of your hands would make things clearer. If all was lost, especially the engine over rough terrain, or above cloud with no navigation assistance, the parachute you sat on was the other way to get home – if, that is, you could get out of the aircraft without striking the wing or tail, had enough height, weren't over water, remembered to pull the D-ring, and survived the landing without breaking limbs or worse.

Those who have received *ab initio* pilot training will be familiar with a sequence of lessons that are pretty much standard worldwide. An outline follows, although to those with a DIY mentality I would counsel strongly against treating these pages as a 'teach yourself to fly without an instructor' manual. My initial intention is to describe for the unfamiliar in some detail what a pilot in the cockpit has to learn to get the aircraft airborne and land it again. Then we'll take a look at other skills that make a professional pilot when, of course, civil and military flying diverge somewhat. A greater understanding of these piloting techniques should prove useful when it comes to describing experiences in fast jets.

Be warned, the detail that follows may depict the pilot as even more heroic than you had thought, as the challenges to overcome are revealed. Or it may cast doubts about a mere human contending with such an array of problems – the weather, the emergencies, the stall, getting lost and the demand to get things right or crash. Don't worry, many pilots relating flying achievements will be prone to bragging, thinly disguised as modesty, and depict the whole thing as the privilege of the brilliant. When learning, the novelty can inflate egos but with experience, practice and currency it becomes second nature to get things right and, as a rule, not crash. Getting to that position relies on good instruction and a touch of self-discipline. For military pilots the handling is taught pretty much like civil schools, since their syllabus and techniques came from the military anyway, but the standard has to be high to move to role training where handling is taken for granted and there is a lot more to learn.

The role of the flying instructor is therefore important in setting student pilots on the right track. After all, someone has to risk life and limb as students reveal their misunderstandings, perhaps inadequacies, by trying to land in mid-air six feet above a hard runway rather than on the ground. I ultimately took up flying instruction and can now reflect on my own response to instructional techniques as I invite you to follow my journey of learning to fly. If memories are too troubling for you seasoned pilots, fast forward to flying operational jets.

The training begins with an easy teacher/pupil relationship in which the confidence and then competence of the instructor becomes evident and the student does what he's told. Not much is expected of the student just yet, other than to complete the required ground school to understand the systems of the aircraft he is to fly and how to use the checklist. More ground school would come later. RAF training and Civil Licence courses call for extensive understanding of the theory of flight with its physics and aerodynamics, meteorology, engine design and operation, air traffic control, aviation medicine and many other topics, all tested by examination.

After a soothing, warm and friendly ground briefing for your first sortie your instructor will get you airborne simply to experience the environment – how things look from the air, how changes in the attitude, direction, power and speed feel, and what a landing looks like – then you start in earnest. The first lesson is about the effects of each control on the aircraft and therefore on you. Stick back raises the nose and you climb, as long as you have enough power to prevent the aircraft running out of speed, which is what the throttle is for. Stick forward lowers the nose to enter a dive which is fun as long as you do not exceed the designed maximum speed (termed Vne or speed never exceed) in which case the wings might tear off, reducing the aircraft to a lump of metal with you in it hurtling earthwards – not good. Stick moved to the right causes the aircraft to roll right and moved left to roll left. It will keep rolling for as long as the stick is displaced so, as with pitch control, you need to neutralise the control to stop in a particular attitude with reference to the horizon. Already you are controlling the aircraft in two planes or dimensions – pitch around an axis running roughly wing tip to wing tip, and roll around an axis running nose to tail. The rudder operated with your feet moves the nose in the horizontal plane to the right pushing on the right pedal or bar and left if you push left and is used in normal non-aerobatic flight to keep the aircraft flying in balance, with no yaw causing unwanted slipstream forces on the tail, or in the jargon 'drag'. Fore and aft stick movement controls the elevator attached to the tail plane while lateral left/right movements control the ailerons that hinge up and down on each wing and the rudder bar, where the feet are resting, controls, well, the rudder. In reality, operating stick and rudder is all about pressures, not movements, until you wish to fly to the upper limits of the aircraft's manoeuvring capability. More detail on all this would require study of aerodynamics on which many wonderful books have been written. Other controls introduced in early lessons are the throttle, giving you more or less engine power, and landing flaps that give you more lift up to the limiting speed together with more drag, both of which are useful in flying slower prior to landing. Finally, there is a trim tab on the elevator that can be positioned using a trim wheel to alter aerodynamic forces such that the control surface stays where it is without residual pressure on the stick, allowing the pilot to only lightly hold the stick to sustain a given pitch attitude – the angle between nose to tail or longitudinal axis and the horizon. The lesson that follows covers how to fly straight and level, mainly using the visual horizon to confirm this attitude but confirming level flight and wings level on the flight instruments which will be covered when we talk about flying in cloud. Next you learn how to turn using ailerons with rudder for balance followed by climbing and descending by increasing or decreasing engine power and adjusting the pitch attitude – above the horizon to climb, below to descend – at pitch angles to sustain a given airspeed.

A key exercise for the student before learning to land is how to handle an aircraft that has run out of flying speed or 'stalled' when lift from the wings that holds the aircraft up collapses. This is a phenomenon caused by airflow over the wings breaking away at high angles of attack (angle between wing and oncoming airflow) due to low speed or turning too hard for the speed and power setting, either of which could occur on final approach to land. This can bring a very sudden end to your flying career and pretty much everything else as the flying machine stops flying and, brick-like, heads for the ground. Most light aircraft with unswept wings exhibit broadly similar stalling characteristics in level flight and a generic recovery procedure is taught, although it is important to refer to type-specific pilot handbooks, checklists etc. for any special guidance. The procedure is to apply full power, keeping in balance with rudder, move the stick forward just sufficiently to un-stall the wings, roll the wings level to the horizon, then, as soon as practical without stalling the wings again, raise the nose to stop any further descent and regain height as speed increases. This is practised with the stages of flap used in the circuit to land and with wheels down on types that pull them up. A stall during a turn on to the final approach to land, uncorrected, can cause a sudden and continuous loss of height, loss of control and even a spin.

The stalling exercise can cause concern for student pilots unfamiliar with the sinking feeling that accompanies the stall as you remove its capability to fly – on purpose. It is for the instructor to instil confidence in students to recover quickly and according to the correct procedure just as soon as they recognise the symptoms of the stall – low airspeed, buffeting, high nose attitude, loss of height, one wing dropping without a control input or a buzzer sounding in the cockpit (stall warner) to indicate 'you are stalling'! In many aircraft types, basic or advanced, straight or swept wings, angles of attack just short of the stalling point produce the maximum lift with the agility of manoeuvre that results. It is indicated by a degree of 'buffet' felt as tremors on the stick as the airflow over the wings is just beginning to break away, with accompanying turbulence and this can be controlled with elevator to maximise turning performance without actually stalling. In advanced types this high angle of attack condition is evidenced by wing tip vortices made visible by condensation as air pressure and temperature over the wings fall.

If this description of how to fly an aircraft begins to sound in any way complex, don't be fooled. It is very close to the way flying instructors describe the in-flight behaviour of any basic aircraft in briefings before each flight using words and diagrams which are readily available. But the real learning comes from an intuitive ability most of us have for translating knowledge into action after the instructor has demonstrated everything he expects you to do, talking you through as you try each manoeuvre. In successive in-flight lessons you will be in control for any manoeuvre you have learned up to that point and this sets the logical sequence of early lessons, beginning with taxi and take off and, with luck, ending with a safe landing. There would hopefully have been a successful landing demonstrated at the end of each of the early sorties and once the basics are covered you will be following the instructor through (hands lightly on the controls without exerting any force) for a landing until he feels you can have a go. Any sign of shyness in putting the aircraft back on the ground, especially as fuel gets low, is indicative of a 'this is not a job for you' outcome since self-preservation is a 'must have' and would be enthusiastically endorsed by passengers or crew who might ultimately fly with you in control. The 'land six feet high' tendency or its counterpart 'not levelling out on reaching the ground' can normally be overcome by a gentle reminder from the instructor that he has a wife and kids who are expecting him to come home, plus some good patter. Patter? It's how flying instructors describe a manoeuvre while at the same time demonstrating it – landing, for example. Good flying instructors are good pilots who fly the aircraft accurately while describing what they are doing with the controls in a calm, articulate, unruffled voice as the student follows through. The less able or less interested instructor might fly the manoeuvre with minimal 'patter' and berate the student when he tries it for not doing it well. Or he might talk too much, speaking faster and faster as he gets behind what the aircraft is actually doing when patter becomes disconnected twaddle.

There are many ways of dealing with student overconfidence but it needs care in military pilot training. A new pilot could be required to operate very expensive equipment to the limits of its performance which requires competence and confidence to do the job, but where exceeding the limits of his ability could kill him, perhaps a crew, or those in other aircraft operating with him. Depending on the role assigned to the student, he may well fly in combat, deliver weapons, or fly in hostile environments and this requires him to be calm under pressure and exhibit a degree of aggression or, perhaps more accurately, determination to succeed whatever enemy action he encounters. Ultimately it's about training to kill people or be killed, when flying the aircraft must be second nature with the primary focus on achieving military objectives set by wise commanders listening to wise politicians … .

But in the halcyon days of early training, whether that's in the RAF or at a country flying club on a summer's day, it is the sheer thrill and challenge of being at the controls of a machine that takes you into the skies and lets you fly like a bird with a feeling of freedom that is indescribable, unless you are a poet. It has been expressed as:

Once you have tasted flight, you will forever walk the Earth with your eyes turned skyward, for there you have been, and there you will always long to return

This evocative quotation has been attributed to Leonardo Da Vinci, but he died in 1519, so it suggests a rather startling premonition or the thoughts of someone living more recently who has piloting experience. Either way it is a perception with which I empathise.

So how do we land the thing? There are significant differences in landing technique between types of aircraft of different weights, sizes, wing forms and structural designs to achieve safe arrivals in varying weather conditions. Some differences between fighter types will become apparent in later chapters but for light aircraft there is much commonality with a few extra considerations for tail-wheel aircraft.

Essentially, a light aircraft needs to be flown to level out or 'flare' just a few feet above the ground, with a small but safe margin of airspeed above the stall, to positon the aircraft for touchdown in varying wind conditions. Descending the last little bit to sink gently onto the wheels is judged with practice by the pilot using the general perspective of the horizon as he looks straight ahead to judge exact height and using throttle to control speed loss down towards stalling speed when lift from the wings runs out and the aircraft starts to drop under its own weight. As the speed falls, the pilot eases the stick back, using pressures more than movements, to achieve an increasing pitch attitude – nose coming up, tail going down – while keeping the flight path in a very gentle descent. For new pilots this last technique is the trickiest, especially for light tail-wheel types. With a tail wheel, the aircraft is designed such that just before it stalls the attitude of the aircraft to the horizon puts the three wheels at about the same height above the ground so that you fly it or gently drop it on to the runway on three points. That at any rate is the classic way 'tail draggers' land with the stick coming backwards to the stop to complete the stall and discourage the aircraft from bouncing back into the air. If this happens more power is applied to avoid a repeat bounce, even a few more bounces, kangaroo style, which is embarrassing at best, and at worst risks a collapsed undercarriage or heavy landing calling for the attention of an expensive engineer. A gentle bounce, sustaining the three-point attitude, is acceptable, especially on grass, and the aircraft will settle quickly onto the ground. Any wind gusts need to be countered with power to avoid an uncontrolled stall and allow another attempt to put it down if the runway is long enough – otherwise it's full power, stay level until the speed begins to rise and climb away for another go.

Nose-wheel types are a little more forgiving and can effectively be 'wheeled' on to the runway without the controlled attitude change tail-draggers need to achieve a 'three-pointer'. Many pilots of tail-wheel aircraft choose to use this 'wheel it on' technique and then lower the tail as speed decreases and you will see this in footage of heavy bombers landing during the Second World War.

Other effects that come into play with light single propeller types include torque from an engine at high power due to Newton's Third Law of Motion which puts more downward pressure on one wheel, creating more friction and a degree of turning towards that wheel (yaw), corrected with rudder. Take off technique for a tail-wheel aircraft requires you to lift the tail by easing the stick forward to achieve a safe flying attitude and this can cause 'swing' (yaw) on take off if you do it too quickly, by exerting a nose-down force on the rotating propeller acting as a gyro which, with precession, is effective at 90 degrees to that force, i.e. yaw.

As trainee pilots on the Provost we studied all these aspects of landing sitting in a classroom. It somehow appeared different when strapped into a noisy, vibrating machine heading for the ground with an instructor intent on avoiding a crash, talking his student through the final moments of an early attempt to land, with eyes widening, heart racing and a voice rising to ever higher frequency as he tried to ensure his own survival. I exaggerate, of course, and the balance between letting the student learn by making mistakes whilst gently correcting and taking back control in situations beyond the student's current level of competence without demoralising him, is the essence of good flying instruction. But any of you who feel apprehensive when flying to your favourite holiday destination should remember that the pilots at the front have every motive to arrive without incident and to deal competently with what are, these days, very rare problems. Pilots are known to have an innate capacity for humanely, professionally and bravely doing their job of looking after you, but there is more. They are not quite ready to die, what with the salary, perks, glamour, uniform etc., and doing something they love. You can be sure they will do whatever is possible to avoid a crash.

To position for landing, trainee pilots have to be taught to set up a final approach with a good chance of arriving at the point of touchdown I describe above. In the early stages of training this is achieved by flying a standard 'circuit' or 'pattern' comprising a climb to circuit height, typically 1,000 feet above the ground, turning 90 degrees for a short crosswind leg then another 90 to fly a downwind leg tracking parallel with and opposite to the landing direction. Tracking means dealing with any wind by taking up the appropriate heading to fly parallel. This correction for wind is required throughout the circuit to describe a rectangular pattern over the ground relative to the runway. Another 90-degree turn sets up a descending base leg before the turn on to a final approach at 500 to 600 feet facing the runway in use. Speeds, power settings, and pre-landing checks are all arranged to establish the aircraft in a safe, controlled descent to the runway for a landing. Debates about the use of power/throttle versus attitude/elevator to establish the right approach path are never-ending amongst instructors. Any technique that works reliably and safely could be seen as OK, with 'elevator for speed' and 'throttle for height' having stood the test of time for light aircraft. Keeping the touchdown point at a constant position in the windscreen with elevator, using power for speed and a 'point and power' technique – pointing the aircraft at touchdown and use power for the correct speed – are also taught. In military flying some allowance is made for the likelihood of flying more advanced aircraft types, with more drag in the landing configuration and better power response, when power plays a greater part in controlling the approach path. The patter will then talk about approach path or angle of approach, demonstrating when the perspective of the runway shows that you are high with too steep an angle to touch down, too low, or optimal, all of which will be further indicated by a lights system at most airfields of AAIs or today VASIs - angle of approach indicators and visual approach indicators respectively. VASIs are also known as PAPIs – precision approach path indicators – with slightly different lights. In practice, a change in pitch attitude to control airspeed will require a power change to maintain the required flight or approach path, and vice versa with a change in power. So with experience they are not treated as separate corrections but controlled jointly with interplay between the two.

Flaps, which change the shape of the wing to produce more lift at a given speed accompanied by more drag, are selected in stages with full flap selected prior to landing unless the wind is strong and gusty, which could cause the aircraft to 'balloon' – rise suddenly with falling airspeed. When this happens the aircraft reacts a bit like a kite, which was a nickname for aircraft in early days of aviation. The wind affects headings and power settings throughout, and strong winds accompanied by turbulence can make the whole exercise more exciting.

If the business of handling an aircraft holds no fascination, and it's the hardware, noise, speed and grunt seen at air shows that gets you going, then these details of early pilot training may not attract your interest. The intention is to make more sense of what pilots are doing in whatever type they will fly since they all start by learning the basic principles of flight and training in a light aircraft before moving to the more complex types. I'll understand if you skip on to the fast jet chapters, but you won't know what you've missed … .

***

After some eleven hours dual flying I went solo at Spitalgate airfield on 9 October 1958. It was a terrifying moment – not for me but for my sceptical instructor as he watched me approach to land. There was another aircraft on the runway lining up for take off as I approached. With no radio control at this satellite grass airfield it was up to me to decide whether to 'overshoot', i.e. climb away and go round the circuit again

I overshot a tad late on my first solo but saw it as decisive… . (*BAE SYSTEMS*)

or to land safely behind an accelerating aircraft taking off. I was, I thought, in control of the situation in my white gloves with narrow-eyed concentration and sharp reflexes honed to react. But I left it a tad late. The guy in front just wasn't moving quickly enough and at the last (and I mean last) moment I opened up the taps and roared away skywards as my instructor, positioned in a runway caravan next to the landing point, opened his eyes to see not a smoking heap of Provost T.1 but his student re-joining the circuit traffic and then completing an adequate landing.

I pressed on with the course but he appeared to remain sceptical about my taking such last minute decisions – but then he came from flying V-bombers (Vulcan, Victor, Valiant) which required a different skill-set from fighter operations. V-bomber pilots did a very serious job, their role effectively being to carry out a one-way journey to create nuclear Armageddon somewhere in the Soviet Union and have very little left of this country to return to. Sometimes they were launched when they didn't know if it was for practice or for real. So perhaps he could be forgiven for being relegated to the comparatively humble job of teaching eager but not necessarily competent young men to fly in a decidedly basic aircraft after the glamour, importance, and status of commanding a V-bomber crew. I felt it would not perhaps be appropriate or in my interest to ask him if he had in fact been a captain or why he had left the V Force. But he looked like a film star, drove a distinctive British racing green sports car and had acquired an attractive young wife who turned every cadet's head, including mine. So he had an image to sustain which I found faintly intimidating, as did others who flew with him, notably his previous student who was chopped just as I was allocated to him. This was not a good omen but it was not enough to dampen my enthusiasm to get airborne and perform well.

We became aware even at this early stage that a posting to fly V-bombers would be a disappointment. This was because V-bombers meant a crew, sitting in the right-hand seat as co-pilot for perhaps years, a rather sedate flight manoeuvring envelope and an intensely serious job. We contrasted it with flying solo in an agile aircraft with the legendary fighter pilot glamour and spirit engendered by films and stories of the two world wars – conveniently forgetting the horrors of killing or being killed. The posting to hope for was to fighters and there was a correlation between assessments at the end of pilot training and selection for this role. It may be that selections were based on more than flying ability as psychologists behind the scenes looked at character traits to distinguish serious-minded leaders with mental stability from wild adventurous types who wouldn't be trusted with a crew (not immediately anyway) but could be expected to fly combat and weapons delivery manoeuvres with the requisite handling abilities and quick thinking.

Whatever the selection criteria, I ended up flying fighters. Vigorous manoeuvring, tactical formation, air-to-air combat, gunnery and weapons delivery, flown in powerful, agile aircraft with one or perhaps two seats engendered a deep-seated team dynamic since aircraft frequently operated in tactical groups or formations where mutual dependence for skill and judgement was fundamental to success. And that was in peacetime. In hostile situations handling skills were taken for granted and tactical competence, keeping focus under fire and a determination to succeed were the key qualities. It could mean being destroyed in the air or having to bale out of a damaged aircraft and face capture by the enemy as so many aircrew experienced during the Second World War. It happened in 1991, during the First Gulf War, when John Peters and his navigator John Nichol baled out of a Tornado bomber over Iraq and were captured and tortured.

Back at Cranwell in 1958 my suitability for fighter operations was not immediately obvious as I moved on without further incident from basic circuits and landings to more advanced techniques. In any single-engine aircraft emergency drills will include instructions on what to do if the engine stops. Perhaps the first thing is not to worry too much. After all there's always the parachute in military aircraft and if you follow the 'forced landing' procedure in the *Pilot's Notes* (aircraft manual) with a bit of luck you will put the machine down in a large flat field with short grass that appears as if by magic just as the engine goes silent and the propeller turns lazily in front of you or stops. If that happens, the extra drag from a stationary propeller slows you down even more and descent rate increases. After I had convinced my instructor that I could land the aircraft, we moved on to dealing with system failures and emergency situations including engine failure or catching fire requiring a forced landing without power. Circuits without flaps simulated flap failure and circuits without using power from base leg onwards replicated the final stage of gliding to a forced landing. Both are practised regularly in any single-engine light aircraft for training and flight checks. Low level or 'bad weather' circuits were practised at about 500 feet to cater for a cloud base below standard circuit height, perhaps with poor visibility, using the compass and watch to fly an accurate downwind course and arrive at a good base leg position.

Even before going solo, such was the enthusiasm of most students that the instructor would commonly demonstrate simple aerobatics since vigorous handling can build confidence and motivate students to fly the aircraft to its limits. It is also exhilarating and enormous fun, although not everyone felt the need to gyrate and cavort in the skies to feel good. The underlying reason for training military pilots in aerobatics

We flew aerobatics early in pilot training. (*Courtesy Lee Howard*)

is pretty clear. In some roles the manoeuvring to position for weapons delivery can be intricate, requiring accuracy and aggression in the face of enemy resistance and enough spare mental capacity to make decisions, perhaps on behalf of formations of aircraft in co-ordinated attacks. After flying and teaching aerobatics I still find 'aeros' the purest and most exhilarating form of aircraft handling. It requires a sound knowledge of the handling characteristics and limitations of the specific type you are flying and in combat this can save your life.

In the RAF and at flying clubs there are five basic aerobatic manoeuvres that have been taught for many years in light aircraft – the loop, slow roll, barrel roll, roll off the top and stall turn. The criteria for accuracy in each manoeuvre are specified to enable the student pilot's ability and confidence to be assessed in the air and are applied equally in judging aerobatic competitions and displays from the ground. There are variations in the manoeuvres that have developed, for example in the US Air Force, but in military flying, whatever the measurement criteria, aerobatics are flown either to develop the confidence and skills of a pilot or for pleasure and demonstration to others. Each manoeuvre requires pilot inputs to the flying controls – elevator, ailerons, rudders and engine power – in a precise and co-ordinated fashion to achieve a predetermined flight path or 'shape in the sky', confirmed from inside the aircraft by pilots with a trained eye, or by observers on the ground. Any vertical element in a manoeuvre is flown in opposition to gravity going up, and with gravity on the way down, which constantly varies the engine power required for a specified speed and flight path, staying within airframe and engine limitations. Roll rate is controlled by ailerons and rudder deflections whose effects are dependent on airspeed which, in turn, is affected by attitude and power setting plus the drag of control deflections, so pilot inputs to the ailerons will vary for a constant rate of roll. When a rolling manoeuvre involves being briefly upside down staying level still requires the lift force upwards to equal the weight but the wing shape is designed for upright flight so the pilot has to push the nose up to present a greater angle to the airflow (angle of attack) to develop the required lift and stay level. You can see that with some set criteria for each manoeuvre – constant rates of pitch or roll and staying level are commonly used measures – the pilot has to constantly vary pressures on stick and rudder whilst adjusting engine power in a co-ordinated way using visual references to attain the required shape smoothly and continuously. Sounds complicated? Well it can be, especially when flying the more advanced manoeuvres but once again the intuitive resources in all of us come to the rescue under the guidance of a good instructor to make it easy, just like riding a bike – upside down.

The most effective way to understand aerobatics is to climb into an aerobatic aircraft with an instructor you like and try them, but I appreciate this is not something that is available, advisable or affordable for all. Perhaps a few words on each of the basic manoeuvres might remove some of the mystery. You can read the descriptions, close your eyes and imagine, have a granddaughter or grandfather hold a model that follows the pattern, go watch an airshow for real or on TV, or skip to the end. Take it from me, they are exciting and stimulating to fly. For those experiencing 'aeros' for the first time they can be intriguing, astonishing, even scary to begin with. After all, man was not designed to fly like a demented bird, or at all come to that, and doing so is something you will never forget. Also worth remembering is that these manoeuvres historically had the very practical aim of training new pilots to explore their own capabilities and those of the aircraft they might fly in a war.

Loop
The aim is to fly a perfect circle in the vertical plane at a constant rate of looping or pitch change. To start, you dive the aircraft with a high power setting – full throttle for a light aircraft – to attain the recommended speed (165 knots for the Provost) then progressively pull back the stick to start a rate of looping you expect to be able to maintain which will initially incur as much as 4 'g'. This means the force on your body is four times normal gravity which restricts blood flow to the upper parts, including the brain, and requires you to clench stomach muscles to counter the effect and avoid a blackout that would do little to improve your flying. 'G' suits that inflate automatically to withstand the effects are used when flying more advanced types. As you approach the vertical, gravity no longer works against the lift force from the wings, 'g' drops off, and stick force lightens to maintain the rate of pitch, the stick barely moving. But as speed falls control effectiveness also falls, so a little more elevator might

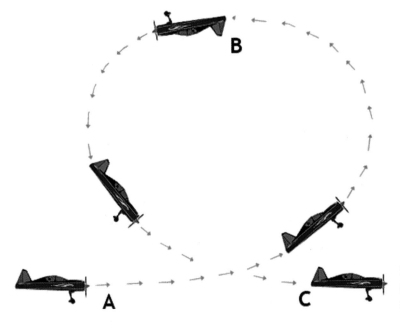

LOOP *RC Airplane.* (*www.rc-airplane-world.com*)

be needed to maintain the rate of looping as you continue to the upside down. A visual check left and right confirms whether you are pulling up straight, with wingtips in the same position relative to the horizon, but only when you reach upside down and see the full horizon again can a confident correction to wings level be made. Here you feel almost weightless as gravity briefly matches centripetal force to keep the aircraft travelling in a circle, then you are diving with increasing elevator stick force as speed increases and gravity takes over again, reducing power if necessary to avoid exceeding airspeed limits. The manoeuvre finishes as it started with a strong rearward stick force to combat gravity and a steady pull to the horizon with wings level. If it is flown well there may be a satisfying bump at the end as you re-enter the turbulent slipstream you left behind when you started. The loop is not difficult to fly but takes practice to fly accurately with forces and control pressures constantly changing to achieve constant pitch rate and a need to look out at visual references to check for a truly vertical circular flightpath.

Slow Roll

The aim is to roll slowly through 360 degrees maintaining rate of roll and height. In level flight gravity effects are constant and the challenge is to co-ordinate the use of aileron, rudder and elevator to avoid descending. The roll is started at cruise speed or higher by applying aileron with a little rudder for balance to avoid yaw. As the roll proceeds past 90 degrees the nose will drop, since lift from the wings is now only acting sideways and an increasingly high deflection of rudder – now controlling pitch – is applied to raise the nose to gain lift from the fuselage which now acts like a wing. At the same time, with speed dropping due to drag from a high angle of attack and control deflections, as the roll approaches wings level upside down the nose needs to be progressively lifted to a high inverted pitch angle to stay level. This means the stick goes forward progressively to achieve an angle of attack that holds level flight – quite a push, with the discomfort of negative 'g'. As the roll

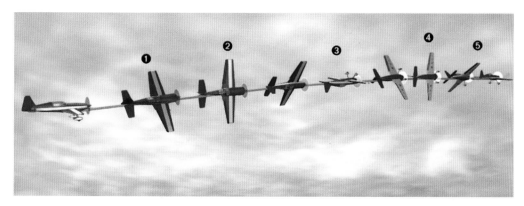

SLOW ROLL *RC Airplane.* (*www.rc-airplane-world.com*)

continues the rudder needs to be deflected the other way to keep the nose up and due to falling speed most of the deflection available is needed, perhaps full rudder on a light aircraft at these modest speeds. Large rudder deflection causes roll as well as yaw due to the advancing wing going faster and developing more lift which will increase roll rate and call for opposite aileron to keep the rate constant. So the manoeuvre finishes with completely crossed controls such that in a roll to the left it finishes with full left rudder and full right aileron speed having fallen. Airspeed has to be watched to avoid a stall which could introduce pro-spin conditions. This manoeuvre is a challenge to many pilots and takes co-ordination, confidence and vigorous but smooth control inputs to achieve the perfect result – all excellent for pilot training.

The advanced and more vigorous version involves stopping the roll at each 90-degree point ('four point roll') or at each 45-degree point ('eight point roll') requiring large deflections of rudder and aileron if the points are to be well defined. You'll commonly see them at airshows. Slow or hesitation rolls start from level flight, which involves significant negative 'g' that some pilots find uncomfortable as blood pools in the head and brain, causing 'red out' when blood vessels in the eyes expand. Commonly pilots crank up the nose a few degrees on entry in anticipation of the nose dropping during the roll.

Barrel Roll
The aim here is to smoothly describe a shape as if flying around the inside of a barrel with constant rate of roll and pitch, flying as much above the horizon as below in the course of the roll. It begins by diving with full power and at least 140 knots

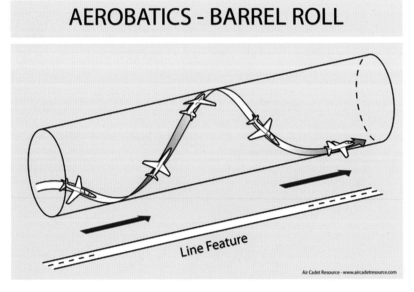

BARREL ROLL.
(*HQ Air Cadets –
6 FTS*)

in the Provost, turning gently to position on the imaginary circle, then reversing the turn, progressively turning and pulling up through the horizon where wings should be level, continuing to turn as the nose rises, reaching the upside down position at the top of the manoeuvre with roll continuing. The nose steadily drops back to the horizon as the roll continues, aiming for wings level when you get there. The idea is to fly an equal half circle below the horizon, arriving back to starting height with wings level again. It is a very pleasant, comfortable, lazy and relaxed manoeuvre where co-ordination of all three flying controls is required to achieve a symmetrical shape in the sky.

Roll off the top

The aim is to co-ordinate aileron and rudder to roll the aircraft to level flight position at the slow speed reached at the top of a loop calling for greater control deflections and care to avoid pro-spin conditions, especially for a beginner. This is one of several variations on the loop where the manoeuvre is modified by rolling during the climbing or descending portion of the loop to describe new shapes in the sky called variously Cuban eight, half Cuban, lazy eight, horizontal eight and a difficult vertical eight, where a second loop is commenced from a roll off the top, with another roll on completion to fly the bottom half of the figure eight This last manoeuvre requires a lot of power and is beyond the capability of most light aircraft.

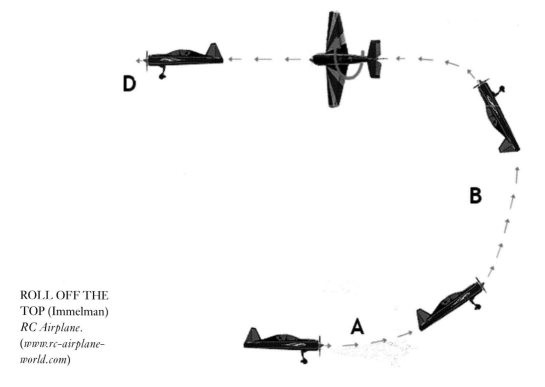

ROLL OFF THE
TOP (Immelman)
RC Airplane.
(*www.rc-airplane-world.com*)

Stall turn

The aim is to pull up to the vertical and execute a lateral 180-degree turn to point vertically down again, all in one vertical plane with a smooth, controlled, ideally constant rate of yaw. It begins by diving with full throttle, pulling to the vertical and holding it there by neutralising elevator, using visual references to check you are flying vertically. Just before the speed runs out progressive amounts of rudder are applied to yaw the nose smoothly towards the horizon, preventing any turn into a different vertical plane with opposite aileron. If you leave the turn too late the aircraft will 'tail slide' or do a 'hammer-head stall', pitching forward and down to the vertical and you have basically failed. Simultaneously – and this takes judgement as to how the yaw is going, if at all – power is reduced progressively to persuade the aircraft, which is now not actually flying, with very little airflow over the wings or control surfaces, to gently cartwheel through the horizon and back to the vertical when recovery to level flight completes the manoeuvre. This can easily go wrong without practice, since you are trying to control the aircraft with very little flying speed.

Mishandling in any aerobatic manoeuvre can create conditions for the spin I have mentioned which is the *bête noire* for young pilots flying solo aerobatics for

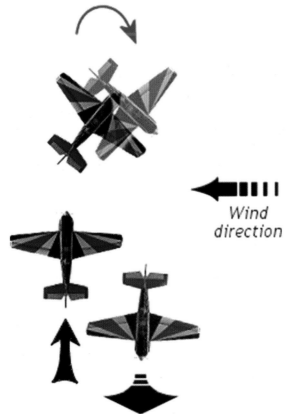

Wind
direction

STALL TURN. *RC Airplane.* (*www.rc-airplane-world.com*)

the first time. The spin is a fascinating phenomenon of aerodynamics which every military pilot is trained to recognise and recover from or, in some types, avoid as we shall see. But first let's briefly digress from learning aerobatics to talk about their impact at flying displays which is where many of you will have encountered them.

Airshows

So what are airshows about? Once you've managed to get into the show, after a hopefully good-tempered queuing experience along with a few thousand other motorists not in corporate entertainment parties, they continue to be a 'sharing with others' occasion as everyone looks up at the displays or down at the packed lunch if they're not already in the beer tent. Various photogenic flying machines, some noisy, some huge, some old, are flown by pilots practised at demonstrating the capabilities, individuality and attractions of their aircraft. I have a preference for the smaller local shows where the focus is on entertainment with a mixture of historic and modern aircraft, ideally topped off by the Red Arrows. But grand events such as the historic Farnborough Airshow, Fairford Air Tattoo or other international shows do have the attraction of assembling a greater diversity of participants and involve intense and important commercial exchanges. Displays here by the latest aircraft are designed to impress senior executives or military officers who have only read the performance specifications or seen a video and need the colour of an engaging in-flight demonstration, enhanced perhaps by a spot of corporate entertainment to refine their judgement.

Large aircraft usually do high-speed and low-speed flybys and demonstrations of manoeuvrability, with military types sometimes dropping things – pretend bombs (hopefully), parachutists, vehicles, flares etc. Helicopters perform unbelievable manoeuvres, demonstrating their amazing versatility in any environment, pretending to be aircraft – a caustic reflection on an early experience in the Whirlwind that convinced me it was a machine designed to shake itself apart and everything in it. Aerobatics are performed in every solo display where the aircraft will withstand the stresses on airframe and engine, so vintage types can be confined to graceful wingovers (turning whilst gently climbing), flybys and occasional mock air battles with more of these fascinating historic machines. Modern light aircraft that are designed for aerobatics gyrate with incredible and stomach-churning vigour – and that's just watching. They climb vertically, rolling continuously, until airspeed disappears and fall tail first or nose first into the next manoeuvre. When near the stall, rudder with opposite aileron applied quickly will cause a 'flick' to add excitement, and perhaps a spin towards the ground recovering briskly to continue the sequence. Flying level while upside down incurs uncomfortable negative 'g' and a loop flown from this attitude, pushing from inverted and known as an outside loop, is not for the fainthearted. Tail slide, Immelmann, Derry turn, eight-sided loop, Lomcovák further extend the repertoire, manoeuvres that you can look up but don't try without help! Much later in my flying career in a BAe Bulldog we performed the 'Prince of Wales' which meant pulling up to the vertical, initiating a stall turn one way but reversing to get the same angle from the vertical the other, still going up, then reverting to straight up and hammerhead stalling forward to dive away – some sort of salute with the three elements creating the Prince of Wales's feathers and a 'bow' at the end. It was vigorous for a student aerobatic sequence but no match for the spirited manoeuvres at today's airshows.

The jets are different. Their power, startling performance – climb rate, tight turns, speed, agility and very slow flight with everything hanging – are thrilling enough. But most impressive for me only a few years ago were the manoeuvres introduced by Russian display pilots when twin-engine fighters with new engine technology and computerised flying controls flew at virtually zero speed and high angles of attack past the crowd, pulled to the vertical with full power, slid backwards without the engines flaming out and accelerated away in afterburner with a roar – amazing at the time.

But things do go wrong and the results can be catastrophic, putting down a sombre marker for enthusiastic display pilots. The break-up of a prototype DH110 at Farnborough in 1952 killed thirty-one people, including the two-man crew, as sections of the engines and airframe ploughed into spectators. It was determined that the wings had less than the predicted design strength and parts broke off in mid-manoeuvre giving John Derry, a very experienced and skilful pilot, no chance. The aircraft did ultimately enter service as the Sea Vixen to enhance and develop the Royal Navy's carrier aviation capability. Over the years since then there have been many crashes, often with fatalities. In my RAF career I became aware that display flying can be very demanding and very exciting for the pilot to a point where effort, tension and professional motivation to give the best possible display can, albeit rarely, cloud judgement if only for a second. There is a pressure to continue with manoeuvres in a set-piece display, relying on practice, currency, and a repetitive routine that keeps the display tight and visible, allowing little room for error. It takes a highly disciplined and skilful pilot to recognise that something is wrong and instantly initiate a safe recovery, even abandoning the display with the loss of face and embarrassment that goes with it. This is something experienced display pilots and their supervisors are very conscious of, hence much practice in flying the display sequence and the need to demonstrate adherence to tight regulations before pilots are authorised to display to the public. But aircraft can, albeit rarely, develop faults and pilots can make mistakes. On 22 August 2015, at Shoreham Air Display, a Hawker Hunter 6 vintage fighter failed to pull out of a loop and crashed on the main A 27 highway near Shoreham Airfield killing eleven people and injuring sixteen. This was the worst airshow accident in the UK since the John Derry disaster. The pilot survived and, when he recovered from his injuries, faced an AAIB (Air Accidents Investigation Branch) enquiry which concluded that the accident was caused by pilot error, entering the loop too low and too slow. I have experienced the adrenalin rush of display flying which can help you give of your best but it is vital to know the limitations of the aircraft and of you and your colleagues and comply with regulations designed to ensure the public's safety but also the pilot's and that of the people they fly with.

Many of us have watched the modern aerobatic light aircraft capable of withstanding 10 'g' positive and 10 'g' negative gyrating at giddy speeds through an impossible sequence of manoeuvres ending in a wild tumbling spin with coloured smoke marking a haphazard spiral path towards the ground, only to snap into recovery and do it all again. A hazard for the unwary, the spin can be a highly controllable manoeuvre as fighter pilots in the Battle of Britain discovered. When outnumbered, they would escape from an attack by entering a spin which was difficult to follow and even more difficult to track with a gunsight. But in training it is treated with considerable respect, even apprehension by some.

The Spin

So what is a spin? The answer is not simple if you wish to penetrate the aerodynamics and physics involved, so we won't. Basic aircraft types with unswept wing forms usually exhibit similar characteristics and recovery is straightforward. Rarely, some types will be reluctant to recover depending on how they are entered, how they stabilise, the control movements made by the pilot and the position of the centre of gravity, affected typically by fuel state, or even overweight pilots. In training an intentional spin is entered by closing the throttle on approaching the stall in level flight and pulling the stick fully back whilst simultaneously applying full rudder in the direction you have chosen. The aircraft flips over and settles into a spin. In this condition one wing is stalled, or more deeply stalled than the other wing, to introduce a rolling and pitching combination that develops into a rapidly descending spiral known as 'autorotation'. The stalled wing is subject to higher drag forces than the other wing to introduce yaw and, with lift having broken down, it drops or rolls to make the angle of attack of the other wing less, augmenting its lift to further increase roll. Unlike a rapid descending spiral *turn*, which will respond conventionally to flying control inputs, the spin is a stabilised stall condition where deflecting control surfaces has abnormal effects that can prevent recovery and doing nothing can result in the aircraft spinning untidily into the ground. Most light aircraft respond to a standard spin recovery procedure which is to close the throttle, apply full opposite rudder to the direction of spin, push the stick steadily but firmly forward until the spin stops, centralise the rudder and recover from the ensuing dive, applying power as the aircraft enters a climb. This works for an 'erect' spin, i.e. flying the right way up at entry. For an inverted spin, which exhibits the same aerodynamic characteristics, the movement of the stick is backwards not forwards. Inverted spins are to be seriously avoided unless you are a display pilot. If during vigorous manoeuvring the aircraft suddenly lurches into what looks like a spin entry with an unsolicited flip over – an incipient spin – neutralising the controls and holding them there firmly can prevent most types from entering a full spin. Similar is the snap entry into a spin and rapid recovery which is the 'flick' manoeuvre flown deliberately by display pilots and, hopefully, not inadvertently by students.

It can take several rotations during an erect developed spin before full anti-spin controls take effect to raise the heart and breathing rate until they 'bite' and the recovery completes. Most pilots manage to avoid spins but they need to recognise when they are in one and apply the recovery actions specified in the aircraft flight manual. Once familiar with the spinning characteristics practising recoveries can instil confidence in the aircraft and in yourself, occasionally adding the excitement of wondering if it will in fact recover as you gyrate towards the ground. In the Provost course we were even put into a spin whilst practising instrument flying to see if we could recognise it purely looking at the dials, and recover. Today, spinning is not normally required for a UK Private Pilot's Licence but is likely to be at least demonstrated on any course to add an aerobatics endorsement to the licence.

Formation flying

I can recall in my first lesson on formation flying how impressive it was to see another Provost resplendent in its silver and yellow livery, apparently motionless against a blue sky, riding along on a cushion of air at 100 knots. Instructors from the world of fighters brightened as we began formation flying. My instructor no doubt flew his Vulcan bomber in formation on occasions but not perhaps with the vigour or enthusiasm of generations of fighter pilots but this did not diminish the exercise. So is it difficult? Not really. If flocks of birds can do it with consummate ease in their thousands why not us? It just takes co-ordination and practice to line up some visual references, a general sense of positioning in close proximity to another aircraft, and the overwhelming instinct to avoid colliding. It does, however, require concentration and a real feeling for the changes of power that go with manoeuvring in formation. This is taken to its ultimate in formation aerobatics that have a grace and satisfaction of their own, pretty much like a murmuration of starlings might feel wheeling and diving in their thousands as they create ever-changing shapes in the sky seemingly as one organism. That is what starlings do. For we humans, thinking as creatures pegged to the ground by weight and an absence of wings, formation flying does have the satisfaction of working with physics and forces but it comes down to a hands and feet thing in the cockpit.

The starting point is 'station keeping', which is staying in a set position in relation to another aircraft in flight. Elevator keeps you at the same height, ailerons and a touch of rudder on slower types maintain the horizontal spacing, and throttle or power matches the speed and moves you forward or back relative to the 'lead' aircraft. Defined reference points on the lead aircraft are lined up to establish a standard position for any aircraft of this type. So it might be positioning in echelon such that the lead's wingtip lines up with a feature or marking on his nose cowling, without wings overlapping,

The Provost in close formation. (*BAE SYSTEMS*)

using throttle and aileron to move in or out along a line forty-five degrees to the lead's fuselage, the references being unique to each type and to the shape of formation required. In line astern, the position is slightly below the lead to be outside the turbulence from the lead's airframe and propeller (or jet) wash, with good clearance between your nose and the lead's tail, especially if you have a propeller! The formations can be varied significantly both for operational reasons and for displays to show the versatility and skills of the pilots and the capabilities and performance of the aircraft. What is not obvious from the ground is how the laws of physics affect station keeping. If you are flying in echelon starboard (on the right of the leader) and he enters a turn to the left, you are flying around a circle of greater circumference than the leader, so flying further requiring greater speed to stay on station, which means adding power and climbing to maintain horizontal perspective relative to the formation and not to the ground. The technique when the leader turns towards you is simply the reverse – less power, turn tighter and hope you are not blinded by the sun having forgotten to lower your sun visor. All flying control movements in close formation are necessarily small, with changes in pressure on the stick more than movements, a guideline that applies across many aspects of flying where smoothness and economic use of controls leads to accuracy and, in airliners, to gin and tonics remaining in the glasses. But some military operations require flying the aircraft to the edges of the performance envelope where confidence and even aggression are somehow more important than comfort. In the RAF strict and consistent procedures, briefed in detail before each formation sortie, are the essence of safety and ultimately operational success. The formation leader is responsible for the safety of the formation and for achieving its objectives whilst in training each instructor is responsible for the safe flying of his own aircraft and the student with him. Once the student is flying formation solo the responsibilities of being a competent and effective member of a team become obvious to the student who has to grow up very quickly. I found formation flying intuitive, demanding, thrilling and, forgive the superlative, cool.

Instrument Flying (IF)

In all the flying discussed so far the pilot uses the visual horizon as the attitude reference. Instruments for airspeed, altitude and heading have been essential since the early days of manned flight which was mainly in good weather with a clear horizon. As aircraft performance developed pilots noticed that clouds are not unusual in our weather, nor is poor visibility, both of which obscure the horizon. Since the 1930s a gyroscopically-driven instrument for showing aircraft attitude with reference to the horizon has been added, followed quickly by indicators for balance, rate of turn, and rate of climb and descent. This set of six instruments in a cluster directly in front of the pilot has been the central feature of cockpit design for many years. It has developed as technology has advanced and today is incorporated into multi-function digital displays broadly referred to as the 'Glass Cockpit', with back-up from a standby attitude reference such as an artificial horizon as a minimum.

The glass (or acrylic) in the Provost merely kept the wind out and covered each of the instrument dials where the analogue symbols and numbers were depicted with luminous paint. Thin amber screens could be slid into place to cover windscreen and side panels which, when the student donned a pair of blue-tinted goggles, eliminated all visual cues except the luminous indications on the instruments. This allowed the instructor to see adequately through the amber screens for safety while the student flew purely on instruments. It was an extremely effective training aid, pitching the student into an eerie blackness with only the instruments showing up with white markings. Later methods of restricting the pilot's view during instrument training were typically a 'hood' or visor to remove any forward view of a horizon – in aviation jargon a 'view limiting device'. In the USAF I was to learn that it meant a white canvas curtain drawn around the windows of the back seat of a T-33 trainer aircraft characterised by Americans in their inimitable style as 'under the bag'.

The six flight instruments in the Provost for flying in cloud, poor visibility and at night comprised the gyroscopic artificial horizon (AH), in later types attitude indicator (AI), driven by a vacuum pump to show pitch attitude and bank angle; airspeed indicator (ASI) fed by pitot tubes measuring static and dynamic pressures from the oncoming airflow; an aneroid altimeter with a subscale to set the datum according to the atmospheric pressure for the day; a rate of climb and descent indicator, also known as a VSI or Vertical Speed Indicator fed from a differential pressure-sensing mechanism; and a direction indicator for magnetic heading known as a DI, later compass or heading indicator, later still integrated with other inputs to a horizontal situation

Instrument panel of Percival Provost T.1 WV562 at the Royal Air Force Museum Cosford showing the six primary flight Instruments.

indicator (HSI) and today part of computer-driven multi-functional digital displays in aircraft so equipped. The final instrument in the basic display is an electrically-driven gyroscopic turn-and-slip indicator comprising a needle or wings symbol to indicate rate of turn – not bank, although the two are linked depending on speed – and literally a ball lookalike moving in a fluid-filled curved lateral tube, such that flying in balance with no yaw centres the ball with rudder correcting any deviation. Flying out of balance in any manoeuvre apart from aerobatics loses aerodynamic efficiency. To learn more you need to study aerodynamics … .

The essence of manual flying in cloud with reference only to these basic instruments is to focus on the AH/AI and radiate out to each of the others in a regular scan, looking at them for as long as you need according to what you want the aircraft to do – stay straight and level, turn, climb, descend, or change airspeed or configuration. Good scanning, attention to trimming out residual stick forces and frequent attention to attitude is the secret of stable instrument flight in cloud. The confidence and comfort that come from practice and currency are essential when there is a task to be accomplished beyond simply handling the aircraft. In peacetime this includes radio communication with air

The rudimentary cockpit of Provost WV606 captures the environment in which student pilots of the 1950s worked. (*Courtesy Newark Air Museum*)

traffic control, following let-down procedures and reconfiguring the aircraft for landing with appropriate power settings, all of which can affect trim. Selection of services such as flaps, airbrakes (speed brakes for some) or undercarriage, when you have one, can shift the centre of gravity and change the lift force profile which, together with reductions in airspeed, can make the trim changes significant. Poor trimming will lead to difficulty when flying on instruments since the tiniest untrimmed residual stick force needed to hold the selected attitude can change that attitude quicker than the pilot can complete his scan should he be pre-occupied with cockpit tasks. This can all amount to a high workload for a single pilot, especially if that smooth, accurate instrument flying is found to be elusive, or there are distractions such as an aircraft emergency or being shot at. Flying on instruments, especially in controlled airspace, or in hostile environments, is perhaps the greatest distinguishing feature of professional flying compared with flying for pleasure, although there are many private pilots who add an Instrument Rating (IR) to their Private Pilot's Licence (PPL). Poor instrument flying can mean inadequate adherence to local procedures to create a danger to the pilot, his passengers and other aircraft whose pilots have to trust that everyone else in the system is competent – a key feature of the worldwide community of professional pilots and air traffic controllers. The advent of AFCS (Automated Flight Control System) and associated avionics has reduced the workload considerably but pilots must be able to fly using basic instruments and have their competence regularly checked. Unlike modern fighters, the RAF aircraft I flew had no AFCS and all cloud and night flying required continuous hands-on flying using the six basic instruments.

So let us return to the predicament of the tender young student learning to fly in this dark and cloudy environment in 1958. Wingless humans are not designed to fly, and certainly not without a visual horizon to look at as any half-intelligent bird will tell you. We are used to orientating ourselves using visual cues and by sensing forces or accelerations that tell us whether we are upright, are falling over, have already fallen over, or are not sure – a condition described as disorientated, perhaps due to medications, illness or one of those special parties from which a taxi home would be wise. The eyes are the dominant information source providing we can see enough. The vestibular system provides a sense of balance and spatial orientation whether standing still or moving and comprises a set of membranes in the ear that detect rotational and linear accelerations, transmitting messages to the brain to sustain control and balance in conjunction with eyes, muscles and limbs as we move around. Gravity is something we are pretty used to after evolving for a few million years and with feet firmly on the ground we can manage orientation pretty well with our eyes and ears, sensitive to weight acting vertically. The vestibular apparatus includes semi-circular canals containing fluid with hairs to detect motion of the fluid in response to rotational accelerations caused by nodding, head shaking, head tilting or linear accelerations such as flooring the car accelerator then stamping on the brakes as the police appear in the mirror. This is all jolly useful on the ground. When we fly, however, extra forces and accelerations are generated during manoeuvring that our bodies do not recognise. We can handle this pretty well using our eyes as we look at the horizon but take that horizon away and the vestibular system gets a little confused which can lead to an insidious phenomenon where a conflict arises between signals sent to the brain from the vestibular system and the information presented on the flight instruments, notably the AH or AI.

To illustrate, let's trace what happens during a level turn to the left in cloud with no horizon visible and orientation as to the in-flight attitude of the aircraft determined solely by reference to the flight instruments. As we enter the turn the head is tilted and the fluid in the semi-circular canals mounted laterally responds to the rotational movement by initially lagging behind due to inertia, moving the sensitive hairs that tell the brain 'I'm no longer upright'. When the rotation stops with bank angle stable, after some 20 seconds the fluid in the canals settles and no longer displaces the hairs and says to the brain 'I'm now upright with respect to the earth' which you are *not*, confirmed by AH/AI, heading indicator and turn needle.

There follows a detailed description of this phenomenon from a pilot's viewpoint. It might throw some light on why it is that pilots, usually flying alone, using basic instrumentation – which is rare in commercial flying – can sometimes lose control for no obvious reason and come to grief. But get ready to concentrate – I had to, to write it!

Once in a level turn the profile of forces on the pilot has adopted a new equilibrium. The turn is produced by tilting the lift vector from the wings to produce a centripetal force component necessary for the turn. The turn is kept level by using elevator to increase angle of attack such that the vertical component of lift again matches aircraft weight or the force of gravity. The force on you, the pilot, is now an increased lift force to balance gravity plus centripetal force, producing the 'g' or increased weight effect which is small at low bank angles and modest speeds, larger at high speed and high rates of turn. Along the longitudinal axis drag is increased with higher angle of attack and balanced by an appropriate power increase with throttle. The new equilibrium between the opposing forces perpendicular to the wings means you don't 'fall into the turn' as many fear when flying in a small aircraft for the first time and at low bank angles the 'g' is negligible. Think of a gin and tonic on a tray in front of you on the way to Majorca. It would be expensive and messy if it sloshed into the aisle every time the aircraft turned, and in fact it stays level in the glass parallel to the table and the aircraft wings – that is the physics.

If the rate of applying bank is less than two degrees a second – that is, very gently – the fluid and hairs do not register the rotation and say nothing to the brain, so bank can creep on unnoticed if you're not looking at the AH/AI often enough. When you do look at the AH/AI it shows bank when your brain says you are still wings level. When you roll the wings level on the instruments it feels like you are turning in the opposite direction and some pilots lean into the original direction of turn to compensate.

Rolling out from a turn to wings level magnifies the contradiction. You come out of the turn by rolling to wings level on the AH/AI. The fluid and hairs detect the rotation, lag behind and say to the brain 'I'm tilting right, no longer upright' which from habit the brain associates with turning right. During the 20 seconds or so that elapses before the fluid settles down again the instruments indicate that you are wings level, which you are, but the brain says you are turning right which you are not. Even when the fluid and hairs settle the mental contradiction can remain. In cloud, poor visibility, at night or whenever the horizon is indistinct, the most powerful orientation sensors – the eyes – can no longer be used to establish aircraft attitude with respect to the earth and this is the root cause of the problem.

These sensations of conflict between messages from the vestibular system and instrument readings in the absence of a horizon can be strong and cause a temporary degree of confusion, even disbelief in the instruments to interfere with accuracy and disrupt mental tracking of what the aircraft is doing. It can prompt erratic control movements to resolve the problem leading in extreme cases to disorientation and loss of control. Professional pilots are made aware of the phenomenon early in their training when the maxim 'always believe the instruments' is drummed into them when flying manually without autopilot. A rudimentary understanding of why the phenomenon occurs helps pilots deal with it routinely. Most pilots encounter the experience at some time in their flying career, perhaps when tired, under stress, or not 100 per cent fit for flight and forced by circumstance simply to deal with it. It is perhaps more likely to be a problem in single-seat aircraft where pilots are used to manoeuvring vigorously. Bank rolled on slowly when flying in cloud or without a clear horizon will not produce conflicting signals as readily as faster rates of roll and the guidance for pilots without recent practice is to turn very gently, limiting angle of bank to perhaps 20/30 degrees. The presence of two pilots, autopilots and the wing-levellers installed in some light aircraft can alleviate the problem. A similar effect can occur when accelerating or decelerating in level flight in high performance aircraft when sensations of climbing or descending can be induced by another element of the vestibular system, the otolith organs, that detect linear accelerations and gravity. This can lead to inadvertently yet instinctively lowering the nose as the aircraft accelerates rapidly with no horizon reference, perhaps during a night take off. The accidents that have occurred citing disorientation might well be related to the phenomena described here when pilots are unaware or out of practice. Distractions can also interrupt instrument scanning to create the problem as can undue reliance on AFCS that goes off line or malfunctions, forcing the pilot to revert to basic instrument flying.

I should add that this account of the problem comes from personal experience when flying aircraft of the 1960s and 1970s and is not offered as an expert analysis. It is also a simplified picture of what are complex responses of the human body to airborne disorientation, involving interactions between eyes, vestibular mechanisms and *proprioceptors*, which are defined by medics as sensory receptors in muscles, joint capsules and surrounding tissues that signal information to the central nervous system about position and movement. Pilots call this 'seat of the pants'.

For military pilots competence in instrument flying is a given although all pilots are regularly checked to ensure they are retaining the standards within tight margins. They have to fly in all weathers to fulfil their specific role – strike attack, air defence, transport, maritime, reconnaissance etc., potentially in hostile environments. Modern aircraft have sophisticated avionics to relieve the pilot of many of the demands of the 'raw' instrument flying described above. Advanced AFCS installations operate the control surfaces to maintain any selected attitude while the crew focuses on weapons-system management, interception and destruction of incoming missiles or aircraft identified as hostile. Navigation and descents and approaches to land can be flown using AFCS but all pilots, civil or military, are still trained initially to fly manually, using the six primary instruments, a skill they might have to revert to if the 'Glass Cockpit' fails or is damaged. The challenge for modern pilots is to stay sufficiently current in using such basic kit when forced by circumstance to do so if the AFCS fails or the weather is outside its design limits, perhaps in turbulence. Much of the practice and testing of professional pilots' instrument flying skills today are accomplished in full motion simulators but this, arguably, does not reproduce the psychological pressures of actually being airborne. The need to fly manually on basic instruments perhaps arises less commonly for fighter pilots than it did, but an awareness of the factors and occasional hazards involved, together with instrument-flying skills, are an essential part of his repertoire to fly safely and effectively, especially in combat situations. In private flying in the UK an intermediate rating – the Instrument Meteorological Conditions (IMC) rating – allows flight in cloud in certain types of airspace where separation from commercial traffic is guaranteed and strict regulatory constraints apply. Here there may well be aircraft that have only basic instrumentation and no automatic attitude control such that pilots flying on instruments must be aware of the 'leans' and stay current to avoid the problem.

***

My debonair flying instructor slid the amber screens into position and handed me the blue goggles as we embarked on an examination of 'Unusual Positions' (UPs) later modified – appropriately I thought – to 'Unusual Attitudes' although both are open to misinterpretation. Recovery from UPs is in part a follow up to the 'leans' story above since it anticipates the possibility of a pilot losing orientation in cloud completely and needing a 'beam me up Scottie' solution to get out of the situation (credit to *Star Trek* TV series). The instructor would gyrate the aircraft vigorously then choose an extreme attitude – climbing steeply with no power, diving turn with high power, stalling, even a spin if he had had a bad day – and hand over control. The simple recovery procedure was standard: level the wings with no 'g', i.e. elevator neutral; using the AH or AI, nose high – apply power and lower nose to the horizon, nose low – reduce power and raise nose to the horizon, believing the instruments, not your ears and brain responses, until things settle down straight and level. The spin is more challenging. It is recognised by feeling the spinning sensation, determining direction by the turn needle, and applying opposite rudder as per standard spin recovery, followed more than likely by a UP recovery. If the cloud base is low and you are approaching it without recovery a parachute ride is the solution – and good luck! Older flight instruments could suffer toppled gyros or power failure and show an 'OFF' flag which should help avoid a UP, but if you only notice this after you are in one then unless you are very skilled you may find yourself up a creek paddleless and again checking your parachute straps. After one particularly sweaty instrument training flight that included UPs, which I thought was productive if not impressive, I climbed out of the cockpit ready for encouragement only to hear 'Lloyd, if you can't fly instruments better than that you'll never make an RAF pilot'! Being the 'bolshie' sort I took this as a challenge and was to confound him with a standard of instrument flying that was to be my ticket to operating what were described in 1960 as 'Night All Weather fighters'.

With its VHF radio fit the Provost could fly in IMC which means in specified conditions of cloud or poor visibility. The aircraft would be talked down through the cloud by a ground controller using bearings requested from the pilot whose radio transmission produced a directional line on his screen, a bearing of the aircraft from his receiver. The line wobbled or disappeared as the aircraft flew overhead the airfield then re-appeared as it flew outbound. Using a watch and adjusting for wind, the controller could give headings to fly a predetermined teardrop pattern from the overhead with descent clearances down to 'safety height', calculated using local terrain or collision hazards, ensuring that the altimeter subscale pressure setting for the day was correct. The pilot would level out at this height and receive magnetic headings to steer for the field. If he missed it or the weather was too bad he could climb again and start worrying about his fuel state and diversion airfields that had been briefed before take off. This form of let down through cloud was known as a 'QGH'. It fitted into a wide range of 'Q' codes originating from 1913 as short form question to ships on position, identity etc. without requiring any specific language for radio communications which were in Morse code when first introduced. In aviation QTE is a 'true bearing' and QDM a magnetic heading to steer to the receiver station. Other significant aviation examples still in use are QNH, current atmospheric pressure at sea level set on the altimeter subscale to give aircraft height above that level in a given region, and QFE, pressure setting to show zero height on landing at a particular airfield. Today radio navigation has been widely overtaken by GPS (Global Positioning System).

There was a landing aid installed in the Provost known as Standard Beam Approach in which two radio signal 'lobes' were coded to transmit A in Morse for one lobe and N for the other to indicate left or right of the runway centreline line where they overlapped with a single tone. But it was not well regarded by operational branches of the RAF; neither was it well regarded by instructors or students and it was, as far as I remember, unavailable at the airfield from which we operated. So to my relief we didn't use it much since instrument flying had enough challenges as it was.

Over many years the primary source of advice to pilots to help them avoid bumping into each other in cloud – and out of it – has been radar. In 1960 radar in the UK was mainly for air defence or as a landing aid at major airports and not readily available to trainee Provost pilots. Collision avoidance was achieved using what in 1960s jargon was known as the 'mark one eyeball' and wartime experience impressed on pilots the need to look out all the time and not into the cockpit unless you had to. Wherever airspace is crowded there are documented procedures for transit, approaches to land and routes for departing airfields and the airspace around them that are monitored and controlled today by air traffic controllers using primary and secondary radar, and radio exchanges. Primary radar transmits a radio signal which is reflected back to indicate azimuth and range and hence position but not, reliably, altitude. Secondary radar uses a transponder installed in all aircraft flying in controlled airspace that is triggered by an interrogating ground signal to transmit the identity of the aircraft together with altitude information. It originates from military 'IFF' technology – Identification Friend or Foe – and has been dominant in conjunction with primary radar in enabling control and separation of civil and military traffic in peacetime operations. Now, new technologies such as inertial and satellite navigation systems can combine with advanced avionics to supplement or even replace radar. Onboard collision avoidance installed in many airliners has the potential to achieve ever greater standards of safety.

Navigation

As a pilot you should know where you are. It helps in finding somewhere to land before the fuel runs out and to remind yourself why you are up there. Are you going somewhere or just 'boring holes in the sky' as some would have it? In early solo flights it was wise to keep something identifiable in sight such as the airfield you just took off from. Look for some unmissable coast line to hang on to, a large river, giant cooling towers, that factory with the bright red roof, or the prominent railway line – you get the picture. But that doesn't work for long, and the techniques of air navigation have to be confronted to avoid the student pilot's nightmare – being lost – or worse, having to publicly admit being lost and prepare to face the shame and witticisms of fellow students.

Navigation is a historic challenge to humankind from seafaring adventurers exploring unknown lands to shouting down the diplomatic guidance from your Satnav. And so it was to Flight Cadet Lloyd in those early training days. I had been a Wolf Cub 'Sixer' and a Boy Scout Patrol Leader, so I had undeniable acquaintance, even confidence, with maps and compasses that should have stood me in good stead over the Lincolnshire countryside and surrounds. It did not. The problem was that I did not have the navigator's passion for calculating logically and calmly under pressure. What pressure? The pressure of getting lost as others arrived on time and on track at every turning point and destination – or so I thought. I later learned that basic air navigation is as much an art form as a process. Teaching starts with the study of changing wind patterns and directions with height, triangles of velocity to assess the wind's effect on the track and speed across the ground, then basic map reading – shades of sick bags in Varsities and Valettas.

There are of course many aircraft flying around and they are often not easy to see until very close, travelling at relative speeds that can be high for jets and more than 200 knots even for a Provost T.1. RAF teaching from the first flight was to look out of the window regularly and frequently to spot them before you hit them. This is not so easy in poor visibility, impossible in cloud and hard at night even with lights showing since they do not indicate range. Aircraft are therefore separated by height difference when cruising, that is flying straight and level. Barometric pressure varies at any height with the passing of weather systems such as the cyclones and anticyclones experienced in the UK. There are therefore 'Altimeter Setting Regions' that provide the lowest forecast sea level pressure for use by pilots known as a Regional QNH. QNH is commonly set when flying close to the surface in order to avoid high ground and obstacles, the height of which is indicated on maps as altitude or height above sea level. The altimeter uses an aneroid barometer to measure local atmospheric pressure changes with height, and by setting a datum pressure on a subscale incorporated into the instrument it indicates height above that datum pressure level, displaying this on the instrument face. QNH set for take off will show the height above sea level of the middle of that airfield. ATC will commonly advise pilots to set QFE on the altimeter subscale when making an approach to land so that the height indicates zero at touchdown. Monitoring clearance from any local high ground or hazards can be done in parallel with a second altimeter if fitted. As aircraft climb and fly over different pressure setting regions a common standard setting of 1013 millibars is used above a transition height specified locally with heights then designated as 'flight levels'. This ensures that all commercial traffic at cruising level is using a common reference.

The story of basic pilot navigation in the 1960s without onboard navigation aids continues. A flight plan is prepared for each flight, marking maps with true tracks to turning points and destinations on the map, then, with a simple hand-held analogue computer, determining magnetic headings to steer using the forecast wind speeds and directions at your planned height and true airspeed (TAS) as opposed to the indicated airspeed displayed in the cockpit. Timing along a stretch of track is determined by calculating head or tail wind to arrive at speed across the ground (groundspeed). Magnetic headings, adjusted for magnetic variation, are what you fly, as displayed on the heading indicator or compass, whilst track is the actual line on the map you want to fly along, the difference being 'drift' caused by the wind. This is all written down on the flight plan together with timings and markings on the map to help you deal with inevitable deviations from the planned tracks. Pioneering air navigators from the early days of flying dreamt up track correction wheezes to test the mental agility of the learner pilot as he tries to fly straight and level on a heading while holding a large map which hides the compass from view. The essence of these corrections is to get back on track from an identified point on the ground (fix) either by the next turning point or by the same time as it had taken to get off track from when you knew you were on it. Hope that's clear … .

The wizardry from past navigators to achieve this is the famous 'One in Sixty Rule' – I prefer *infamous*. It is not about the number of RAF pilots in a bar that don't drink but the fact that at 60 miles from a start point, if you are one mile off track, it means an error of one degree from your planned track. At greater or lesser distances along track you can interpolate to calculate a heading correction back to track or to fly to your intended destination, known respectively as double track error correction and closing angle technique. This is a very neat system but it has dependencies: you must fly on an accurate heading, with compass/heading indicator synchronised; your in-flight mental calculations must be accurate; you must maintain altitude and speed; and it's best to look out of the window to avoid colliding with other aircraft, even a colleague flying the same route – quite a lot to ask, I always thought. Failure to make the appropriate corrections risked departing even further from planned track, requiring even more drastic corrections, this time from an even less certain position. If you then discovered that the DI had not been recently aligned with magnetic compass (a wobbling indicator in a glass case floating in fluid) and that you had been steering the wrong heading anyway, a dilemma arose. Was it the wind that had been poorly forecast or your inaccurate flying and which correction would be appropriate? And why am I in this situation with my instructor in the right seat looking slightly amused as he drafted the trip report in his head that might suggest I never fly alone.

I was even more disheartened on a night navigation flight searching for my turning point of Kings Lynn when my New Zealander instructor (a stand-in for my regular instructor who was no doubt out in his staggering beautiful car with his staggeringly beautiful wife at a truly amazing party) laconically queried 'can you swim mate?'. 'Yes thanks.' I answered with a false cheeriness to which he replied, 'Well I bloody can't so get over the land!' I had drifted further off track to the north than I realised and was over the Wash – all down to trying to use the track correction techniques that didn't seem to work any better in the dark, with the lights of one town looking very much like any other. Perhaps I wasn't cut out to navigate myself around, perhaps I would need a navigator, perhaps I was destined for 'heavies'! This prospect jolted me into some serious study of geometry, drift calculation, closing angle technique and other dark navigator arts, and I got better. Just as well because I was to train many fast jet pilots navigating at 420 knots and 250 feet, and subsequently *ab initio* pilots in the RAF and at flying clubs at 1,500 feet and 100 knots without navigation aids.

We advanced to using radio bearings for navigation to cover flying in or above cloud which served to confuse the situation further for we trainee pilots as we endeavoured to draw 'cocked hats' using intersecting bearings from different stations whilst flying the aircraft. Only later did I learn to develop a situational awareness that integrated the many factors affecting pilot navigation derived from experience, commonsense and a sense of calm and confidence that comes with currency – hard to explain but natural to all we adaptable humans. In addition, avionics developed to confine these very basic pilot navigation techniques to General Aviation, which covers anything that is not a commercial airliner or military aircraft, and then to less sophisticated types without onboard aids, only to find that GPS is now available to anyone with a phone in range of a mast.

Flying at Night

My first experience of flying at night was magical. Outside the cockpit on a clear night the world is a panorama of twinkling lights with clusters to mark cities, towns and villages, a brilliant starscape stretching from one horizon to the other, any moonlight revealing a ghostly outline of the terrain. Inside the Provost cockpit is darkness relieved only by red and ultra-violet lights to light up the instruments and controls with dimmer switches to turn brightness down to a minimum to make you feel at one with a tiny vessel seemingly travelling the vastness of space, an ethereal experience akin to the spiritual. High above clouds the stars are even brighter, the moonlight shining eerily on a soft, silvery expanse of cotton wool hiding the world below to leave you alone with the grandeur of physics and light. The machine is insensitive and merely responds to the controls at your fingertips to become part of you, suspended in the blackness. It really was that kind of experience, and for the many hours I was to fly at night alone or with a navigator or student I never lost that sense of awe, even romance, immersed in this natural, physical wonderland.

Night circuits and landings in the Provost were not difficult. After all, you were just flying the daytime pattern but referring more often to flight instruments to achieve the heights, speeds, attitudes, and using runway edge and approach lighting for perspective of being high or low on the approach to land. It was introduced by a 'flare path demonstration'. The instructor flew level towards the landing point from a couple of miles out on final approach at perhaps 500 feet to show the changing perspective of the runway lights as he flew from low on an ideal approach path to high on the approach as he continued to fly level. To this day, lights are positioned near the touchdown point in various configurations to shine at specific angles to show the pilot on a straight-in approach whether the aircraft is low (red) or high (white) to provide a reference 'glide-path' angle suited to the aircraft, typically a red/white combination. Early tri-colour versions called angle of approach indicators (AAIs) had a green light to indicate a 3-degree glide-path but the red and white lights combination has become the most recognised international standard.

The night landing was no different from day as far as the Percival Provost was concerned but for the fledgling pilot not being able to see the ground as he tried to land was something to consider. The small landing light mounted on the undercarriage strut shone dimly in the general direction of the runway just before the flare but since the attitude for a three-point landing was nose up he had to look elsewhere for help. The approach was straightforward enough with the lead-in runway approach lighting or simply a red 'T' to show the threshold and runway edge lights to give direction and height perspective. Flare to just above the ground was judged using the peripheral cues of runway edge lights to achieve wings level and the correct height as power was reduced to reach the required speed and attitude for a hopefully gentle touchdown. If you got everything right the aircraft would sink gently to the runway without the dreaded bounce. As in daytime a bounce happens when descent rate is too fast with speed a touch high and heavier contact compresses the oleos and tyres to launch the aircraft back into the night sky close to stalling speed which threatens the embarrassment of an even heavier landing if nothing is done. What *is* done, and quickly, is to apply power sufficient to hold an attitude that sustains flying speed and avoids a stall, then gently lower the aircraft back to the runway – if it's long enough. If in doubt initiate a full-power climb away on instruments to try again. By the time a student had reached the night-flying phase any attachment to repeated bouncing had usually either bounced the student off the course or been trained out of his psyche.

The chances of a successful forced landing in the event of an engine failure were limited since fields have no lights in them and cannot be identified as fields, just uniform darkness unless the moon appears. If you were lucky enough to be over an active airfield with its lights on then the daytime pattern might work. But the options were a bit stark, and tightened parachute straps and engine tests prior to take off took on more significance. Flying in cloud at night, which we did very little of in the Provost, is an eerie experience with aircraft lights reflecting back off the cloud to cause a distraction, especially in close formation which, somewhat surprisingly, is practised by some, notably in the USAF, as I was to discover. Visual navigation, as I have hinted, was for me a dark art anyway but techniques at night were no different, just a question of deciding whether very similar looking clusters of lights were your turning point or not. I felt I should have been forgiven for having taken my non-swimming instructor from New Zealand out over the Wash after missing Kings Lynn when you look at how many towns surround the Wash and it is hardly a conventional coast line, which I might just have spotted – well that's my story.

Low Flying

In marked contrast to the mysteries of the dark, the serious business of instrument flying and a need for the skills of an albatross to navigate, low flying was *fun*. The sense of speed, even at 120 knots in a Provost was noticeable at 500 feet where the exercise typically began, and more so at 250 feet which was as low as we flew. Height above the ground is maintained visually with the altimeter set to show height above sea level (QNH) which does not change with undulating ground and might show 250 feet as you fly over a 200-foot hill, 50 feet above the ground. Looking out of the cockpit is vital to avoid bumping into hills, pylons, other aircraft etc. and the map used for low flying in the UK is covered with annotations of areas over which you are forbidden to fly on pain of prosecution as a civil pilot, or court martial for a military pilot, depending on whether it's a live-firing range in action (big) or bird sanctuary (not so big unless you are a bird). Navigation is different, not so much in the flight planning as in the range at which you can see ground features that are less recognisable when seen from an oblique angle. Tracks can be related to features distinctive enough to provide a fix but can also be routed directly to such features from which less obvious points can be found by simple dead reckoning using winds, speeds and headings just like ancient mariners – but a bit faster. Winds at low level are less predictable than at 2,000 feet and above where our early navigation exercises in 'Pigs' were flown. This is due to surface friction that reduces wind speeds and changes their direction, especially near undulations in the surface terrain or near rain showers, where gusts and downdrafts can change the local wind significantly. An effective demonstration when learning the effects of wind at low level is to pick a day with a strong surface wind and fly a figure of eight relative to features on the ground, then watch the student try. Rates of turn have to be constantly varied to avoid being blown off the required pattern, accelerating or decelerating across the ground as the wind changes from headwind to tailwind.

The Provost was sturdy with a good performance for its time but still a light aircraft that could be subject to turbulence in hilly areas. To be avoided in aircraft with limited power is flying through a narrow valley with cloud sitting on the surrounding hills and no visible exit route as the ground ahead rises. Limited engine power could mean that a turnabout is impractical and climbing into the cloud means sight of the ground disappears – so might you if it's hiding a tall hill. Faster aircraft are less affected by wind which makes navigation with map and stopwatch easier and they have the power to escape clouded valleys but everything happens that much faster.

Throughout the year's basic flying course life as an officer cadet continued with days split between academics and flying. Social life during the week was confined largely to male pursuits since there were no female cadets until 1970. These pursuits ranged from preparing kit for the next parade to academic study and comparing notes for the next assignment or parading for 'Strikers'. This was the jargon for a succession of parades during evening hours as punishment for some misdemeanour such as blanco on the brasses, a dirty rifle or inadequately polished boots, all clearly vital for the defence of the nation. There was much sport, such that those with talent could take advantage of superb facilities and carry on where they left off at schools where sporting ability was developed as part of education. At Wandsworth Grammar I played rugby fives, second eleven rugby and chess, all without distinction. At Cranwell I preferred flying to any other activity and for sports sessions a like-minded friend and I opted for rowing which was the least supervised sport and where taking sandwiches and a bottle of wine to laze by the river attracted no attention. The key non-flying, non-academic non-sporting activity was either moping about missing girlfriends, guardedly relating what the last scented and very private letter said, or making arrangements for the weekend to meet local girls. Retford Teachers' Training College (alas no more) and a dance hall called The Sherwood Rooms in Nottingham (gone posh) were the main targets. Occasionally it was planning a sortie to London and deciding where to meet for warm-up drinks and which party to go to.

People did get chopped for many reasons. Some found they did not have the aptitudes and skills for military flying and were in some cases more suited to the civil world. Some found the airborne environment psychologically uncomfortable or stressful and couldn't deal with the pressures of training. Some did not match up on OQs (Officer Qualities) or academics and just didn't make the grade. Failing check flights was the route to failure in pilot training but there were options to retrain as a navigator or for other branches of the RAF. My abiding image to epitomise a fear of failure was walking out to the Provost on a cold winter's morning, grass crackling with frost, completing external and cockpit checks, then trying, unsuccessfully, to start the Leonides engine before my instructor arrived. It required pulling up a lever to load and fire a cartridge that cranked the engine, pressing a priming button at the right moment before and during start (bit like using a choke in a car) whilst setting the throttle in an attractive position to catch the engine if and when it fired. The fact that this might be the fifth or sixth week of Lincolnshire fog since this engine had run and this morning was still foggy with minimal chances of actually flying might have played their part in putting the Leonides in a bad mood. But the ignominy of failing to start up as my instructor strolled towards the Provost after leaving a warm instructor's crewroom was painful. All around me were the noises and smells of every nearby Provost as they thundered into life in throbbing chorus in the cold morning air and warmed up exuding that intoxicating smell of aviation fuel. But timidity was not a good recipe for success and when the instructor couldn't start it either, lamely suggesting I might have 'flooded it' (overfuelled by over-priming) when in fact it just didn't like the weather, I looked blankly out of the window pretending to hide a grin that was short of 'smug' but visible to the instructor. OK if he had a sense of humour, risky if he was having a bad day, and was cold … .

The Percival Provost was a very pleasant aircraft to fly and a successful trainer designed to be more difficult to operate than its predecessors in anticipation of the rapid growth in performance of jet aircraft. I never saw an assessment of my performance on the Provost basic pilot training course. There were 'Handling Tests' that paved the way for a working life of constant testing even after training but I have blanked out most of them as nerve-racking experiences that forced you to produce your best under the spotlight of 'he who could bring your flying ambitions fluttering to earth' – failure being anathema to most pilots and most people. You will have gathered I passed and was destined to fly the de Havilland Vampire jet.

The de Havilland Vampire

For most of us, a jet is either the shiny machine that carries us quietly and smoothly on holiday or an exceptionally noisy machine that rushes around airshows and impresses us with its power, manoeuvrability, speed and fuel consumption. Inside, even in full afterburner (reheat for the older reader), all is conversation quiet, although if the

De Havilland Vampire. (*Courtesy Cameron Sys*)

pilot is pulling 9 'g' the conversation becomes a little stilted. The Vampire cockpit was certainly much quieter than the Provost with its throbbing nine cylinders firing in sequence, vibration from the propeller and wind noise from an unpressurised, unsealed cockpit. Side-by-side seating, a development of the single-seat version, was cosy, especially when fitted with ejection seats as were those at Cranwell, and pilots virtually took turns to breathe. It was powered by a Goblin 35 engine that used a centrifugal compressor, an early development of Sir Frank Whittle's 1937 design for one of the first turbojets to fly. It developed 3,200 pounds of static thrust at ground level, measured with no forward speed.

A major difference from the Provost was a slow rpm response to throttle from idle. Jet engines developed the greatest thrust in the top 10 per cent or so of the rpm range with a need to spool the engine up slowly to avoid over fuelling, meaning throttle movement had to carefully track rpm increase. Open the throttle too quickly for initial take off and the engine protested alarmingly with a loud shuddering that could loosen teeth, rapidly send JPTs (jet pipe temperatures) over the limit and stall the compressor, resulting in no thrust at all. Careful throttle opening was quickly learned. Another consequence of this characteristic was a need to set a minimum rpm on approach to land to ensure a quick response to throttle when extra thrust was needed, especially in turbulent conditions. Piston engines give an immediate rpm increase in response to throttle like a car, producing instant thrust from the propeller. The design of the jet requires feeding in fuel at a rate to match the increase in the mass of air passing through the engine in exactly the right ratio and acceleration is constrained by engine

The T.11 with side-by-side seating. (*BAE SYSTEMS*)

design. Increases in thrust are therefore not instant but progressive with rpm increase. Today's designs allow the pilot to 'slam' the throttle fully open to maximise the rate of thrust increase with fuel/air ratio controlled automatically. Do consider buying a more comprehensive and knowledgeable explanation of the jet engine for bedtime reading if curious, but it may be a thickish book.

Slow engine wind up for initial take off was OK with a long runway, but could create a little tension when taking off again after a 'touch and go' ('roller' in the 1960s RAF) from a short runway, especially if you had landed a tad long. But, after take off, the power of the jet engine was exhilarating as speed simply kept on rising to a climbing speed of 250 knots to Mach 0.6, the ratio of true airspeed to the speed of sound in the local atmospheric conditions, notably the ambient temperature. The Vampire handled beautifully despite having none of the power-assisted flying controls of later jet aircraft that I flew. It was responsive, fully aerobatic and could reach 30,000 feet in twelve minutes and 40,000 feet in twenty minutes where the engine was running out of puff. It was also very quiet, almost as though you had left the sound behind you, which in later types you did.

Landing the Vampire for the first time after flying with a propeller was a smooth, quiet affair, flying the aircraft over the runway threshold in a gentle descent at 105 knots, checking the descent just above the runway, and reducing power to 'fly it on' with elevator barely moving, to achieve a controlled touch-down on the two main wheels compared with the Provost's three points. The technique of flying it on while reducing power to idle by touch-down meant that the weight of the aircraft and softer undercarriage oleos made a bounce unlikely. The nose wheel was allowed to sink on to the runway and braking could commence using a stick-mounted brake lever (bit like a bicycle brake lever turned into the vertical) distributing braking to the main wheels using the rudder pedals. The circuit and approach to land were straightforward, provided you remembered to lower the undercarriage, having flown with the Provost's wheels permanently down and locked. Most important when turning finals to land was to be sure to set a minimum RPM of 5,500 (max was 10,650) to obtain a quick enough response from the engine to counter a loss of airspeed and, at worst, an incipient stall, which could result in a very noisy and uncomfortable arrival short of the runway or, as we say in the business, a crash.

Practice landing patterns simulating an engine failure were regularly flown, gliding at around 170 knots into a descending spiral over the airfield, with key target heights to arrange for a speed over the runway threshold sufficient to avoid landing short and low enough to avoid running off the end, ideally close to the normal 105 knots if that could be arranged. It did, of course, rely on the good fortune to find an airfield within gliding range when it happened. The alternative was ejection using the Martin Baker Mark 3B ejection seat that relied on the thrust from a 50 feet-per-second explosive ejection gun that would risk back injury. Later seats used more progressive rocket thrust. It could be used down to minima of 200 feet and 120 knots. The pilot's legs were restrained by cords that pulled the legs to the seat on ejection to avoid losing them on exit or having them blown apart by the airflow after leaving the aircraft at what could be very high speed. Time-delay mechanisms and a barometric device prevented deployment of the parachute if speed or altitude were too high. The whole sequence from pulling the blind over the pilot's face to initiate ejection to full chute deployment was automatic, but there was an override 'D Ring' should the pilot have any doubts.

My instructor surprised me one day after discussing re-lighting a flamed-out engine by inviting me to close the main fuel supply cock. As the engine ran down and the Vampire became a glider he talked about the reliability of the engine re-light system which we were hopefully about to demonstrate. Happily the engine restarted. He had recently been flying with the RAF's 2nd Tactical Air Force in RAF Germany, notorious for a spirited, gung-ho attitude to flying, possibly a product of the fatalistic mindset originating in low expectations of survival during the Second World War reinforced by the threats of a third world war, which all of us in the 1960s lived with. The result of feeling that life could be curtailed sooner rather than later was a fun-seeking approach that disguised a dedicated commitment by a highly professional military to counter the Soviet threat.

Emergencies' training is an integral part of any type conversion but the main focus in the Vampire course was to explore a flight envelope that manifestly extended the

The Vampire jet was popular with pilots used to piston-engine fighters. (*BAE SYSTEMS*)

Provost experience to prepare for more advanced aircraft coming into service. With a maximum sea level speed of 350 knots rising to 455 knots above 10,000 feet, 'g' limits of plus 6 and minus 3.5 and well-balanced controls it was a magical experience at that time. Aerobatic manoeuvres were executed easily, even lazily, with plenty of power to sustain steady pitch rates during 4 'g' pull ups for loops which were longer in duration and took up more sky than the less powerful Provost. All the basic aerobatics were eminently flyable to include loops, barrel rolls, slow rolls, Derry Turns, stall turns, rolls off the top, Cuban eights and so on.

Spinning was exciting in the Vampire. It was a fast rotation and had a significant pitching element quite unlike many types I was to subsequently spin. In most aircraft the spin is a vigorous manoeuvre that the unfamiliar can find stomach-churning, even scary, until they learn how to recover, which in the Vampire was happily to use the conventional standard recovery procedure. On some types I flew spinning was not practised due to the unpredictable behaviours of the aircraft observed during flight testing at Boscombe Down prior to entering service, or deduced from the unfortunate experiences of pilots failing to recover after it entered service.

Formation flying in jets requires the same basic techniques as for lower performance types. But there are differences. The piston engine gives an instant power response with an immediate 'bite' of the propeller, especially with variable pitch which adjusts the angle at which the propeller blades meet the oncoming airflow to optimise the ratio of lift to drag. Reducing power quickly brings an immediate drop in rpm and thrust, the propeller now acting like an airbrake, and immediate deceleration. Jet aircraft even with straight wings are more streamlined and heavier, thus sustaining momentum. The Vampire maximum all–up weight without stores (bombs rockets etc.) was 11,194lb while the Provost T.1 was some 4,400lb. Higher speeds mean higher drag (increasing at the square of the speed) so power increases with early jet engines brought a smoother, less immediate speed increase for station keeping. Later, with more powerful engines, this effect became less noticeable. But the higher operating speeds also meant greater inertia which, combined with a lower drag profile, meant that reducing power to move backwards to stay in position needed more anticipation. I discovered this during an early solo formation sortie when joining up on my instructor leader just after takeoff. The technique was to establish an overtaking speed, judge the closure rate to synchronise speed on arriving most commonly at the echelon position, slightly behind the lead aircraft, using airbrakes if required. If overtake was too high the 'escape route' was to descend to just below the lead aircraft keeping him in view as you gently bank away from him and try again. Inexperience led me to realise rather late that I was closing too fast and I instinctively pulled up and away in a steep banked climbing break to avoid collision. This was effective but dismayed the leader as he looked at the underside of a Vampire 'close enough to count the rivets' he recounted later in a rather serious debrief.

Single-seaters in formation. (*MOD Crown Copyright via RAF College*)

The effect of inertia is more prevalent at higher altitudes. The aircraft handles in response to indicated airspeed, which means to the pressure of oncoming air due to speed or dynamic force from the airflow, with the static pressure element taken out of the calculation within the instrument. Indicated airspeed drops off as you climb due to falling air density but in the thinner air the aircraft also goes faster at a speed defined as True Airspeed (TAS). So at 40,000 feet the speed on the ASI might be 250 knots, but TAS around 450 knots. Airliners fly high to take advantage of this phenomenon and because fuel consumption is markedly less at height. It also means, incidentally, that speed across the ground will be this value adjusted for windspeed which at high altitude can reach 200kts in a jet stream. Since kinetic energy is a function of mass and the square of speed, in this case TAS, closing the throttle at 30,000 feet does not slow the aircraft very quickly relative to the lead aircraft, nor does an airbrake work as well in less dense air. I found I had a natural aptitude for formation flying as did several others on the course and instructors recognising this were happy to fly simple formation aerobatics with students on each wing – a demanding and exhilarating experience at 20 years old, so exhilarating that I'll digress for a moment to look at it more closely.

Formation aerobatics are not a terribly useful fighting tactic; in fact I cannot think of a more attractive target for an enemy pilot having a bad day than nine or more aircraft packed tightly together concentrating not on you but on each other. However, display teams do present the skills of a nation's pilots and the handling virtues of their aircraft. They are also effective in portraying pilots as flying ambassadors with team members chosen, one assumes, for their good looks as much as their formation skills – or so hiss the unchosen.

Formation aerobatics have been a spectacle to fascinate crowds since the days of the RAF Hendon air displays and 'Pageants' of the 1920s with their Avro 504s, Hawker Harts and Vickers Vimys. The large jet-fighter formations of the 1960s and '70s set the scene for a proliferation of national aerobatic teams with the RAF Red Arrows setting the standard (I'm biased). With safety of the crowd and display aircrews paramount, following some early disasters, there is a tight regime of regulations and currency requirements for participating teams in their preparation and work-ups. The weather on the day is critical in deciding on a 'flat' show – no looping manoeuvres to take the formation into cloud for more than a few seconds – or a full show under the cloud base. Surface wind can blow the whole display away from the crowd, or towards it, and this means the leader has to compensate by tightening or easing the rate of turn and adjusting looping manoeuvres during the manoeuvre to stay on the display line that avoids flying over the crowd and presents them with a good view. Good displays are required to be as close to the crowd as possible, meaning tight turns that are manageable by aircraft and pilots on the edges of a formation where those on the outside of a turn need to use more engine thrust than the leader and those on the inside less. Each display has been rehearsed to reliably reach reference heights and speeds to make the display smooth and flowing for all pilots, with the leader's flying ability and radio calls critical for a safe and spectacular show. He must fly smoothly and predictably as he pulls tight turns and looks over his shoulder for orientation while avoiding any sudden movement of the control column which would ripple through the formation to disrupt the symmetry. And his radio calls to the team need to be crisp, short and the same each time to have the team execute the command together. Other factors include judging the rate of pitch change and 'g' loading for each vertical manoeuvre to avoid significant cloud and, on the descent, to stay above a minimum height cleared for the display. It requires a very special pilot to do this job and someone who has flown in a team and knows the demands on pilots in each position. Among the most famous leaders of the Red Arrows was Ray Hanna with whom I had the privilege of flying on several occasions to observe the master for myself from the back seat of a Gnat. But this was beyond my imagination as I focused on making the grade of RAF pilot in a Vampire T.11.

The Vampires we flew had just a simple VHF radio and navigation was by map and stopwatch with steers and bearings for fixes. Instrument approaches were by QGH or a radar-monitored descent into either an ACR-7 radar approach to the runway or by precision approach radar (PAR). For an ACR 7 the controller provided headings to

The distinctive twin-boom Vampire was photogenic in 1960. (*BAE SYSTEMS*)

steer to maintain runway centreline and advisory heights for each range he provided, to fly a 3-degree approach path. In a PAR approach the glide-path was displayed on the controller's screen enabling him to advise the pilot to increase, decrease or maintain his rate of descent. The instrument final approach configuration when descending through cloud was 30 degrees of flap, undercarriage down and 140 knots. When the runway came into view at maybe a mile or two, depending on cloud base and visibility, more flap was lowered and speed progressively reduced to arrive over the runway at threshold speed.

During basic training students were not let loose on their own when there was a significant 'crosswind' which means that component of the surface wind at an airfield that blows at 90 degrees to the direction of landing. To fly along the centreline of the runway the pilot must introduce a correction to counteract this wind component blowing him sideways. Basic students were taught the 'crab' technique which meant an approach to the landing with the aircraft heading into wind at an angle to the runway sufficient to maintain the centreline, then 'kicking it straight' just before touchdown. Kick off the drift early with a few too many knots and the aircraft will not settle on the runway but head sideways for the grass as the crosswind takes over and it's full power for a 'go around' and another try. Fail to take out the drift and you may lose or damage the undercarriage which is designed for travelling forwards not sideways. The use of rudder requires opposite aileron to keep the wings level and avoid a wing striking the runway which would also have consequences. The stronger the crosswind the more challenging the landing which is why aircraft have crosswind limits, as do pilots during training. Another technique used by some more experienced pilots in certain aircraft types is the 'wing down' technique. Here the pilot turns the aircraft into wind with bank according to the strength of the crosswind component whilst applying opposite rudder to maintain the runway centreline, flying rather awkwardly out of balance. At touch down one wheel will touch first with rudder then centralised or used to control direction as normal. These techniques are routine and in everyday use by pilots, sometimes in combination, but in limit conditions it takes high concentration and for lighter aircraft a second attempt can be wise if the wind gusts threaten to disrupt a safe landing. So when you arrive back from the sunny Costa Brava to a wet and windy UK airport have respect for the pilot who plants the aircraft firmly, even very firmly, onto the runway and establishes safe three-wheel ground contact, which gives him immediate nose-wheel steering and will break through any surface water that might cause aquaplaning when braking and steering are reduced. This might be more likely in a comparatively light fighter jet than a large airliner but when operating near the design cross wind limit these factors come into play. 'Just part of the job' is what most pilots will say, and I would worry if they didn't!

Life at Cranwell in the third year was still challenging with some cadets faltering and re-streaming to navigator training. But for most the refreshingly friendly approach of advanced flying instructors, many of whom were not much older than we were, was to make us feel part of the piloting fraternity. They came out to the pub with us to sing songs and took us on Staff Continuation Training sorties where they revisited their low-level ground attack profiles learned in the Tactical Air Force in Germany from which most had come. The **d, p** and **b** continued but we were the senior entry and were treated as such in expectation of passing out, for which read graduating with a ceremonial 'Passing Out Parade'. We duly passed out in July 1960 with the enormous privilege of having as reviewing officer Her Majesty the Queen.

As I write, RAF pilots receive about four months elementary training to include flying the Grob Tutor aircraft (being replaced by the Grob Prefect), then for those streamed to fly fast jets twenty-one months flying the Tucano (being replaced in 2019 by the Beechcraft T-6 Texan 11), amassing some 300 flying hours before training on the type each pilot is destined to fly, typically another seventy hours. The process takes at least two years and often more while waiting for allocation to a course. The coveted pilot's wings or brevet is awarded at the end of the Tucano/Texan course. In 1959/1960, I flew 150 hours on the Provost and 130 on the Vampire, taking two straight years with wings awarded on graduation. My posting was to the 'Night All Weather Fighter' role which meant the Gloster Javelin FAW Mk 9. It was a tribute to my first flying instructor's caustic comments on my early instrument flying that prompted a determination to prove him wrong and set me on the road to very good results in that department, essential to success in air defence operational flying.

These were the very early days of jet fighters. The Me 262 and then the Gloster Meteor proved the concept and the rapid increases in performance were to transform professional aviation. But there were setbacks. In civil aviation the unhappy story of the de Havilland Comet which suffered three fatal crashes in twelve months due to metal fatigue indicated that there was a great deal to learn about operating in this new environment. The Comet did not perhaps have the success its imaginative designers deserved and the Boeing 707 arrived to take jet transport to airlines worldwide and lead the market for some years. The development of military jets was driven predominantly by an arms race. It meant that timing for newly-developed RAF jet fighters to enter service was driven by urgent operational need, not necessarily when their designs had been adequately refined ... .

***

20 Jun 1963 RAF Akrotiri Cyprus

We'd briefed for a pairs take-off, so I lined up my 29 Squadron Javelin Mk 9 in the number-two slot, wound up the two Armstrong Siddeley Sapphire engines against the brakes, and watched for the leader's hand signal. Brakes release, up with the power and we're rolling – 80, 90, 100, 110 knots, nose wheel coming off, and BANG. A loud graunching noise behind me, lots of smoke and a smell of burning, loss of thrust, then loud cracks as rounds from two loaded Aden 30mm cannon cooked off and whistled across the airfield at a rapid rate. I had suffered a catastrophic engine failure attributed to 'centre-line closure' where the compressor blades fouled on the shroud surrounding them and became detached, causing the engine to disintegrate. More common when flying into cumulonimbus clouds with rapid cooling, this episode was at high ambient temperatures with the blades under maximum strain on reaching full power. Why it happened was somehow less important than saving the respective rears of my navigator and me from the burning aircraft as I managed to bring it to a stop. The somewhat unsophisticated engineering fix was an abrasive coating on the shroud to 'sandpaper' the blade tips and coax them into becoming a little shorter rather than breaking up. My navigator and I leapt some twelve feet or more off the wing and got away with it. The aircraft didn't and was a write off.

Was this incident a surprise? Well it was when it happened! But failures were by no means unheard of in those early jets. There were military and commercial pressures to bring ever more advanced aircraft into service at a time of confrontation between the West and the Warsaw Pact with air forces on both sides expanding rapidly. Inevitably, aircraft came into service with unresolved design problems that today would be eliminated with computer-aided design and sophisticated testing. Knowledge of materials, fatigue life, engines, avionics and the many other aircraft systems advanced quickly, much of it coming from failure reports and accidents. The need to stay ahead of the enemy brought a relentless demand for more performance, more lethality, more

I inspected the damage to the Javelin after the explosion.

operational effectiveness and, of course, more value for money. The result was that aircraft were in some areas of design still in their experimental or developmental stages as they came into the hands of RAF pilots.

***

The wise men of the Ministry had decided that no first tour pilot could possibly handle a nineteen-ton monster that came with two engines and a navigator and live. They would first have to fly the dream fighter of all time, the Hawker Hunter, for three months at the holiday town of Barnstaple in sunny Devon to come up to speed. You can imagine the response of two Cranwell colleagues on the course and myself – 'Oh well, if you *insist*', with a poorly disguised whoop of *Hoorah*. It might have been Air Ministry (now MoD) caution, even guilt (no, perhaps not), at putting tender young pilots into new fighter aircraft whose designs were incomplete, judging by the accident and incident rates reported in the RAF's monthly magazine *Air Clues* and the rate of aircraft modifications. Most likely was the perception of MoD boffins emerging from the age of propellers that entrusting modern, highly expensive hardware to naïve, over-enthusiastic pilots who didn't know better would be embarrassing if they crashed. Later selection of first tour pilots to fly the Javelin's successor, the English Electric Lightning, which they did with ease, might suggest they were overcautious. So it was that after a period of 'holding' at RAF Valley flying the Vampire for continuation and currency, three naïve, overenthusiastic pilots showed up at RAF Chivenor to begin the three-month Hunter Operational Conversion Unit (OCU) course. We just had to grin and bear it.

Chapter 3

The Hunter

The Hunter was for many years the epitome of a fighter pilot's aircraft, a modern day match for the Spitfire. After straight-wing Vampires, Venoms and Meteors, the swept-wing Sabres paved the way for the Hunter with its sleek, streamlined airframe and powerful Avon engine. It was, of course, designed to kill and destroy but for those nevertheless fascinated by the ingenuity of design, power, speed and versatile manoeuvring it was a delight to watch at airshows, displaying as a singleton or in the famous mass formation teams of the day. The Black Arrows, formed by 111 Squadron were perhaps the most ambitious aerobatic team at the time, looping twenty-two Hunters in close formation at the 1958 Farnborough Air Show, followed in 1961 by the Blue Diamonds of 92 Squadron team of sixteen Hunters who flew a seven-aircraft line-abreast loop – a very difficult manoeuvre to fly accurately. So we knew the reputation of this fantastic fighter aircraft that every pilot wanted to fly and we were not to be disappointed.

Hawker Hunter in flight.

Looping 22 Hunters brought new ideas to airshows. (*BAE SYSTEMS*)

The first and most memorable exercise in converting to the aircraft before actually flying it was the trial by procedures trainer. This was not the sophisticated moving type of flight simulator developed later but a fixed sweat-box affair that was an accurate mock-up of the Hunter cockpit with all warning lights working and enough instrumentation, switches and controls to manipulate in handling any emergency.

Hunter Mk 6 in Black Arrows livery. (*BAE SYSTEMS*)

It was operated by a simulator instructor who might also be a flying instructor or, if your luck was out, an embittered ex-Hunter pilot set on testing the mettle of young students by bombarding them with every known – and unknown – emergency situation that could occur in three lifetimes of flying the machine. Fail these tests and you didn't fly the aircraft. This was not the most subtle way to ensure that you knew the *Pilot's Notes* cover to cover and backwards, especially the emergency drills, but it worked. It was perhaps another example of preparing pilots for those airborne emergencies that did actually happen during this stage of jet aircraft design as new aircraft types, new systems, new components and materials were constantly being introduced to maximise operational effectiveness.

We were soon strapping into the Hunter T.7 two-seat trainer for conversion. The reputation for smooth handling and impressive performance were easy to understand once airborne. Power controls, swept wings and a Rolls Royce Avon engine were a considerable advance on the Vampire and, with a high visibility cockpit, it really was a delight to fly. Extremely sensitive and responsive flying controls took a little getting used to after the Vampire's manual system. Take off was simply line it up on the runway, select full throttle and watch the speed build rapidly to 125 knots, stick back to raise the nose wheel and fly off at 150 knots depending on weight. Climb speed was 430 knots clean (no external 'stores' such as rockets, fuel tanks etc.) until reaching

Mach 0.85 and it was supersonic in a dive. It had an airbrake which was a sort of board that lowered from under the fuselage and was only moderately effective for such a clean aircraft, albeit better at higher speeds due to the V-squared rule for you budding physicists. Flaps were very necessary due to the low drag design, not only to configure the wing for the landing, as in all types with flaps, but to slow the thing down a bit on finals since it felt like it only wanted to fly fast, too fast to land. Speed for the circuit was around 200 knots reducing to 160 knots for base leg and a threshold speed of 135 knots depending on weight.

After four sorties, each of forty-five minutes, I strapped into the Hunter Mark 4 for my first solo flight. In these early jets there were detailed check lists to learn and, in the RAF of the 1960s, perform from memory, moving around the cockpit in a set pattern, checking that everything was in an attractive position before starting. The bubble canopy and snug cockpit made it feel that the aircraft was part of you with excellent visibility and no wasted space. The transition from Provost to Vampire meant a significant change of sound environment from very audible engine and airflow noise and vibration to a smooth subdued whistle. The Hunter was another order of silence and smoothness, the radio calls being clearer as a consequence. Solo flying in the Hawker Hunter was one of the early highs in my flying experience with exhilaration, challenge, achievement, satisfaction and a sense of privilege all coming together. I was 20 at the time.

The two seat T.7 trainer on approach to land. (*BAE SYSTEMS*)

The contrast between the rarified atmosphere of Cranwell, where staff were dedicated to grooming officer cadets for stardom and beyond, and the commitment at Chivenor to the job of operational flying was profound. We were coached at Cranwell to aspire to senior rank and display the behaviours and attitudes that go with it, even though we were as liable to seek fun, mischief and rule-breaking as anyone else just out of adolescence. Lots of saluting, raising of hats, ceremonial parades and interaction with important people, mainly very senior officers of any service or nationality, were seen as good for cadets' motivation. At Chivenor, the thin blue braid depicting Pilot Officer rank drew much less attention than the pilot's brevet or wings on our chest which were the same size for all ranks. The entire station was dedicated to the operation of the Hunter jet. All OCU aircraft can be deployed operationally, so the fact that pilots were being converted did not detract from the operational role, even if some instructors would have preferred to stay on a squadron. Any notion of distinctiveness from our Cranwell training dissolved rapidly as we embarked on conversion flying alongside those following a more conventional route with everyone focused on passing the course.

Some of our Cranwell training was to come in useful however. Grooming by the advanced ex-RAF Germany instructors had honed our capacity to consume prodigious quantities of beer in the pubs of Lincolnshire while singing songs of questionable taste, local drinkers having become inured to such extrovert behaviour exhibited by generations of RAF officers. But this was not Cranwell; this was the real RAF where such fun had to be balanced with concentration on the job in hand. So we visited local hostelries to research that balance of fun and exuberance, enlisting the assistance of such young ladies as might be interested, of whom there were many. Social life thrived but the dominant motivator was the Hawker Hunter Mark 4 jet.

The easy bits were the pure handling exercises to include different circuits with various simulated system failures. One of the more challenging of these was simulated hydraulic failure which required the aircraft to be flown in 'manual' when ailerons were very heavy to use, especially at higher speeds. Pitch was controlled by more limited elevator responses, although a switch in the cockpit could operate an electric actuator to position the tail plane to follow up elevator movement as it would automatically in powered mode.

Rejoining the circuit to land was invariably a 'run in and break' rather than the rectangular pattern flown in basic training. This originates in spending minimum time at a lower and more vulnerable speed in landing configuration were hostile air attacks to be a threat. The technique, introduced during Vampire training, was to fly parallel to the runway at perhaps 350 knots or more and break (hard turn) with airbrakes onto the downwind leg, continuing the turn through what had been the base leg. Flap was selected in stages as required to roll out on a short final approach, allowing for the wind, with speed reducing throughout to achieve threshold speed whilst retaining a minimum engine rpm to respond to any need for power.

Visibility from the cockpit is apparent in this Mk 9 of 54 Sqn. (*BAE SYSTEMS*)

Formation flying was a doddle with such precise, responsive controls and a powerful engine. The opportunity to lead formations of two and, later in the course, three aircraft was new. The primary aim of a formation leader in military flying is to successfully carry out an operational task. The effectiveness of different formations has been trialled and debated since the advent of aerial warfare. In the Second World War there was much debate about the merits or otherwise of mass bomber raids flying in defensive formations to minimise losses to enemy fighters, and whether to fly in daytime or at night. Fighters flew in tactical formations that provided mutual cover, concentrations of firepower, and a vehicle for less experienced pilots to follow their leader's instructions. The anti-ship attack profiles of the Buccaneer called for low-level formations of typically six aircraft that would split into smaller sections to attack from different directions using anti-ship missiles. In the Hunter era 'finger-four' formations were employed as well as close formation 'vics' (three aircraft, one on each of the leader's wing), pairs and 'box fours' (adding an aircraft in line astern), a formation used in flypasts. The finger four was a loose formation, one in echelon, two in echelon on the other wing, with greater spacing to allow attention to look out for the formation without the demands of flying in close. In bad weather, pairs or vics could recover to base through cloud as one unit, as far as the air traffic controller was concerned, thereby increasing the rate of recovery when fuel might be running low. The formation could then break cloud and land individually or land in formation if the cloud base was too low for visual circuits.

In training the emphasis was on briefing thoroughly, including what to do if things went wrong and, once airborne, flying smoothly enough to allow the wingmen to stay close without difficulty. The leader is responsible for decision making, look out and safety of the formation, together with calls for formation changes or radio frequency changes and check-ins. He always restricts power use to allow the wingman a margin of excess power, especially during a formation take off and climb. Smooth flying is especially important in thick cloud since the wingman can sometimes barely see the leader's wing and contact can be lost, requiring him to make a positive turn away to avoid a collision and then revert to flying his aircraft on instruments. The wingman flying in formation is obviously not looking into his cockpit and tracking the attitude shown on his instruments and he can experience the 'leans', feeling he is turning when in fact level. This will induce instinctive yet unwarranted throttle adjustments to interrupt smooth station keeping. The trick is to concentrate on staying close to the leader and trust his skills of flying in the weather, whilst staying relaxed and keeping station regardless of attitude. This element of trust is endemic in all fighter operations and in all weathers where operational tactics require everyone to fly accurately and rely

The bulges under the fuselage for holding expended shell cases from the 30mm cannon were called 'Sabrinas' after a shapely actress, popular at the time.

on everyone else to do the same. It has been a characteristic bond amongst pilots in fighter squadrons since air warfare began. Other roles perhaps have more opportunities to fulfil their tasks alone or in co-ordination with others rather than operating as one fighting unit. However, this might beg the question of whether the Dam Busters attack of 1943 was 'one fighting unit' or not, so it could be a fighter pilot's myth … .

Flying in close formation is always exhilarating with the sight of other aircraft very close up in flight, sometimes at high speed at low level with the ground flashing by, sometimes seemingly motionless at altitude, sometimes in approach configuration with wheels and flaps down and 160 knots ready to land. Aircraft in flight are very photogenic. But being pretty is not what military aircraft are for.

The Hunter course provided the first opportunity to fire guns. To the sceptic, the pacifist or the fainthearted this might not have seemed the most uplifting prospect but when everything else in international relations had failed it could be necessary. We practised air-to-air firing, leaving out ground-attack techniques that pilots destined for day fighter squadrons would learn. This meant arranging to meet up with a lone Gloster Meteor towing a cable on the end of which was 'banner' or 'flag' which was a sturdy piece of white cloth about six feet or so in width and thirty feet long held flat in the vertical by a spreader bar. It presented to the aspiring pilot a long rectangle to attempt to hit with 30mm bullets that left a coloured dye mark to identify the guns that fired them and assess the pilot's score of hits. In the cockpit the pilot had a gyro gunsight with radar ranging that, in theory, made the task of hitting the target easy simply by tracking a 'pipper' on the target, getting into firing range and pulling the trigger for a short burst. More important than hitting the flag was not shooting down the Meteor. How close student pilots came to doing this was apparent from the cine films of each attack initiated with the same trigger. The trick was to achieve sufficient 'angle off' to present a bigger plan view of the flag, supposedly making it easier to hit. If the angle off became too low the Meteor appeared in the frame of the film so there was no escape from a tongue-lashing from the instructor on debrief. Happily the Meteor pilot landed elsewhere and was not made aware of his close calls. However, whenever I subsequently met a tow pilot I couldn't help but notice a nervous look and a twitch after surviving another day. High enough angle off was achieved in training by flying a 'quarter attack' pattern from 2,000 feet above the Meteor, flying parallel and displaced by a mile or so, overtaking until directly opposite. We then flew in a descending turn towards him, reversing halfway to establish a healthy angle from which to fly the 'pipper', a white dot projected on to the gunsight glass, onto the flag pulling perhaps 4 'g' and hoping the gunsight did its magic as you opened fire, rapidly breaking away over the flag to avoid the cable and banner. It was exciting but difficult to get hits without regular practice. I was assessed as 'average' which perhaps justified my posting to the night all-weather role – although the Javelin did have four 30 mm cannon … .

Note the fuselage gun-ports under the nose and the Hunter's capacity for carrying underwing stores which could be extra fuel, rockets, bombs or missiles. (*BAE SYSTEMS*)

Navigation at medium and high levels was visually or by using Distance Measuring Equipment (DME), providing range from the selected beacon, radio bearings and ground radar guidance. At low level it was by map and stopwatch. This was a well-used technique operationally, flying at 250 feet as a finger-four and speeds up to 420 knots or more, but on the pre-Javelin conversion course the syllabus was more concerned with handling at low level in formation than attack profiles and weapons-delivery techniques which would be more comprehensive for those heading for the day-fighter role.

It was a privilege to fly the famous Hawker Hunter. The lighthearted but dedicated instructional staff motivated students to sustain that glamorous dare-devil image to emulate young fighter pilots of the Second World War with their spotted scarves, and squadron spirit. For them a fatalistic party-going lifestyle could hide the apprehension, perhaps fear, at being pitched into mortal air combat with minimal training and experience. For us it was the ever-growing threat from the Soviet Union and Warsaw Pact that focused our minds on attaining a high professional standard – although the parties were fun … . The three Cranwell graduates all passed the course and were to find a very different atmosphere and mindset in the world of night-fighter pilots, flying with a 'navrad' – short for navigator/radar operator – who put his life in your hands. We headed off to RAF Leeming and 228 OCU to begin our conversion to the Gloster Javelin Mark 5.

Chapter 4

The Javelin

The Javelin was a big aircraft for a fighter, certainly after flying Vampires and Hunters, and it was the first delta-winged fighter to enter RAF service. The final FAW 9 version had an all up-weight of over 40,000lb, a wingspan of 52 feet, powered by two Armstrong Siddeley Sapphire engines of 11,000lb of thrust each – 12,300 with reheat. Its maximum speed was 610 knots at sea level and Mach 0.93 at altitude. Armament was four 30mm Aden cannon and it could carry four pylon-mounted air-to-air Firestreak missiles. It also came with a navigator.

Acceptance of the aircraft into service with the RAF was a tortuous business. There were many limitations and modifications, including prohibition of stalling or looping the aircraft after test pilot Peter Lawrence lost his life entering a 'deep stall' at more than 45-degrees pitch angle and reducing speed when the large delta wing blanked off airflow over the tail-mounted elevators used to recover. They became

I flew the Javelin Mk 5 at 228 OCU RAF Leeming. (*via B. Mayner*)

ineffective and the aircraft just fell out of the sky. In later flight testing of new fighter types at slow speed, tail parachutes were introduced to offer another means of recovery, especially in spins. These were unpredictable in swept-wing aircraft such as the BAE Jaguar whose spinning characteristics reported by test pilot Jerry Lee are worth reading.

After arrival formalities at Leeming the assembled course members inexorably drifted into the bar. The pilots and this new breed of co-trainees, *navigators,* eyed each other up, having been left to make their own choices of whom to fly with as a crew during the course. We were in a 'blind date' situation, having to shyly make an approach to a pilot or a navigator to take the plunge together as a crew who would need to co-operate closely both to survive and pass the course. It was not an immediate choice so, like the ritual courting dances in nature, we continued to circle potential mates, warily testing strengths and weaknesses – confidence, sense of humour, drinking habits, enthusiasm and, for the navigators, piloting competence as perceived but not yet demonstrated. I was duly approached by an intelligent and clearly discerning Scotsman who drove the same model of Jaguar as Inspector Morse in the TV detective series which weighed heavily in his favour since cars were an interest of mine and an essential asset to make pursuit of romance practical. My first car was a 1934 Singer Le Mans sports car purchased from my elder brother for £90, of which I ever only paid him £50. But

Vortex generators on the Javelin to avoid boundary layer breakaway – one of many modifications introduced after entering service.

the love of my life, having not yet met my wife, was my blue MG TC which I learned shortly after buying it had been in some kind of accident, which would explain a crab-like tendency to lurch sideways with no steering input. But it completed the image of a young, available pilot hero which was to pay dividends – in social terms anyway. I never let my wife forget that, as we rushed towards marriage a couple of years later, I had secured a bank loan to buy a Triumph Spitfire which was trumped by purchases of bed linen and saucepans.

Ground school was serious and comprehensive, covering all aircraft systems and the theory and operation of the radar equipment operated by the navigator but acted on by the pilot. Conversion was in the T.3 two-pilot aircraft which did not have radar but was armed with four 30mm Aden cannon. This was straightforward and I soloed in the T.3 after three hours. It was an easy aircraft to handle with fully-powered controls that gave positive responses, albeit not as light as the Hunter. Landing on the cushion of air generated by the large delta wing was a gentle business as the power to balance high drag was reduced to idle crossing the runway threshold at 135 knots, and the aircraft sank to the ground with a sigh of relief at not having to fly any more. Then came the new experience of flying with a crew, my brand new navigator, who had thought that flying with me might be no more risky than flying with the other dubious characters he had looked over in the bar. No pressure there then.

The sports car (MG TC) was part of the image.

On my birthday, 4 February 1961, I taxied out at RAF Leeming in a Mk 5 Javelin for my first flight in the aircraft with my new, sceptical (about everything) Scottish navigator in the back whom I'd never flown with and dearly needed to impress. Without nose-wheel steering differential braking was provided by toe brakes on the rudders which meant bracing heels rigidly on the rudder bar to keep it central and rotating the ankles to apply brake to the relevant wheel a somewhat ungainly arrangement having been used to stick-mounted brake levers. I understate 'ungainly'. I approached the holding point after reciting checks with a flourish, assuming a 'this is your captain speaking' voice when, for some unaccountable reason, the aircraft left the taxiway with a thump and stuck in the mud. 'Brake failure', I cried petulantly to no one in particular as my navigator quickly considered who else he might trust with his life during the tow back to dispersal. You guessed it, I hadn't braced the rudder pedals firmly enough when applying brake and had inadvertently forced the opposite brake on. This was the cause of many a burst tyre when correcting drift for a crosswind landing and old hands (me after this episode) called 'feet off the brakes' over the intercom with every finals 'three greens' gear check. As if lack of nose-wheel steering and playful brakes weren't enough to think about when taxying, the engines at idle emitted an ear-piercing howl to prompt irate calls during night flying from station married quarters about waking babies, so we had to up the power a bit and risk brake failures from excessive braking to avoid scary taxying speeds. The Lightning reverted to a stick-mounted brake lever ... .

The OCU course lasted six months during the 1960/61 winter, practising interceptions of all shapes and sizes and at heights of 500 feet to 40,000 feet, evenly split between day and night. We flew in all weathers down to the limits of our instrument ratings, which could mean long climbs and descents in cloud often at night and approaches to land with cloud base down to 600 feet. There was no autopilot, so our instrument skills developed quickly. All sorties were debriefed using a wire data recorder which showed the radar screen that the navigator was seeing for each intercept, to provide for coaching by an instructor. Confidence of the navigator in his pilot relied on two tests: 'Is it looking like he'll get me through the course' and 'is he flying the aircraft and getting back on the ground without scaring me'. Some didn't pass the tests and left the course as the navigator found himself another pilot. One pilot but no navigators on my course failed but I am sure others did since it was a very demanding job.

In the cockpit the deal was that the pilot did the handling (not a lot of choice with one set of flying controls) and made the decisions while the navigator controlled the interceptions. The radar controls were all with the navigator who issued instructions to the pilot once he had radar contact with a target – starboard gently, starboard, starboard hard, starboard as hard as you can go, corresponding to turns using 15, 30, 45, 60 degrees of bank (or on the buffet) staying level. Then up gently, down gently etc. using set VSI readings of rate of climb or descent. More speed, less speed

Javelin front cockpit straight out of Pilot's Notes.

completed the set of manoeuvring parameters which all had to be flown accurately and in combination to allow the navigator to predict and control the intercept. The pilot controlled the weaponry if there was any. The final stages of the night intercept for a guns attack meant closing to around 200 yards on radar, trusting the navigator completely, then peering upwards to see the unlit silhouette of the target against the night sky for identification, pulling up for a simulated guns attack and announcing 'splash'. The target was usually the other Javelin you had taken off with and the first thing you would see would be the glow from the jet exhausts. Missile attacks would be at longer range having identified the target as hostile. It was all in total darkness with minimal instrument lighting selected to protect night vision, then just stick and throttles. The memory of climbing up through cloud on a murky night, breaking cloud at perhaps 30,000 feet in a moonlit, star-studded night sky with just the ultra violet light on a minimum setting and all red lights off is vivid and reinforced my Vampire experiences. You were as one with the aircraft in a man/machine embrace within a hostile environment where the physics of the upper atmosphere on the edge of space with its unblinking stars brought a strange mix of harsh physical reality and unearthly perceptions of grandeur in the brief moments you could think about it. Temperatures outside the cockpit were perhaps minus 56 degrees, while inside you were pressurised to 20,000 feet breathing 100 per cent oxygen and wrapped in an immersion suit to prolong life for a few minutes were you to plunge into the North Sea seven miles below. The navigator was an integral part of delivering results but it was the pilot who flew the machine and got you both back safely. Close crew co-operation was vital, whether that closeness translated into close friendship on the ground or not. It often did.

Social life proceeded much as before for the bachelors on the course, seeking out the hotspots of Ripon or racing down the A1 to London for further research on responses of the fair sex to young, dashing and pretentiously modest RAF aircrew in a party environment.

With the course completed I was posted with my Scottish crewman to RAF Middleton-St-George near Darlington, County Durham (now Durham Tees Valley Airport, but rumoured to be reverting to 'Teeside International') to fly Javelin FAW Mk 9s with No. 33 Fighter Squadron – my first operational posting. Most of the crews had converted from the Meteor NF.14 night-fighter and were somewhat older than me, doing the families and children thing. Unwisely, in retrospect, I decided after a familiarisation sortie to make my mark as a young new arrival by carrying out a screaming low pass over squadron offices to rattle windows and catch the attention of anyone dozing in the crew room. My dour Scottish navigator was not with me on this sortie or would probably have talked me out of it. My flight commander, a certain Bunny Harvey, successfully talked me out of it for the future in a surprisingly serious interview with safety, responsibility and self-discipline coming up amongst other heatedly explored topics. But I persuaded myself that he was hiding a secret grin of admiration at the 'spirit' my exuberance showed. I lived with this justification for many years during which I saw plenty of spirited low flying and 'beat ups', as these low passes were known even at the flying instructors' school I was to attend later. Working routine settled to flying at least thirty flying hours each month alternating between day and night intercept sorties over the North Sea where the Soviets might be expected to route on their way to bombing UK.

As a pilot on my first tour the most exciting and demanding flying in the Javelin was in the primary role of intercepting targets in bad weather and at night, with no lights showing, perhaps facing ECM (Electronic Counter Measures) and potentially defensive weaponry. At 21, with just three months on my first squadron, it was the feeling of being operationally ready, trained and competent, mixed with exhilaration, excitement and challenge, all set in the tensions of the Cold War. The mission was to preserve the peace by training with sufficient conviction to sow doubts in the minds of the Soviets as to their chances of eliminating our power to retaliate with sufficient speed to avoid mutually assured destruction. We were all fully committed to this objective but in the crew room it was '*well, this is what we do, so what!*' The blasé attitude contrasted with the V Force boys who didn't know if 'scramble' was another practice or the Third World War. The Cold War was a time of tense readiness without the actual combat that would have meant nuclear war, somewhat different from life-threatening RAF missions in the war zones of later years. Most of the time this underlying awareness of a threat was subdued but it has been suggested that the 'Swinging Sixties' lifestyle for young people released from wartime pressures and National Service (conscription) was a fatalistic response at a time of anxiety to go out and enjoy life while we could. It is perhaps music that has best defined this enthusiasm for parties, adventure and freedom to do what 'turns you on'. Rock and Roll had appeared in the 1950s and many groups and bands appeared on the scene to portray Britain as a leader of pop music culture with all the reputedly decadent lifestyles it encouraged – drink, drugs, new dances and more. The Beatles, Rolling Stones, Beach Boys and many more bands competed for the top spots engaging with young people across the globe as they twisted, jived and hopped about to the music with abandon. Parties in the RAF were no exception.

Unlike modern jets there were things that could go wrong for which there was no warning system. Pre-flight checks were split with the pilot checking the bottom half of the aircraft and the navigator the top half, including looking into eight inspection windows to check that latches securing the very heavy, independent, pilot's and navigator's sliding canopies were secure. On 8 September 1961, shortly after arriving on 33 Squadron, I was teamed up for the day with a new navigator – my usual crewman was elsewhere. Another day, another pairs take off, ho hum … . As we lifted off, out of the corner of my right eye I sensed my canopy lifting from the right-hand rail. It ripped off, sucking all the accumulated dust and detritus from the cockpit floor, temporarily blinding me and making station-keeping somewhat difficult as the canopy struck the tail. The navigator still had his canopy and started calculating with his pencil the beers he would owe me, as I slowed to 170 knots in a very stiff breeze, flew past the tower for a check, burned off fuel and landed with raised eyebrows and a red-eyed glance at him as we got out. Moral? You decide!

Social life was punctuated by 'strikes' on local teachers' or nurses' colleges where students seemed well qualified to teach less mature souls to dance, drink, party and understand women. If these targets were out of range or out of bounds, weekend life was centred on the Officers' Mess. The advantage here was that the risk of being caught drink–driving, crashing after driving, or split from one's driver in pursuit of romantic opportunities were low. Mess members who were married displayed more interest in drinking, talking loudly, even playing darts or snooker than dancing with their eager young wives. Step in the dashing, nearly sober, confident, courteous young pilot or even navigator to comfort these frustrated dancers by – wait for it – yes, dancing the night away with no fear of large angry husbands bent on reprisals, only friendly smiles all round. But the colourful life on 33 Squadron was shortlived due to a shortage of crews further north and my navigator and I were posted after six months to 29 Squadron at RAF Leuchars, Fife, Scotland, my remarkably well-connected Scottish colleague strongly denying any undue influence. Life continued in similar vein, with only the Haar (sea fog) offering variety in terms of weather to fly in.

These Javelin Mk 5s at RAF Leuchars in 1957 show the heavy duty separate canopies. (*via B. Mayner*)

Any whiff of real operational flying was intoxicating. As part of UK readiness, aircraft were held on a continuous two-minute Quick Reaction Alert across the country, meaning that both crew were strapped in and connected to tele-brief (direct connection to base operations), to be scrambled on detection of unidentified intruders into UK airspace. Two-hour shifts flashed by for me with eyes wide open and fingers poised over engine-start buttons while my navigator slept under a blanket, assuring me, without conviction, that he, too, was fully strapped in and ready to go. Tedium and stiffness gradually replaced adrenalin and keenness on most of these stints. But one day the call came '*SCRAMBLE* vector 140 degrees, climb to 36,000 feet.' At last! Engines started OK and everything began to come on line ... *except* that a main inverter doll's eye stayed white. These were indicators that changed to black when successfully converting DC from the two generators to AC for instruments and, crucially, the radar system. Then I saw the red light showing that one generator had not come on line – the one that powered the radar. 'We can't go,' shrieked my nav, 'We have no radar!' But I wasn't going to let a duff generator or a redundant navigator prevent me from finally doing the job I'd been trained for, so we roared off with just one generator in gin-clear weather and daytime, so not that brave. It was a stray Valiant bomber not showing identification which we decided not to shoot down. The bar bill to smooth my navigator's ruffled feathers was sizeable ... .

During the late 1960s and early 1970s the Javelin was the mainstay of UK strategic air defence against the Soviet threat. Some 436 were built, equipping fourteen squadrons based in Germany, UK and the Middle and Far East. RAF Akrotiri had become strategically important with many squadrons of Canberra bombers and troop-carrying Hastings transport aircraft positioned in readiness for operations across the Middle East and Africa. They needed air defence which had been provided by the Hunters of 43 Squadron but was now provided by Javelin squadrons on rotating three-month detachments from the UK. Happily, the flight plans to refuel at friendly bases and carry enough to reach equally friendly diversions along the route meant a first stop at Wattisham, still in the UK, and then any number of exotic stopovers – Orange-Caritat, Istres, France; San Guisto (Pisa), Italy; Grossetto, Italy; Luqa, Malta; El Adem, Libya. This was a master-stroke of aircraft design for young unmarried pilots hungry for adventure thanks to two very thirsty Sapphire engines and a shameless drag profile. An ungainly looking refuelling probe was later fitted to avoid stops and scotch these tourist aspirations. In any case three-month detachments for each UK Javelin squadron were seen to be more expensive than having a squadron permanently based on Cyprus, and it was 29 Squadron that got the job. So, in February 1963, the squadron moved to Cyprus, families too.

Social life at Akrotiri during detachments had been frenetic, enlivened by the married guys away with the boys enjoying cheap drink and cigarettes. At the end of an unhealthily alcoholic evening I was all but persuaded to take up smoking in order to save large sums of money buying duty-free fags but the penny dropped, pretty much as I did after so much booze. As it became known that I and other bachelors had moved into our single rooms at the Officers' Mess, local 'schoolies' vied for a relationship with a young flier that might lead to love in a sunny climate. They staked their claims by leaving their sports cars with us on the base for us to use, a generous gesture which produced two marriages, one of them for my navigator who, at the age to justify 'marriage allowance', gloated not infrequently how much more than me he was earning just for playing with the radar. It could get a little alcoholic at weekends in the kebab restaurants of Limassol, with dubious red wine served in copious quantities from recycled lemonade bottles; lunches at the Kyrenia Harbour Club at Sunday lunchtime; and Greek men dancing on the tables in cafes with handkerchiefs in their mouths. Or it could be dancing in the Officers' Mess at parties, or anywhere else really, to the music of those wonderful 1960s' groups – Herman's Hermits, Gerry and the Pacemakers, the Beatles, the Rolling Stones and many, many more. It was a jolly time to be young and in the RAF.

But my declared ambition to delay getting married until the age of 29, should the opportunity arise, was shattered. During one of the detachments, as we lazed on the beach exploring common interests with girls working for the Foreign Office, I met the one who was to become my wife a year later, at the age of 23. I had succumbed to the inevitable but it was, and still is, a great success! It made little difference to the job but social life was transformed after a wedding back in UK and a move into a house in Limassol. My wife continued with the job she couldn't tell me about. At that time, after a recent history of anti-British violence, the atmosphere in the town was remarkably peaceful with Greek and Turkish communities living side by side, albeit in separated areas or 'quarters'. The diversity of cultures was a delight to experience but, shortly after our time on Cyprus, the Turks invaded and the island separated into Turkish and Greek regions which are retained to this day. Unforgettable was an instruction, not request, from my wife one day to pack up the car at our Limassol home and head for the RAF station on the Sovereign Base Area in the knowledge that local civil unrest and inter-communal hostilities had broken out. It was not a time for British military people to be swanning around Limassol or any other town on the island. This was the local environment the squadron had to accommodate and the job of flying to be ready for any military threat went on with exercises in defence of Cyprus and Malta conducted over the skies of the Mediterranean as preparation.

The Javelin Mk 9 was easy to fly, had a good instrument platform, and was fitted with a capable radar for its time for the navigator to enjoy. While taxying still required an unnatural bracing of the legs on the rudders, there was a degree of self-centring to bring the rudders and the nose wheel back into the straight-ahead position without enticing the pilot to press on the opposite brake and burst tyres. Wing-mounted guns

While never a classic it was easy and pleasant to fly. (*BAE SYSTEMS*)

relying on radar lock-on and ranging from the rear seat meant almost ramming a target to ensure hits but it was a good Firestreak missile platform to spoil the concentration of any Soviet attacker.

Performance wasn't startling and only subsonic but the Javelin was astonishingly good at slowing down, hence its nickname 'Dragmaster'. Deltas at high angles of attack collect all sorts of drag – induced, profile, form, skin, interference and any others available. Add highly effective airbrakes and, with throttles at idle for an 'operational descent', you literally hung in your straps, a bit like a Stuka pilot. Another slowing-down manoeuvre at low level was to engage reheat. Reheat increased thrust at high altitude by taking the fuel you saved in lower density air, spraying it into an expanded jet exhaust nozzle and setting light to it. The extra thrust was a relief when manoeuvring at altitude but fuel gauges were a blur with the consumption. At low level, engaging reheat starved the engines of fuel due to limited pump capacity and the aircraft slowed down but the *WHOOMPHA* noise and flames they produced on lighting up was very engaging and it did so impress one's friends at air shows until the Lightning arrived to scupper the ploy with its amazing displays in full reheat with lots of extra thrust and noise.

Exhaust nozzles opened for extra thrust at height to provide reheat, or afterburner as it's now known.

After three years practising forced landings in Provosts, Vampires, and Hunters, frequently monitoring the one engine you relied on for making the bar each evening, it was sheer luxury to have two big engines to play with. They only rarely exploded and were straightforward to operate – well, apart from starting them. Engine starters used a volatile fuel called AVPIN to run up the engines to self-sustaining revs and this had a habit of catching fire in the starter bay, making ground crew waiting to close the hatch more than a little nervous. Worse was the starter's annoying habit of shedding its turbine blades and over-revving to destruction with a banshee scream meaning *run for it guys*! This all added interest for the aircrew as they waited to see if starter fires or disintegration occurred to prompt speedy vacation from the cockpit – bravely of course.

Asymmetric was easy with engines mounted side by side and we routinely practised single-engine operation. On one such practice, descending into Akrotiri, after shutting down the port engine at 25,000 feet I set up for a PAR approach, levelled at 1,500 feet and lowered the gear and flaps, speed quickly settling to 160 knots. As we commenced our descent with the glide-path the starboard engine ran down. Now, as I've explained, the Javelin was fantastic at slowing down, so to keep control I had to dive the aircraft steeply – from 1,300 feet ... . You will appreciate the ensuing problem. With some rapid prodding at the levers I got the port engine restarted at around 600 feet and preparations for ejection were cancelled as we climbed away. My navigator was both relieved and proud of his hero for saving his life and wasted no time in proclaiming this to a crowded bar that evening as I basked in the glory and admiration with due modesty. That is until our late PAI (Pilot Armament Instructor) Brian Carroll opined quietly, but for all to hear, 'did he read the latest Air Staff Instruction (ASI) changing "shut down" of an engine below 20,000 feet to "set idle power" for asymmetric practice?' Like Cinderella's carriage team I was transformed in one gulp of beer from stallion to mouse. It taught me to be cautious, not just about handling jets but staying up to date with changes from on high ... . But I was secretly pleased with myself for handling the situation. And my navigator stayed utterly loyal! He hadn't read latest ASIs either.

Did I experience more than my fair share of incidents? Not really. All pilots of those early fast jets had to cope with many, shall we say, idiosyncrasies that didn't appear so much in later types with their computer designs, sophisticated systems and, of course, price tags. Canberra/Meteor asymmetric, BAC Lightning engine fires, F-104 handling all presented challenges many pilots were unable to meet. There was great pressure and expenditure to equip a large air force and bring successive types into service quickly to sustain technological and lethal counters to perceived threats. So you had to be ready if things did happen – and learn the lessons. The expense of losing aircraft and pilots also fed into greater flight safety awareness derived from experience and accident reports.

33 Squadron Mk 9 operating with Hunters and Lightnings of Fighter Command. (*BAE SYSTEMS*)

Mk 9s in formation. (*via B. Mayner*)

The Lightning brings a new approach formating on a Mk 9 Javelin. (*via B. Mayner*)

29 Squadron crews pose during a Missile Practice Camp at RAF Valley firing Firestreaks at Jindivik drones. (*via B. Mayner*)

Air gunnery practice followed the same procedures described for the Hunter OCU, but the handling was different. The four guns mounted out on the wings rather than in the fuselage, as in the Hunter, were harmonised to concentrate fire at 550 yds where they would impose most damage. For any chance of actually hitting the banner described earlier the firing range had to be spot on and fed to the gunsight together with lead derived from rate of turn, range and gravity drop of the bullets. The pilot had to set up his quarter attack ending in a tight turn with sufficient angle off to avoid frightening the Meteor pilot, very much like the Hunter techniques I had learned at Chivenor. The navigator had to find and lock onto the banner, with its metal spreader bars, to enable the radar to feed range to the sight. Then it was a matter of flying the 'pipper' smoothly, steadily and quickly onto the banner and squeezing off a short burst before executing the escape manoeuvre over the cable and banner. While it was not easy to score highly with hits on the banner it was encouraging to think of a concentrated cluster of rounds in a pattern very likely to fatally damage enemy targets at the ranges we closed to during intercepts. However, it was more practical to rely on the Firestreak heat-seeking missile which could be fired from as much as six kilometres and needed no active guidance from the launch aircraft. But it was ineffective in cloud and the UK does seem to be cloudy at times.

It was the spin-off from air gunnery that gave me the chance to fly the famous Gloster Meteor. Famous because it was the first RAF jet fighter to enter service in 1944 and was produced in large numbers for British and foreign air forces before being phased out of the RAF in the 1980s. My first close-up view of the Meteor had been at Cranwell where it was used to train tall pilots. It was truly an early jet with none of the sophistication that came later with swept wings, power controls and air-to-air missiles. The squadron Meteor 8 was powered by two Derwent engines producing 3,500lb of thrust each and sported an ejection seat not available in earlier marks, plus a bubble canopy providing superb visibility compared with the T.7 two-seat trainer used for conversion. Meteors were used to tow banners for air gunnery practice and only a few pilots elected to fly them in this role, despite most having flown many hours in the night-fighter version prior to conversion to the Javelin. Perhaps it was naiveté, perhaps ignorance, but more likely sheer enthusiasm to fly the famous aircraft that motivated me to go for the conversion. There were 3,875 Meteors built for the RAF and for export during the 1950s and its early design limitations and hazards were infamous, calling for many modifications. Accident statistics vary but one report suggests that some 900 Meteors were lost during its service with the RAF, 145 of these in 1953 alone. Among the factors that caused those accidents were undercarriage failures, difficulties flying on one engine, high fuel consumption, causing pilots to run out of fuel more often, no ejection seats on earlier models and occasionally the 'Phantom Dive'. This occurred on the T.7 and some other variants when forgetting to retract airbrakes on the break to land, then selecting gear and flaps which combined to disrupt airflow over the wings and control surfaces to cause loss of control, especially if the wheels came down asymmetrically. The aircraft could simply fall out of the sky from circuit height with no time to recover. More common as a cause of accidents was the high rudder forces with one engine failed (or throttled back for practice) as power was increased. On approach to land at around 120 knots it took considerable strength to keep the ball in the middle (i.e. no yaw) and sustaining this for the duration of an approach could cause a 'leg tremble' familiar to Meteor pilots as they ran out of push with increases in power. Indeed, it was too much for some pilots and caused many accidents, some fatal.

All that said, the Meteor was a wonderful aircraft to fly and I took every opportunity to sign out the F.8 single-seater and enjoy low flying along Cyprus beaches which, in 1963, were deserted in the heat of a summer's day. It was fully aerobatic, albeit with heavy controls at the higher speeds. But giving pleasure to new young pilots, oblivious to its chequered history, was not what the public were paying for. I flew the Meteor to tow banners while other pilots fired bursts of 30mm ammunition that would, with luck, miss me and hit the banner I was towing or, more likely, the sea far below.

I flew this 29 Squadron Meteor 8 towing banners and low flying along deserted beaches. (*via B. Mayner*)

I signed out the Meteor 8 at every opportunity, here taxying out.

Towing required techniques that had to be learned carefully. The banner was laid out on the runway and its cable attached to a latch on the rear underside of the Meteor's fuselage. On a signal from the control tower, take off commenced with one-third flap, lifting off at 95 knots to enter a steep climb at 125 knots that would haul the banner

The 29 Squadron Meteor 7 two-seat trainer, with framed rather than bubble canopy, can just be seen in the background.

off the runway cleanly, raising the gear and flaps and climbing away to the firing range levelling at perhaps 5,000 feet or more depending on cloud. If you survived an hour or so of being shot at you recovered to base and flew along the 'dead side' at about 120 knots and 700 feet, parallel and close to the runway on the opposite side to the live circuit. A steady track across the airfield was maintained until the air traffic controller called 'drop' or 'release', whereupon you operated the latch to drop the banner and its cable to the ground. If the controller had judged the wind correctly the banner would land on the grass and not the runway. My memories of flying the Meteor, nicknamed the Meatbox, are all good ones, no doubt linked to the exhilaration I still felt in my early twenties for any kind of flying, especially solo.

The role of defending RAF Akrotiri from air attack was not an arduous one since the only threat at the time was perceived to be from the Greek Air Force eager to upset the Turks and reclaim the island. That, of course, is simplistic and the politics of this disputed island with its long history and strategic position were and still are complex. Were there to have been situations in the Middle East or elsewhere to raise the focus on air operations from the strategic base of Cyprus the threat would have been very different. So, when a flight of Greek Air Force fighter-bombers decided to do a Hi-Lo-Hi flight profile to sneak up on the base at low level over the sea to test

29 Squadron: from closest aircraft, Meteor 8, Meteor T.7 trainer, Javelin T.3 trainer, Javelin Mk 9 and one with the ungainly refuelling probe fitted to extend range for deployments. (*via B. Mayner*)

our reaction the response was somewhat comical. It was the day of a visit by the Air Officer Commanding – a large 'cheese' – with a formal lunch attended by all the top brass on the station. With summer working hours of 0700 to 1300 it meant that very few were at work. For some reason I was not invited to the lunch and was on a five-minute readiness at the airfield, more as a token of watchfulness than anything. As the foreign planes were picked up on radar and a scramble ordered I had someone call the Officers' Mess to alert the hierarchy and ran for my Javelin with my navigator. We got airborne by which time the visitors had cheekily 'buzzed' the base to the surprise of the Station Commander toasting his VIP at the time and we escorted them away from our airspace meekly, belatedly and unarmed, shaking our fists aggressively. The lunch went on unabated with no response to what was regarded as unbelievable and perhaps even a hoax laid on for the AOC's entertainment. It was a bizarre incident, not so very different in principle from Russian flights near the UK even today to test air defence responses and happily not to be compared with Pearl Harbor.

More serious was the build-up of tension associated with the Cuban Missile Crisis of October 1962. The history of the American responses to the positioning of Soviet nuclear missiles on Cuba, raising a clear threat to all of the United States, is well known. The Soviets were concerned at US missiles stationed in Turkey and Italy, and responded to a Cuban request for missiles to defend against any further invasion attempts by the Americans following the failed Bay of Pigs operation. It has since been regarded as the closest we came to all-out nuclear war between the West and the Soviet Union with the prospect of grotesque, devastating and unimaginable destruction on both sides. The nuclear deterrent would have failed. All military units of the Western powers raised their readiness status to a very high level and that included all units at Akrotiri. It was very sobering, having grown up with the constant fear of confrontation turning into war, to find that it might actually happen, and now. We watched breathlessly as events unfolded and it was with enormous relief we saw the Soviets blink first – as it was portrayed publicly. But a secret deal had been done to remove the missiles from Turkey as part of the apparent climb-down. Life returned to normal. We sweltered in hot cockpits at 30 degrees ready to scramble in minutes as part of regular exercises. We flew by day and night at all heights in summer heat and winter rains to sustain our readiness. It was great fun compared with that awful sinking feeling as leaders of the great powers glowered at each other and horrifyingly raised the stakes in vitriolic rhetoric when all we could do was watch and wait.

I recognised that the Javelin Force was ageing, as were most of the people flying the aircraft, and I fancied the idea of becoming a flying instructor. I applied successfully to undergo the famous Central Flying School (CFS) instructor course at RAF Little Rissington in Gloucestershire. It was a turning point in my flying career, indeed in my exploration of something else I might do well – that childhood need to achieve. I had sold the crooked MG before leaving UK, driving an MG Midget and Riley saloon in Cyprus, but fortunately my father-in-law in UK handed my wife the keys to his pre-war Rover 14 saloon, the original long black car. It sported a handle to wind out the front windscreen for ventilation and a notorious freewheel device that disconnected the drive-shafts from the engine, leaving you at the mercy of drum brakes that faded without warning on steep hills. The air blocks in the carburettor that stopped the engine on a hot day, the playful slack in the steering, the blue smoke from the burnt oils that brought a new fragrance into the interior added a magic of their own. It was our 'wheels' for some months after returning to UK and it joined a car pool taking colleagues to Little Rissington each morning from various points around Moreton-in-the-Marsh in early 1965, routing up and, more challengingly, down the steep hill in Stow-on-the-Wold, where snow would add to the excitement of trying to slow the monster down.

Chapter 5

The Gnat

Everyone on the CFS course flew the Jet Provost Mk 3, which felt like a child's toy after the mighty Javelin. Switch on the engine, point it upwards and it flew. Point it downwards and it landed and you switched it off. It was an uncomplicated and highly suitable aircraft for training pilots and therefore learning how to teach – instruct if you prefer. Curiously, its airframe design was based on the Piston Provost and equipped with one Viper jet engine rated at 1,750lb of thrust, side-by-side seating, manual controls, a tricycle undercarriage, ejector seats and an oxygen system. The later Mk 5 was pressurised. Everything about it was conventional and predictable. It was not built for speed but for stability, ease of handling, docile stalling and spinning, and an awareness of fuel management. It enabled pilot training to become all-through jet for a period with both primary and advanced stages flown in the JP as it became known.

After a brief conversion to type, the flying followed the conventional basic pilot-training syllabus. Each exercise was demonstrated by a staff instructor. Next, flying with a fellow student, you 'gave' the lesson while the other played the student role – sometimes outrageously incompetent, cack-handed, even argumentative, just for fun, especially if his colleague was finding instructing too easy. The roles were reversed for the follow-on sortie and the same game was played, albeit with more serious intent, since on the next sortie it was 'give back' time when the staff instructor was the student for the lesson. This long-established system flying 'mutual' sorties with fellow students for practice worked well. The patter to describe what you were doing with the controls, accurate flying of the demonstration and clarity of the learning points were the initial aims. As things happened quicker – perhaps during aerobatics or on approach to land in a turbulent crosswind – patter from the less able student instructor could descend into high-pitched gibberish that described, unsuccessfully, what the aircraft was doing a few moments before which, at 120 knots, was not much use to a student. The ability to fly accurately whilst describing techniques calmly and succinctly and then give appropriate verbal encouragement and guidance when the student was doing the flying is the essence of good instruction. During the course I was introduced to the regular 'beat up' or high-speed low pass over the airfield by the lucky instructor tasked with flying a weather check as everyone emerged from the morning 'Met briefing' just to remind everyone that flying was fun despite the seriousness of the task.

I did find the JP rather ordinary, and it was good to fly with someone who took an unconventional approach. I flew a mutual sortie with a certain naval lieutenant who came from flying off and, with luck, back onto carrier decks. This was a skilled affair with a short strip of deck on a ship that pitched and rolled as your target, flying a very specific approach to land, helped by men with bats, succeeded by lights and mirrors, with an eagle-eyed flight-deck audience to see whether you caught the wire and avoided breaking the undercarriage, all unnecessarily dangerous I thought. But naval pilots are different. Grudgingly I can now admit I found them even more fun than many RAF types, perhaps due to the copious quantities of 'Horse's Necks' that they drank with any excuse. As we returned to Little Rissington after a routine exercise, the naval lieutenant was clearly missing the thrill of successfully landing back on his tiny ship. He asked if I would mind if he practised a MADDLS approach. 'Why not,' I said lightly, not revealing my ignorance as to what this could be. He flew us on a downwind leg prior to turning on what would normally be base leg as taught to students. Instead he set up a gentle continuously turning approach descending throughout, muttering about mirrors. It was of course a Mirror Assisted Dummy Deck Landing as we all know. It seemed necessary to fly just above the stall throughout this approach so that when the power was cut the aircraft would fall with a thump onto the imaginary deck without bouncing and catch an imaginary cable which would prevent an amphibious landing. But there was no ship, no mirrors, no man with bats, the speed was hovering above a stall, and the lieutenant hadn't quite mastered the technique yet, hence practising in a non-naval aircraft with a non-naval pilot on board who managed with difficulty not to seize control. The shy grin from the naval lieutenant as we walked back into the crewroom and a comment, sotto voce, that he 'hadn't quite mastered deck landings yet' perhaps said something about why he was on the course. On completion of a very enjoyable and stimulating three months flying the JP and absorbing the instructional techniques, I was selected for advanced instruction and continued the instructor course flying the Folland Gnat T.1 out of RAF Fairford, recently vacated by B-52s of the USAF.

My first sortie was a familiarisation ride to get the feel of the aircraft. My new instructor taxied out and lined up on the runway, checked that my seat harness was secured tightly, opened up to full power and released the brakes. The aircraft shot forward, rotated at 100 knots and rapidly accelerated as he held it down at 300 feet until we reached 480 knots, then pulled smoothly up into a vertical climb with the altimeter winding very fast to 12,000 feet where he levelled off and casually said 'what do you think?' It was truly exhilarating, so I said 'Yeah, pretty good', thinking I had never experienced such breathtaking performance. Remember this was 1964 and I had yet to fly the Lightning that routinely exhibited this behaviour for longer, higher, faster and with much more noise.

The Gnat was originally designed as a fighter and used as such by the Indian and Finnish Air Forces. The RAF version was the Gnat T.1 powered by a Bristol Orpheus engine with 4,520lb of thrust, maximum speed 535 knots at sea level, maximum height of

Folland Gnat T.1 in the livery of the Yellow Jacks display team which preceded the Red Arrows. (*BAE SYSTEMS*)

48,000 feet, a range of nearly 1,200 miles and supersonic in a dive, much like the Hunter. Pilots sat in tandem with the instructor's view from the back somewhat restricted, being at the same level as the front seat, with instrument panel and student blocking all but a peripheral view of what was ahead. The elevated rear seat of its successor, the BAe Hawk recognised the need for a better forward view. Sitting in the front seat felt very much like a sports car ready to race with legs extended horizontally to the rudder pedals and superb visibility all round through a bubble canopy. An innovative feature of the ejection seat, based on a Saab design, was a safety lever at the top of the seat that dug into the pilot's neck in the unarmed position. It had to be rotated through 90 degrees to make the seat live, which was difficult to forget with a pain in the neck. It also dispensed with safety pins that could drop to the floor to create a loose article hazard. The level of competence needed to fly the Gnat effectively and safely to its limits was appropriately high prior to flying contemporary fast jets such as the Lightning, Harrier, Buccaneer, Phantom, Jaguar and also V-bombers. Its design and systems were unique to the Gnat and subsequent transition to operational types meant learning new systems from scratch. Two examples serve to illustrate its many idiosyncrasies.

Lowering the undercarriage caused a significant trim change in the pitching plane, so much so that the tail plane incidence was adjusted automatically, with no pilot input, to accommodate the shift in centre of gravity as the wheels retracted backwards. Selection of airbrakes partially lowered the undercarriage when the doors provided the necessary drag to lose speed with little trim change.

The feel system was interesting, even quirky. In aircraft without powered flying controls, the stick is connected by cables or rods directly to control surfaces, and the pilot can feel the aerodynamic forces on them according to indicated airspeed and the control deflection he applies. This builds up an intuitive sense of how the aircraft responds to inputs through his hands and feet. During landing, manoeuvring, delivering weapons or flying in formation, this 'feel' is a vital part of manual handling by the pilot. In modern fighters with fly-by-wire systems a computer translates pilot control inputs into control-surface deflections or engine-power changes to match environmental conditions and deliver accurately what the pilot has demanded without exceeding aircraft limitations. The design will include an automated feel system to retain that intuitive sense of aircraft responses to the controls. Such sophisticated systems do more than simply fly the aircraft, they allow levels of aerodynamic instability in manoeuvres that would be difficult for a pilot to work with manually but improve performance. Flight controls in early jets such as the Hunter, Javelin, and Harrier were hydraulically powered with pumps and actuators or screw-jacks that responded directly to the pilot's stick movements. But they also needed to replicate the feel that manual controls had offered. In the Gnat the power controls system and feel arrangements were complicated, adjusting the stick pressure for tail-plane deflection according to airspeed and other variables using a system of springs, pulleys and cams. In the event of hydraulic failure, the all-moving tail plane was immediately trimmed to a specified central position using a tail-plane position indicator and elevators were unlocked from the tail plane by the pilot with a lever in the cockpit to provide limited pitch control. If you had successfully trimmed the tail to the optimum position before hydraulic power ran out when it froze, the unlocked elevator was adequate for an approach to land as long as you set up to need little pitch correction – so straight in and shallow. You wouldn't want to run out of elevator just as you check the rate of descent for touch-down. Hydraulic power could be switched off with a cockpit lever to practise 'manual' handling when the feel system no longer operated. If future military aircraft need no pilots then the 'feel' issue will disappear and computers, even robots, will take over. The competence in playing computer games shown by most young children today will make flying them child's play.

Despite these oddities of design the Gnat's performance and handling were superb in preparing pilots to operate at high speed and be right on top of the aircraft, and it was an excellent vehicle to instill the determination and tenacity that fighter pilots need. I did not hear Lightning or Harrier pilots complain about their experience on the Gnat, or find any difficulty in adapting to new systems and the flight instruments display was at least very similar. It was an absolute delight to fly and to instruct in, despite the limited view from the rear. The rate of roll was so fast that a restriction was introduced via the famous removable Fuse 13. Without this restriction, it was possible to achieve up to 420 degrees a second which, with mishandling, induced roll yaw coupling that could, and for some did, lead to loss of control and structural failure. In the right hands however, this fuse could be safely removed as it was for the Red Arrows to achieve sparkling twinkle rolls in air displays. Even with the fuse in place response to the flying controls was more than positive.

The advanced pilot-training course covered conversion, emergency handling practice, formation at all heights, aerobatics at medium and low levels, low level navigation and night flying. The students would have covered all the basic exercises in the JP and these were repeated on the Gnat at higher levels of performance and complexity. They were supplemented by handling at 45,000 feet to explore aerodynamic effects of flying at or close to the speed of sound when shock waves transform the airflow around the wing to affect handling and stability as drag increases and trim and stick forces change.

Demonstrations of circuits and landings after simulated hydraulic failure were a challenge for some instructors since the approach was practised flapless with a high nose-up attitude on finals and an even more limited view of the runway from the rear seat. Another demanding demonstration was a sustained six 'g' descending turn at 360 knots on the buffet whilst delivering a patter that would help the student when he tried it. Slow speed flight was a cautious business since the Gnat was unstable near the stall and would readily enter a spin from which recovery was not guaranteed, confirmed during my tour by a colleague and his student having to eject when a demonstration got out of hand. With such responsive controls and a high power-to-weight ratio it was a delight in formation at all levels.

Low level flying at 250 feet with speeds rising from an initial 240 knots, so four miles a minute, through 360 knots to 420 knots or seven miles a minute, using a map and stopwatch, was tremendous fun and extremely satisfying. At that time it was how air attacks against Warsaw Pact targets were envisaged, evading radar detection by staying low. The typical training profile was a 'Hi-Lo-Hi', flying at fuel-conserving height to the target area, typically Scotland or Wales, descending for a low-level route, then climbing out to recover using minimum fuel. The Gnat was very fuel efficient at altitude. Navigation at medium and high levels was under ground radar direction or using TACAN, a UHF Tactical Air Navigation System, which provided range and bearing to a transmitting station plus an offset facility to nominate a specific point to home onto, similar to way points in modern SATNAV. ILS (Instrument Landing System) was installed to provide the purely pilot interpreted runway approach aid with azimuth and glide-path clearly displayed on an HSI-style heading display. This is still widely used for instrument approaches with radar monitoring when available.

Towards the end of the flying instructor course we could enter for a low-level aerobatic competition, competing with pilots flying the Jet Provost. After a check by a staff instructor we were let loose down to 1,000 feet above the ground, flying with another student instructor, taking turns to perform our display. This was a very sweaty and demanding affair, especially if you were with an overeager showman flying close to the limits of the aircraft to achieve as tight a display as he could which meant being subjected to repeated 6 'g' and constant vigorous manoeuvring in all attitudes. Rolling in air displays is meant to be fast, with crisp well defined finishes or hesitations, as in a four-point roll, or on entry to the next manoeuvre. This needed full aileron deflection with some rudder, then a spine-juddering, head-banging full reversal to stop the roll precisely, with more abuse of the controls. That's OK if you are flying the aircraft but gruelling to be subjected to it by a pilot you may not have come to trust completely yet, since he, like you, had no experience of flying aerobatics this vigorously and this close to the ground. But it was a way of losing a few pounds from physical effort, nervous tension and intense concentration to make sure you went home that night. My partner for this masochism went on later to be the lead Lightning display pilot for several seasons.

The Gnat at altitude over North Wales.

After a three-month intensive course at RAF Fairford I was posted to the only student-training Gnat base, RAF Valley on Anglesey. Two of my course mates were from Hunters and Canberras respectively, with one straight out of training to instruct on his first tour having demonstrated above average potential. Such first tour QFIs, creamed off to instruct, were affectionately known as 'creamies'. My wife, now pregnant with our first daughter, became a little tearful in July 1965 as we crossed the Menai Bridge in steady rain with sheep crouching for cover from a 40-knot wind that bent trees to 45 degrees in a slate grey landscape. We took up residence in Llanfairpwllgwyngyllgogerychwyrndrobwllllantysiliogogo, which aficionados of the Welsh language will recognise as 'Saint Mary's Church in the hollow of the white hazel near a rapid whirlpool and the Church of Saint Tysilio of the red cave'. It was known to us as 'Llanfair PG'. Our daughter was duly born shortly thereafter in Holyhead after a breathless twenty-mile drive along a bumpy A5 road, only for the baby to make her entrance (or exit) the following day. I was airborne in a Gnat T.1 at the time, not at the bedside – how things have changed.

The job of teaching aspiring fast-jet pilots settled into a routine with plenty of flying, teaching the syllabus we had gone through at Fairford. The difference was that these were real students needing good instruction, guidance to fulfil their potential, and be safe enough to survive their early piloting years until experience was built up. They were occasionally overconfident which, for their sake, had to be addressed. To concentrate his mind on his limitations, I took one such student for a low-level navigation sortie in the Welsh hills which were, of course, new to him. I knew them well by now, including the pass through which we sometimes flew to give students experience at low flying over and around hills to simulate evading radar or to stay under the cloud base. As we recovered to Valley I took control and flew at 250 feet and 400 knots along the A5 road towards Snowdonia. I knew there was an escape from the pass at the end of the valley just before arriving at a very solid piece of granite called Snowdon. He did not. Nothing was said as I roared towards the rock until, at the last minute, I routinely turned the Gnat on its side and pulled hard to follow the route to the right that led to the pass exit. It was a calculated squeeze on the student's confidence to show that he didn't know everything, combined with a measured debrief to compliment him on his competence and spirit which he needed to be a fighter pilot. But he also needed to survive and be ready to learn all the time. Trite, but worth repeating, is an old adage: 'There are old pilots and there are bold pilots. But there are no old and bold pilots.'

We were at 45,000 (I know, I know, 'nothing on the clock but the maker's name' goes the saying, but bear with) where I was demonstrating the effects of high altitude and compressibility on turning performance when there was a loud bang from the engine and many warning lights came on – happily not the fire warning light – and I made the MAYDAY call, went through the drills of shutting off fuel etc., and set up the glide towards Valley in manual controls with hydraulic power off. I dismissed the option of trying to restart the engine for fear that anything mechanical that had failed could cause a fire once the fuel was turned on. Vivid memories returned of the compressor disintegration of the Sapphire engine in a Javelin two years earlier during a take off that I managed to abort. That was not at 45,000 feet, nor in a tiny, lightly-built craft, where we sat with the engine between our legs. The subsequent descent and landing pattern went according to the practices we flew regularly and the weather was gin-clear. So it was 5,000 feet for high key, just upwind from overhead the touch-down point, to head crosswind, 3,000 feet at low key opposite touch-down, then a curved gliding approach allowing for wind and rate of descent that would end up touching down well into the runway. I had briefed the student in the front about ejection should I order that and he was not only remarkably calm but seemingly enjoying the experience. The approach was fine, with touch-down a fraction shorter than I had planned but rolling to a stop safely on the runway. As was traditional in those early days of jets, all the pilots had gathered at some high point to watch the whole thing and see if we made it, with the crash crews and ambulances ('blood wagons') strategically positioned to deal with fires and help us to escape from the aircraft if it crashed … . We hadn't crashed and, on arrival at the crewroom, I was hoisted high on the shoulders of colleagues and transported directly to the bar where we celebrated two more survivors of a forced landing, a rare but not always successful event in those early days of jet flying. I was duly commended, only to discover that the engine fault was not mechanical failure but a serious compressor 'surge' and I could in fact have re-lit the engine. All very well to know that afterwards, but putting a match to high-pressure kerosene, sitting astride an engine with a noisy malfunction in such a tiny aircraft, with temperature outside at minus-57 Celsius in clear weather, and responsibility for my student was, in the circumstances, a 'no brain needed' decision.

The weather factor at Valley – an indication of the number of days in a year when an airfield would be open for landing or as a diversion – was among the highest in Britain but the weather could be a little rough. The Gnat could take a 20-knot crosswind component and we flew to that limit with winds of 50 or 60 knots not uncommon. I can recall being 'duty QFI' supervising flying from the air traffic control tower when the wind was gusting up to 70 knots, but blowing straight down the short runway at Valley with turbulence that was hopefully within the capabilities of instructors, and we carried on flying, dual that is, with an instructor on board. The responsive controls and engine of the Gnat inspired confidence in those in current flying practice.

We moved to live in a married quarter on the base at RAF Valley where life style was enlivened by spirited students. On the occasion of a formal dinner attended by the Station Commander they built a life-sized mock-up of the rear section of a Gnat and planted it with the tail sticking up out of the lake outside the Officers' Mess to gauge his reaction on arrival. It was one of momentary shock, a private grin of relief, then the necessary stern reflection. Announcements the next day indicated the required disapproval but it was before the advent of dispiriting health and safety admonishments we could expect today. Long live a mischievous sense of humour.

A QFI friend and I were so keen to get airborne in anything when activities slowed between courses that we pitched into summer camps for ATC cadets, typically at RAF Shawbury, to give them air experience in the Chipmunk. This was a nostalgic return to the dainty, aerobatic aircraft I first flew, and during ground tours was happy to fly again at a number of AEFs (Air Experience Flights).

In the RAF flying instructor world there were categories of instructor to indicate experience and performance. After the CFS course everybody started as a probationary B2, then upgraded to B1 after about six months with quite a jump to reach an above average A2 category. The pinnacle was be an A1, seen by some as a dyed-in-the-wool instructor person dedicated to teaching forever, as opposed to those with operational experience doing a short instructional tour – I couldn't possibly comment, although A1 instructors were highly respected. Preparation for 're-cat' to A2 was extremely intensive, covering the theory of everything remotely connected with flying generally, and flying the Gnat or instructing in the Gnat. It was deemed essential to describe in painful detail how all Gnat systems worked, the engineering science behind them, the faults they could suffer, how those were fixed, what the designer ate for breakfast and more. We covered each of its flight instruments down to how precession of the gyros in the attitude indicator occurred, its effects on instrument accuracy and how it was automatically corrected. In-depth study of aerodynamics, meteorology, air traffic control operations and reference documents, engines and thermodynamics were all explored to anticipate the most obscure questions that a student could ask, were he to be unhealthily inquisitive. However, the 'student' for re-cat was a CFS standards instructor whose day job was to check all CFS staff instructors for performance and adherence to prescribed teaching methods. In 're-cat' mode this meant assessing briefings, lesson formats, clarity on the objectives of a lesson etc. to cover any part of the course syllabus plus a technical lesson with probing questions. He could in playful moments throw a searching even outlandish query that would hit the limits of the candidate's knowledge, who would then be sent away to learn more and come back to try again. And this was just the ground school examination! If the candidate got through this sweaty session without being sent away he would be asked to deliver a complete lesson chosen by the examiner on any exercise from the teaching syllabus which had to briefed, flown and debriefed not just to the level expected of everyone doing the QFI job but to standards that might be seen as above average by the CFS examiner who supervised the standard of CFS staff QFIs, who were training new QFIs who would teach the students at Valley. Hope that's clear. These were the people who tended to have 'A1 QFI' against their name. Every emergency procedure that might be thrown at a candidate was practised and honed while in standards flight. Since no candidate from Valley sent for upgrade to A2 in the previous two years had passed, the lengths to which my coaches in standards were prepared to go to achieve a pass were extraordinary. On the ground this was excruciating if enlightening, and in the air highly stimulating. I flew to Little Rissington for the test with more knowledge at my fingertips than ever before which was in danger of leaving me en route. I passed, flew back to Valley as an A2, threw a victory roll in before landing and accepted handshakes, beer, and warm words more appropriate to scoring a goal for England. This re-cat was to prompt a posting back to CFS to become a staff QFI teaching pilots to be Gnat instructors, flying out of RAF Kemble, Gloucestershire, alongside the Red Arrows. It also meant a family move to a cottage in the village of Great Rissington.

I flew with Ray Hanna, the Red Arrows leader, a number of times and saw just how utterly suited he was to the job. He had a wonderful combination of piloting skill, leadership, flair and New Zealand modesty that endeared him to everyone I ever met. He set an example of flying near the limits of both aircraft and pilots but with the discipline, judgement and infectious sense of humour that inspired the same standards throughout the team. They could then produce flamboyant showmanship whilst staying within the bounds of safety at public events. However, practice at Kemble was not a public event and this was probably just as well as they honed their low flying by occasionally pruning the tops of taller trees and executing stream take offs a few feet above the ground whilst turning to join the leader who was slightly below

Flying solo out of RAF Kemble. (*Courtesy Ray Deacon*)

them, a manoeuvre I watched wide-eyed from the back seat of Ray Hanna's aircraft. I had occasion to deliver Lou Wilcox, the team manager and commentator at the time, from RAF Abingdon, where the team had refuelled, to position at Biggin Hill for a display on a cloudy day in September 1967. I cleared the flight with London Zone Control, who were accustomed to providing special routes for the team to circumvent London, took off and was instructed to level at 2,500 feet in cloud and 'expedite' to avoid upsetting the routine stream of flights heading for Heathrow. Having spent a career avoiding all forms of controlled airspace – airways, civil airports, busy let-down and climb-out areas – it was an eerie experience flying at 380 knots in thick cloud within a mile or two of Heathrow, guided by radar to descend and pop out of the cloud on a three-mile straight-in approach to RAF Biggin Hill with a large crowd watching. After flying with Ray Hanna in the display I flew back to RAF Little Rissington by a more conventional route.

RAF Kemble, now Cotswold Airport, is in a delightful part of Gloucestershire close to the Roman town of Cirencester. Set in the countryside and away from controlled airspace, it was ideal both for training and for largely unobserved Red Arrows practice. They could indulge very privately in the sort of flying they needed to work up for a season of displays to sustain their reputation for perhaps the most exciting, innovative and impressively professional team anywhere. The confidence to fly fast and low

Ray Hanna the master at leading formation aerobatics in action. (*Crown copyright via Andrew Thomas*)

Ray Hanna upside down leading the team over the top of a loop. (*Courtesy Ray Deacon*)

in formation or as a pair hurtling towards each other, passing feet apart, to excite the crowds – and certainly the pilots – came from constant practice and meticulous rehearsals of new manoeuvres. It was a private airshow spectacular on most days, not only a joy to watch but prompting pride to be working alongside the team flying the same aircraft.

I was one of five instructors taking mainly experienced pilots through the Gnat QFI course prior to instructing at RAF Valley. The flying followed the Valley syllabus and was the same pattern that I had experienced at CFS two years earlier, but sitting in the front seat more often. The students were a pleasure to fly with, having flown operationally yet keen to add flying instruction to their skill base which would look good on anyone's CV in military and, particularly, civil flying. Some had reservations about leaving the operational world but it was usually for just a tour of two or three years – unless of course you were so thrilled with instructing that you went for the A1 category. Their experience was invaluable to student pilots who relished the opportunity to fly and talk with cool Canberra pilots and their hairy Harrier contemporaries.

I had by now come to regard the Gnat as a thrill to fly and a workhorse to teach in. We flew out of Kemble because the runways at Little Rissington, our parent station, were a bit short for the Gnat in a training role. It was also an accident waiting to happen if we mixed circuit speeds of 200 knots and 115 knots downwind and threshold speeds of 135 knots and 90 knots. The preference for Kemble was endorsed one day when

The Reds continue to show formation aerobatics at its best with BAe Hawks replacing the Gnat. (*Crown copyright MOD*)

I dropped off a visiting VIP at Little Rissington and taxied out for the flight back. On clearance for take off, aware of the limited runway available, I opened the throttle smartly and rapidly accelerated. But, as I reached full power, there was a sudden surge in the engine and thrust dropped off at about 90 knots with the end of the runway in sight. One choice that flashed up on my notional 'what do I do now' screen was to stay down, raise the undercarriage and hope for the best on an airfield that sat on a 600-foot hill with downslopes all around – basically a sticky end to the sortie. The other, which on impulse I chose, was to close the throttle and open it again steadily, hoping the airflow through the engine would sort itself out with a 'reboot'. Happily it worked, and I eased off the very end with a few yards to spare and flew gingerly back to Kemble just twenty miles away. Many pilots at the time had such experiences; some got away with it. Not much was made of the incident, just an engineering fix to adjust the fuel/air ratio settings.

One morning in March 1968 the phone rang in the Kemble crewroom. It was our Squadron Commander wishing to speak to me. 'Ron, how would you feel about six weeks flying Spitfires in a film about the Battle of Britain?' Astonishment was followed by excitement at the prospect and I tried to sound nonchalant as I asked what it involved before metaphorically biting his arm off. Six weeks was to turn into four months that I would treasure for all the reasons you can imagine, not least the privilege and good fortune to fly some of the most famous fighter aircraft of all time.

Chapter 6

The Battle of Britain

The Battle of Britain has come to symbolise the courage, determination and fighting spirit of the British in the summer of 1940 as the RAF held out against a Luftwaffe bombing campaign intended to achieve air superiority prior to Operation SEALION, the invasion of England. The name derives from a speech given by Winston Churchill on 18 June that year in which he said, 'the Battle of France is over … the Battle of Britain is about to begin.' The film is a historical record of the battle in the air at a dangerous and threatening stage of the war which some suggest marked a psychological, if not strategic, turning point.

It was directed by Guy Hamilton and produced by Harry Saltzman and Benjamin Fisz with a budget reputed to be $14 million. Many distinguished actors were in the cast, including Lawrence Olivier, Trevor Howard, Michael Caine, Robert Shaw, Susannah York and many more. But the real stars of the film were the hundred genuine vintage aircraft that were acquired or hired, some flyable, some not. They ranged from Spitfires and Hurricanes to Messerschmitts, Heinkels, Junkers and a B-25 Mitchell bomber adapted for filming, painted in Day-Glo bright colours for conspicuity, to stop

Spitfire, RAF Debden 1968.

dozy pilots crashing into them in search of stardom. Of the twenty-seven Spitfires acquired, some had been mounted on poles outside RAF station gates, twelve were made airworthy and the rest either capable, supposedly, of taxying or used for static shots to make up the numbers when depicting aircraft lined up at airfields or filming them being destroyed. Many full-scale mock-ups were constructed which were difficult to distinguish from the real thing until you looked closely.

You might be curious as to why it was me who got the phone call. I was too. One could imagine that there were many pilots – commercial, private, stunt – who would be more than interested in getting their hands on a Spitfire. But it seemed that RAF pilots were seen by the film's producers, investors, and insurers as a better bet. Could be true and I would certainly have agreed had I been asked. They are more skilled, more sociable, better trained, better disciplined, just nicer all round – and they were free. This latter feature was a coup for the film company as was the free use of active and non-active airfields owned by the MoD. There were some ageing RAF pilots who had flown the Spitfire in anger but the MoD in its wisdom thought that were pilots' faces to appear on the screen in the film these guys would not be sufficiently representative of the 20-year olds who flew in 1940. A signal (message) went around all the RAF's fast-jet squadrons looking for pilots with the right profile and I heard it said that some would have physically maimed competitor candidates, sold their houses, left the Air Force or their wives to get their hands on a Spitfire. But fast-jet pilots on operational squadrons were in short supply at that time and none could be released. 'Shame really,' I gloated later. A trawl of Training Command came up with an assortment of pilots who fitted the bill in one way or another: available, i.e. doing nothing useful; currently flying propeller-driven types, but they must have been antiques – the planes that is; film star visage but narcissism does not fit well with teamwork. Often in life it's 'who you know' that brings success, they say. They would also say that I knew no one of any importance. However, I was an A2 QFI (knew it would come in useful one day), I was current on a fighter type aircraft, I had many hours of tail-wheel piston types with currency on the Chipmunk and, as for young and handsome, well I was 28 anyway. Nine RAF pilots were seconded to work with Spitfire Productions on recreating the Battle, of whom two were flying the Gnat at the time, the others coming from Jet Provost instruction or various other roles in Training Command. This did not include the Battle of Britain Memorial Flight (BBMF) pilots who joined us later, with public display commitments to work around. I never found out exactly how pilots were selected but had no complaints. While our faces did appear in various television interviews, my particular face was never to be revealed to the film-going public, which was no great loss but confounded MoD boffins who had ruled out using highly deserving older pilots. My considered reflection was to sympathise with the MoD in having to make such a difficult choice – not.

The twelve airworthy Spitfires rounded up by Group Captain 'Hamish' Mahaddie came from a variety of sources, including Rolls Royce, who lent a Mark 14 with its

Griffin engine. This rotated in the opposite direction to the Merlin, requiring any swing on take off to be controlled using the other rudder pedal. This characteristic and some nervousness that having all pilots fly it would increase the risk of mishandling and damage meant that only one pilot was nominated to routinely fly the aircraft. The BBMF provided Mark 5 and Mark 19 versions, the latter with five-bladed propellers. Neither of these types flew in 1940, but in air-to-air shots this difference was not obvious. Indeed the only aircraft of the twelve that did fly in the Battle was the Mark 2a. Some of the more dilapidated machines were completely renovated at RAF Henlow to make them airworthy and legal. That is where I showed up for a conversion ride where, conveniently, a two-seat version, a converted Mark 9, was due for collection. We had been issued with *Pilots Notes* so I had a general idea of how to operate the aircraft – starting the engine, speeds, limitations, emergency procedures etc. I strapped into the front seat with a certain Wing Commander Elliot in the back from Headquarters Training Command, who had apparently flown Spitfires and Hunters in his early years. He advised me that this was a delivery flight to RAF Debden, and that I should take us there and get used to the aircraft on the way. That was it. He didn't feel the need to give any instruction and in any case the intercom that worked OK on the ground became intermittent once airborne. Apart from the occasional shout of encouragement from the back there was no conversation. I flew it to Debden, using the notes on speeds etc. that I'd made, did a 'touch and go' landing and a final landing and that was my conversion.

One of the two-seat Spitfires in which I converted. I wore more when flying!

Two-seat Spitfire cockpit with 'spade' grip stick visible.

What was it like to fly? Well, so much has been written already. In 1940 the thrill, the glamour, the pride that went with selection to fly the Spitfire was evident amongst many young pilots. But there are accounts of inadequate training, shortages of aircraft and instructors, and a lack of flying hours for pilots joining squadrons in 1940. This was epitomized by Churchill's words 'Never in the field of human conflict has so much been owed by so many to so few', a speech that has resonated in the minds of analysts, writers and historians ever since. Other reports suggest that the numbers of pilots arriving on squadrons with inadequate training might have been a little inflated to sustain the legend. If you were an experienced pilot with combat experience, the Spitfire would represent a robust fighting machine to make the odds against their Luftwaffe counterparts of similar competence close to even. However, if you were newly trained with no combat experience, barely having fired a gun, let alone practised air gunnery, it was certainly a different prospect and that would apply equally to new recruits in the Luftwaffe. The glamour of flying the Spitfire or other fighters would quickly give way to fatigue and a fatalistic acceptance of the odds of not coming back – by air at any rate. The statistics on surviving were not great for such pilots. Yet personally I can imagine a preference for flying a fighter, being in control as much as you could be of your own destiny when compared with the task of bomber crews as they penetrated German defences at night, frequently in bad weather, often sustaining damage, with many hours flying to get home – if they could. They had a different kind of courage.

Above left: The aircraft was very photogenic whichever pilot stood in front!

Above right: I did feel pride and privilege at flying such a great aircraft!

For a pilot spared from such fears, with 2,000 flying hours, having trained on the piston-engined Provost and with 150 hours on Chipmunks, flying the Spitfire was a privilege, not a problem. It was a delight to fly, handling like a high-performance Chipmunk, with well-balanced controls, responsive and powerful engine and good in-flight visibility. The cockpit is snug, with a sliding canopy and a drop-down side door for access. The spade-grip control column was easy to get used to, with its brake lever attached. The undercarriage selector, curiously labelled 'Chassis', was somewhat agricultural, that is large, with a long fore-and-aft rotational movement by a lever that felt that it was going to stick halfway around the curved quadrant, and I found I did sometimes have to recycle to get it to work smoothly. Visibility for landing was quite adequate using a curved final approach, looking down the side of the nose, and then peripheral references for attitude and height at the flare. I usually landed on three wheels ('three-pointer') but gently since any extra load on the tailwheel due to the attitude being a fraction nose high, touching tail-wheel first, could cause minor damage, requiring its replacement. 'Wheeling it on' by touching the main wheels first then lowering the tail was a technique used by some pilots, uncertain about the three-point attitude, feeling more in control, and it was also used when landing heavier tail-wheel aircraft. The narrow track of the main wheels has led some to suggest difficulty in staying straight on landing and taxying but it seemed fine to me with just the usual precautions of using aileron to hold a wing down in a crosswind and care not to over-control with rudders or overheat the brakes to keep straight.

Three Hurricanes were made available for filming. One was flown by its Canadian owner, one by the BBMF and the third from Rolls Royce, again flown by just two RAF pilots chosen arbitrarily. The Hurricane was arguably the easier aircraft to land with greater forward visibility and handling that some compared with the Gloster Meteor for stability. More importantly in 1940 was its reputation of being a good gun platform, with four guns mounted close together, not spread out like the Spitfire.

The Messerschmitt 109s in the film were in fact Spanish Air Force aircraft manufactured under licence with the designation HA-1112-M1L *Buchón*. They were based on the Bf 109 but, ironically, fitted with Merlin engines. Seventeen were acquired for the film and used in the shooting of the Luftwaffe scenes in Spain, after which they were flown to England for the air combat sequences. I shall call them Messerschmitts, hoping that purists will half-close their eyes and imagine them as such in the summer of 1940. Spanish Air Force pilots were seconded to fly them, a number having flown the F-104 Starfighter. It emerged that four of the airworthy Messerschmitts were owned by the American-based Confederate Air Force, a group of wealthy vintage aircraft enthusiasts, who agreed to lease them on condition that they flew them. After the filming in Spain, these four colourful characters joined the Spanish pilots to ferry

Right: The view from the Spitfire cockpit was
quite adequate for landing.

Below: The narrow track undercarriage
caused no difficulty using brakes and rudders
with care.

The Hawker Hurricane had better forward visibility and guns closer together than the Spitfire.

the aircraft to England, a considerable news story for front pages in the UK at the time. Only one of them, Wilson Connie Edwards, remained flying with the film, a pilot I was to see a lot more of in the USA.

I had no opportunity or inclination to handle the larger types but did have trips in both the colourful B-25 Mitchell camera ship and in the Heinkel 111s, again manufactured under licence and designated CASA 2.111. Thirty-two of those aircraft were lent to the film company with their pilots at no charge. There are reports, however, that a large donation was made to the Spanish Air Force Benevolent Fund. The Heinkel was especially interesting to me as I watched the pilot in the left-hand seat operate flying controls mounted on a single horizontal arm protruding from a central vertical control column that could be swung over to the right seat to hand over control. This would have originally been to the navigator/bomb aimer in the event of pilot incapacitation or in other crew arrangements to a second pilot. It was resourceful German engineering.

As we got used to flying the Spitfires we became more aware that some of them had been renovated extensively, using by no means new components and that made us cautious however skillfully the work had been done. We agreed amongst the RAF pilots that we would set ourselves some limitations both to preserve the precious machines for posterity but more importantly to preserve our respective posteriors for

Hispano Aviación HA–1112–M1L Buchón.

CASA 2.111 Based on Heinkel 111.

Dual controls Luftwaffe style.

the sake of our families and friends, and to fly another day. Since the RAF was handing us over to the film company, and the aircraft were civil registered, there appeared to be no appetite for regulating, restricting, even guiding us on flying in a film. So we were on our own which rather suited us. We agreed on a limiting airspeed of 350 knots, 4 'g' positive and minimal negative, maximum boost for normal operations of +4 psi and to co-ordinate aileron and rudder carefully when manoeuvring to avoid undue twisting of the aircraft structure – something we should be doing anyway. Few shots called for much in the way of vigorous manoeuvres since that would make filming a challenge and we were often in formation. Most of the scenes we flew required passes in front of the relevant camera, flying solo or in formations of two or often more to add impact to the shots by bringing more aircraft into the camera frame. Occasionally, solo scenes would need to do something special to respond to the storyline and this is when we saw some spectacular flying to take us back to the realities of the Battle.

**

It is June 1940 at a small airfield in rural France overlooked by a beautiful château, its roofs, turrets and facades glowing in the sunlight. RAF pilots are evacuating the field in their Hurricanes in advance of the German *blitzkrieg*. Not all aircraft were serviceable or had pilots to fly them and many courageous ground crew and army troops had the task of torching these and anything else of value before the Germans arrived. Suddenly they heard the unmistakable whine of a high-speed fighter entering a steep dive, the rising pitch of the sound and the roar from its engine increasing rapidly with its approach, putting fear into the hearts of the men as they ran for cover. The German Bf 109s came in low and fast in a strafing attack. They flew at treetop height, their machine guns and 20mm cannon blazing, ripping into the hapless men with a ferocity that was merciless yet coldly efficient. Many died.

**

That was the story line of the film. In May 1968 it was among the opening sequences that included some impressive, no doubt highly enjoyable, low flying by Connie Edwards, with the château resplendent in the background. Through the camera lens it looked very French and authentic with its impressive and elegant architecture but it was in fact a cleverly painted two-dimensional hoarding at Duxford. An everyday fake for the film makers, it was intriguing to see how imaginatively they arranged it. Hiring a château on location in France would have presented all sorts of problems – money for example. These solo shots were clearly recognisable in the completed film,

The splendid Château at Duxford.

The Château was a hoarding.

whereas much of the footage of our flying ended up either on the cutting room floor or being edited, spliced, mixed, cut, pasted, however film people describe it, so that it was often difficult to spot where you as an individual were the pilot. But I did have my moment.

It was one of the rare sunny days in the summer of 1968 at RAF Hawkinge where we had positioned with our aircraft to film scenes at a grass airfield that typified fighter stations on the south coast in 1940. There was a brief lull in the daily filming schedule and we RAF pilots lounged on the grass near our aircraft, not unlike pilots in 1940, playing cards, exchanging war stories, making dubious jokes and thoroughly enjoying the idleness. We were far away from the film crews, who we assumed were setting up ground shots on the far side of the field, and we were happy to revert to RAF lifestyle if briefly. A film company car appeared in the distance, drove fast towards us in a cloud of dust and drew up next to us. A colourfully dressed youth from the Aerial Director's team jumped out and strode across to us. 'We need someone to do a roll at very low level – like a victory roll,' he said cheerfully, and stood waiting for a reaction. Either the rest of the group of six or seven were just not into low-level aerobatics or I was just a bit quicker off the mark in saying, 'I'm quite happy to do the shot but I'd like to get a bit of practice somewhere.' Furtive glances at the rest of the group for other bidders met with self-conscious disinterest.

We positioned Spitfires at RAF Hawkinge as a representative wartime grass airfield.

In fact, they looked slightly relieved, perhaps thinking 'I wonder if he knows what he's letting himself in for, he does have a wife and kids.' For those of you unfamiliar with the story in the film Jamie, one of the new pilots, returns to base after what he claims as his first kill (as do several other pilots) and is sufficiently elated to carry out a spirited victory roll over the field. His reward is a third of a kill and a rather serious debriefing by his boss, which is an understatement, covering accident risks, aircraft shortages, a sense of responsibility, indiscipline and a few other things. In the jargon of the day he was 'torn off a strip' and in the vernacular he was given something beginning with 'B' ending in 'ing'.

I called RAF Manston, less than twenty miles to the north, to ask air traffic control if they would mind if I brought a Spitfire over and practised rolls over the airfield. They were very enthusiastic and contacted all their mates to arm themselves with cameras and head for the field. I flew the Mk 9 up to Manston and started the rolls at 2,000 feet to see how the aircraft behaved which, unsurprisingly, was conventionally, the nose dropping during a roll, using full aileron and a touch of rudder for a higher rate. I quickly lowered the start height until I was only a few feet above the runway, flew in at around 250 knots or so, cranked the nose up and rolled quite safely ending up higher than I started. Back at Hawkinge we briefed for the shot which was with a Spitfire in loose formation on each wing, flying from Eastbourne and climbing up towards Hawkinge, which is set on high ground, where the cameras were positioned. 'Action' cried the director person as we approached and I rolled as briefed, the other two aircraft staying clear. 'Too low.' came the cry, so we circled for another take. Several takes later, it was apparent that the cameras were not well positioned to film a low-flying Spitfire and the scene became, from my point of view, not as exciting inside the cockpit as it could be as we raised the height but they got their shot. It was enormous fun for just a few seconds in the film but good for numerous free beers in the years to come.

Filming for the nine RAF pilots started in May 1968. Each day a printed programme was circulated which set out the flying sequences we were required to produce. There was an aerial unit with its own aerial director to arrange each scene to match the story line. This was largely irrelevant to us since each shot or sequence was defined in terms of what they wanted the camera to see, and it was for us to decide how to position and fly the aircraft to achieve that. This was ironed out at a planning session held each morning after weather briefing.

We quickly gathered that the aerial director suffered from air sickness, at least according to members of his team. Once airborne, it seemed he could manage between bouts to transmit 'action' but that was about it and, to be fair, we didn't need much more. Another minor complication during pre-flight briefings was that

The first rolls I flew were too low for the cameras.

I could easily recognise this as my moment of fame.

the Spanish pilots spoke very little English and what they did speak was mainly around ordering drinks and asking someone to dance, which did not fit well with establishing heights, speeds and how to avoid collisions. The leader of the Spanish group of pilots was, happily, a very experienced colonel who appeared to relish command and believed in tight discipline – a good thing, we thought. After some discussion among the pilots he would get together with our leader, who, for hands-on flying, was Squadron Leader Mike Vickers, my friend and colleague from the Gnat FTS (Flying Training School) at RAF Valley. The wing commander seemed to deal rather more at the political level and I didn't see a great deal of him. Mike would then brief us in normal RAF style on the whole sortie including take offs in formation, manoeuvres, safety, emergencies, and recovering back to Duxford where we were based for most of the flying. Once airborne, dialogue with Messerschmitt pilots over crackly radios, even assuming we could all arrive on one frequency and in the same piece of sky, did not contribute much, so the single word 'action' had to be sufficient to capture the shot, although I had never looked over my shoulder and everywhere else so often for other aircraft.

There were many types of shot and many different camera arrangements. Take offs in singletons, pairs, threes and sometimes as a 'gaggle' simulating an urgent scramble when the field was under an air attack were all filmed on many miles of film with perhaps just a few seconds finally being used. Many airborne passes were made on a helicopter which presumably provided more freedom of movement for the cameraman, especially when he chose to dangle in a harness fifteen or so feet below the aircraft clutching his camera. This was the technique of the famous Johnnie Jordan which he used in several Bond films to get that special shot. In filming *You Only Live Twice* he had a leg taken off by the rotor blade of another helicopter using this daring technique, but his luck finally ran out when he was sucked out of his helicopter by the slipstream of another aircraft passing close by. He was a great cameraman.

The main airborne camera platform was the B-25 Mitchell. Cameras were mounted in what would have been a tail gunner's position, now an open air platform, to get uninterrupted action shots if the cameraman could stay warm enough to operate the camera. The nose position also incorporated a camera mount for head-on shots. Other cameras could shoot through fuselage gun positions and by lowering a camera through the open bomb doors. The paintwork on the B-25 made it difficult to miss, which was what the pilots – Jeff Hawke and Duane Egli – had in mind as they watched countless scenes of excited pilots with unknown reputations hurtle towards them to miss by only feet to get 'That Shot'. More technical resourcefulness resulted in mounting other cameras on anything that moved or could fly to get shots, including the Heinkels and Messerschmitts.

Johnnie Jordan preparing to film from the helicopter.

It could be chilly filming from the tail of the B-25 Mitchell camera aircraft.

A courageous camera position for head–on shots.

The paint scheme was designed to make sure pilots missed it!

Plenty of glass in the Heinkel nose to shoot film through.

We had two Spitfires with two seats installed in tandem. In one a camera was fitted in the front seat pointing vertically upwards into a prism which captured a pilot's eye view ahead. A gunsight graticule could then be superimposed in the frame. Current in flying the Gnat, with its view from the back seat decidedly limited, I found the two-seat Spitfire straightforward to fly from the rear and settled occasionally into instructor mode, sitting VIP visitors in the front seat, camera removed, for introductory flights. The staff officer at MoD responsible for the project was among the first to come for a ride and relished this distinctive day out away from his desk, no doubt to tell all as a dinner party piece. It was also a sound investment in the continued provision of airfields, aircraft and pilots for film company use.

Among the special effects line up was the installation of smoke canisters on the side of a Spitfire's nose to simulate the results of enemy hits. I did some test flying with the canisters attached which seemed to work pretty much like the smoke selection in the Red Arrows' Gnats except that selections of red white and blue was replaced with black or white. These shots usually involved rolling lazily into a spiral dive and disappearing earthwards for the cameras, not waiting for the director to say 'pull out now' in case he was feeling queasy. What might have been mischievous banter amongst his team had made us cautious but most of us had not flown with him.

Skeets Kelly checks the camera set up in the front cockpit of the two-seat Spitfire.

I got pretty used to flying visitors from the rear seat after flying the Gnat.

Smoke pots attached to the nose to simulate fire.

The most difficult shot was producing a realistic looking dogfight that could be captured within the letter-box Panavision frame. It required as many aircraft as possible to fly close to the camera at the same time which creates an obvious hazard. With weather hold ups, technical problems and the natural caution of perhaps twenty pilots converging on one spot of sky, keen to live a long and satisfying life, it took six weeks to get anything 'in the can' that looked remotely like air combat.

The set-up for the dogfight shots taken from the B-25 was pretty standard. Ten or more Messerschmitts would take up a 'perch' position 2,000 feet higher than a formation of Heinkels and on their port side, flying a parallel heading at the same speed. A similar number of Spitfires and Hurricanes would adopt the same perch on the starboard side of the Heinkels. A short distance behind the Heinkels, a single Spitfire and single Messerschmitt flew in formation with them at the same height. On the Director's familiar croak of 'action', both formations would wing over into line astern and dive towards the Heinkels, simulating attack or defence – which looked pretty similar – with the singleton Spitfire jiggling to indicate an attack and its pursuing Messerschmitt doing very much the same.

The rest of us would by now have arrived in the same spot to create a chaotic swarm of aircraft with the primary aim of avoiding a collision. This took a great deal of spatial awareness, cranking of the head around to look everywhere for other aircraft and

Spanish pilots taking turns at the controls of the Heinkel.

wild manoeuvring to avoid them, before fleeing to the edges of the piece of sky and reforming to do it all again – many times. This, it emerged, looked remarkably like a real dogfight and was edited into the film accordingly. Equipment on the B-25 enabled the film crew to see the progress of the shot in real time and in replay mode, so they could keep striving to get an attractive shot for as long as our fuel lasted. It was tiring work but exciting, with a touch of risk, but there were no collisions and we finally had some good footage. There were no bullets, no threats, with only simulated gun flashes and smoke to simulate hits on selected aircraft that would dive earthwards for the cameras. We retained the thought at the backs of our minds that this was very different to the summer of 1940.

There were many advisors to the film company including some very famous names recognised as 'aces' in the Battle who could comment. Those included Douglas Bader, James 'Ginger' Lacey, Robert Stanford Tuck and Adolf Galland. Ginger Lacey was often to be seen during ground shots advising on how faithful the set-up was to the 1940s RAF fighter stations. But it was for us to translate the story line and the Director's attempts to specify flying manoeuvres into practical sequences along with our Spanish friends with whom we used pictures more than words. At one of these briefings we were privileged to have in attendance Lord Dowding, who was Commander in Chief of Fighter Command in 1940, now in his nineties, monitoring briefings closely from his wheelchair.

Second World War ace 'Ginger' Lacey contemplates on set.

I did wonder how the shot would work as 'Ginger' Lacey discusses it with Directors Guy Hamilton and Derek Cracknell and me. RAF colleagues in the background also ponder.

Above: Ground shot filming was conventional and fascinating to watch.

Left: Michael Caine awaits his call to film another scene.

Lord Dowding, ex- C in C Fighter Command in 1940, monitors the dogfight briefing from his wheelchair.

There were, of course, shots in the film of aircraft being damaged, shot down, set on fire and exploding in a ball of flame. An impressive production line of full-scale static models and scaled-down radio-controlled flying models was established at Pinewood studios. A Junkers Ju.87 'Stuka' belonging to the RAF Museum was examined for its potential to fly dive-bombing shots but would have been too expensive to make airworthy. Two Percival Proctors were modified to look like Stukas but were not used on-screen, with the radio-controlled models fulfilling the role. In addition to the twelve airworthy Spitfires there were eight or so 'taxi only' machines which were to provide us with some hair-raising experiences during the numerous ground shots. These supposedly taxi-capable aircraft had engines that more or less ran, with some coaxing, but would easily overheat. Flying controls that were needed to exert downforce on the tail to avoid nosing over, or to counter crosswinds that could dig in a wing, worked only partially. But the main problem was the brakes. They did not work well, if at all, and since some shots called for just short of take-off speed, bouncing across the grass in close proximity to a number of other marginally controllable Spitfires, it was, to say the least, exciting. Some found it very exciting, notably one of the lead actors who stood on the brakes while the aircraft was moving slowly and the aircraft tipped onto its nose. As I recall, taxiing was only carried out by professional pilots after the incident. Thankfully, the aircraft we actually flew were maintained by RAF ground crews and engineers who were as chuffed as we were to be working on a film and were utterly dedicated to keeping our aircraft serviceable. They were as safe as they could be.

Above: Some of the shots of taxiing and simulated take offs were more than exciting.

Left: Finishing touches with the file make a replica look real.

More carpentry. RAF groundcrew maintained the airworthy aircraft.

While we were not involved in ground shots that had no flying or taxiing, after a tip off we all assembled in front of one of the original aircraft hangars at Duxford for a scene that was, we understood, to show the hangar taking hits in a supposed air attack. What surprised us, and perhaps the RAF officers liaising with the film company, was to see most of the vintage hangar destroyed at a cost, we heard, of £50,000. It illustrated just how far the film people would go to get impact in the shot.

We became familiar with the Messerschmitts (again *Buchóns* for you purists) as the weeks went by. The Spanish pilots were very pleasant and friendly, displaying the camaraderie all professional flyers share. Unsurprisingly, they spoke in Spanish with only occasional attempts at English. 'Thank you mine's a pint of bitter', they could manage with fluency, plus a few other niceties but that was about it. They stayed in hotels and therefore socialised together and not with us who were ensconced in the Officers' Mess at RAF Debden which, during the week, housed officers running the RAF Police Dogs Training School and at weekends was deserted. We could hardly have been further away from the RAF environment as we cavorted in old aeroplanes, living in the world of crazy film people, maniacal special effects enthusiasts, celebrity film stars – and dogs.

But I eyed those Messerschmitts with curiosity, admiration and, finally, an ambition to fly one. What other chance would I get? Our leader, my friend and colleague Mike Vickers, was the only one of the RAF pilots to be checked out in the aircraft. After some

To our surprise they blew up the entire hangar.

I took a fancy to the Messerschmitt.

lobbying of Mike and much 'oooh-ahhing' near any Messerschmitt within earshot of Spanish pilots, I got my conversion. It was a challenge and a pleasure I was never to forget. It is now fifty years ago, so memories are beginning to fade but a few things stood out that I shall not forget.

There have been many accounts of flying this aircraft to extol its virtues as an agile, fast fighter that in the right hands could match or outmanoeuvre the Spitfire and other fighter types. Others have learned to approach the aircraft with a measure of caution, discovering what advocates would call *characteristics* that you became familiar with over time. Critics would refer to these as *vices*, harking back to the (anecdotally) high accident rate amongst inexperienced Luftwaffe pilots in the Second World War. This was arguably due to training inadequacies as much as any fault of the aircraft, but it was thought to be a handful for the unwary. My own experiences were a blend of these impressions.

I was handed some typed notes on flying the aircraft which provided me with the most important speeds and not much else, being in Spanish. Happily, there was a two-seat version affectionately known as 'The Dublomando' which enabled the highly-experienced Colonel and a very pleasant Captain Artega to sit in the back seat for two thirty-minute check-out sorties. These amounted to demonstrations rather than instruction since conversation was rather limited, but take offs and landings and bits in between showed the aircraft to be straightforward to fly in all stages of flight and I soloed after the hour in perfect wind and weather conditions. Then I got to know the aircraft better.

I inevitably compared the Messerschmitt to the Spitfire which, despite its obvious capacity for violence in combat, handled like a lady with no vices. Ladies need careful handling, of course, and the Spitfire could misbehave in the wrong hands if you opened up the power or raised the tail too quickly on take off and encountered a cross wind while doing either or both. But that is a characteristic of many tail-wheel aircraft. It was powerful, responsive, predictable, and had a balance of stability and manoeuvrability. The Messerschmitt was of a very different character from the time you first looked at it. It sat squat on the ground with a high nose restricting forward visibility even more than the Spitfire. The cockpit was, to say the least, snug if not cramped for all but the smallest, most slender of pilots. The heavily engineered canopy hinged sideways and the windscreen was made of tough green glass, crazed due to age, that together, even on a sunny afternoon, changed the cockpit into a fish tank, or worse a coffin.

Being briefed on the Messerschmitt cockpit by Captain Artega.

The Messerschmitt cockpit was snug with good visibility once airborne.

Taxiing was a challenge with much weaving to see past the nose, peering through the thick glass to follow the correct route to the runway, avoiding damage to accompanying expensive machines. Mishaps of any kind involving expense could incur untold levels of displeasure amongst senior film people. For one unfortunate colleague it did just that, causing a return to his day job after damaging a Spitfire in a landing accident caused by an encounter with a wire fence stretched across the undershoot at North Weald which, not unreasonably, had escaped his notice.

The characteristic that caught my attention, as it did for others who flew the aircraft – including, it later emerged, the Spanish pilots – was the aircraft's behaviour during take off and landing, especially with a touch of crosswind. There have been many stories about uncontrolled swing, ground looping and general difficulty keeping it straight during take off. These come more from pilots unfamiliar with the aircraft than those who have flown it for a few hours and become inured, fond and faithful. I was, of course, more than familiar with tail-wheel types and current on various types of Spitfire. But the Messerschmitt was certainly more 'skittish' in that it seemed directionally less stable than other types I had flown and I was under-briefed on its idiosyncrasies. The confidence of youth was to be confronted with the challenge of reality

The geometry of the undercarriage is one such idiosyncrasy. The legs cant forwards and retract outwards. The wheels are not mounted vertically but with inward facing

Damaging Spitfires was expensive and the pilot went home.

The Messerschmitt was a great fighter but it could bite the unfamiliar.

camber. The whole arrangement was supposedly designed to take up less space and reduce the weight of fairings in the wings, enhancing performance and ammunition capacity. But more downward force on the left oleo, caused by torque from the Merlin engine's clockwise rotation, makes the left tyre on its cambered wheel 'bite' more, creating drag and yaw to that side. The effect is common to many light tail-wheel aircraft with a high power-to-weight ratio during the early part of the take off, but their wheels will normally be mounted pretty much vertically (like the Spitfire) and not 'dig in'. It was said (not to me!) that in flying for the film, the Messerschmitt's left oleo was slightly over-pressured by Spanish ground crew to counter this effect and that pilots would taxi back in if they detected a soft left oleo. The yaw caused by the rotating slipstream from the propeller striking fuselage and tail fin and the gyroscopic precession effects of raising the tail too quickly, mentioned previously, are also common to all tailwheel types with a powerful engine but they will vary between types to catch out those unfamiliar with a specific aircraft. I could talk about asymmetric propeller loading as another effect but don't let's go there. Looking at parked Messerschmitts I was struck by the shortness of the fuselage and smaller fin area compared with the Spitfire, suggesting diminished directional stability. One report claimed that the asymmetrical tail fin design of the Luftwaffe's Bf. 109 had not been adjusted to allow for the change of engine rotation from the counter-clockwise German Daimler-Benz crankshaft to the clockwise Merlin, which would exacerbate the effect of torque and its consequent swing at take-off speeds with high power. All of these characteristics have been much debated as to their explanation or otherwise of the difficulties some fledgling pilots experienced during take off and landing. Ultimately it becomes a matter of a keen awareness of these effects acquired by flying the aircraft and dealing with the effects intuitively. That is the flying instructor in me talking. But relying on intuition when flying the Messerschmitt is like betting heavily on your team winning a penalty shoot-out against a seven-foot goalie guarding a hockey net.

I found the take off to be straightforward since my experience of handling any tail-wheel aircraft that was unfamiliar encouraged me to bring up the power slowly but steadily initially and, once more or less straight, more quickly, avoiding large rudder corrections and allowing minor directional deviations. Sudden use of elevator to raise the tail is also asking for trouble in any tail-wheel type. These survival techniques tend to quell pilot induced oscillations that can develop with over-controlling. Any unhappy weaves whilst accelerating will then, with luck, become irrelevant since you are airborne before there are any embarrassing deviations from the intended take-off direction, such as the in-use runway. This would be less critical on grass where a wiggle or two is fine. I later learned that more experienced Messerschmitt pilots would apply right aileron as they started take off to offset any tendency to overload the left oleo and cause a swing.

Landing I found was a bit less predictable and, of course, more critical since you are decelerating through a zone where any directional instability, whatever the cause, becomes more difficult to control as flying control effectiveness drops off. I found this to my embarrassment on my first landing in a strong crosswind on a narrow hard runway where controls are crossed to kick it straight, and the aircraft decided to take a short detour via the grass. So much for the hotshot pilot with tail-wheel experience! It just did not land like a Spitfire, an impression strongly endorsed by the Spaniards who were furtive, even shy, about their own experiences of controlling impetuous directional departures. Some likened the Messerschmitt to a highly strung thoroughbred racehorse straining to do its own thing, while you attempt to coax it to do your thing – not crash. All these smiling, hitherto unforthcoming pilots, I came to realise, had either had their own educative experience or had relished watching someone else as the aircraft went skitzy on landing. Many young Luftwaffe pilots in training or on operational units came to respect the aircraft for both its temperament and its effectiveness in combat. Once familiar with the aircraft, its skittish character became an attraction as it impressed its pilots and its enemies with agility, solidity, speed and sheer character.

Once airborne it was a delight to fly. While visibility was not that of the bubble-canopied Spitfire (earlier Bf.109 developments in Germany had a higher visibility cockpit) it was adequate once off the ground. Controls were responsive and it was a pleasure to handle. To improve manoeuvrability and lift, it sported automatic leading-edge slats which popped out at around 100 knots straight and level or at the equivalent angle of attack in a turn. These surfaces are not unlike the leading-edge flaps you see on modern airliners during take off and landing, but extending on rails to produce a gap to allow oncoming air to accelerate flow over the wing at higher angles of attack. If the aerodynamics interests you look up boundary-layer control. They didn't necessarily come out at the same time, however, since each wing could be subject to slightly different airflows not meeting the pop-out criteria. This caused degrees of yaw and roll that you got used to but it could disconcert the leader of a close formation when his wingman appeared to wobble alarmingly to stay on station around 100 knots. Indeed it could disconcert you if you were doing the wobbling but again you became wise to it after a few hours. Surprising to me was how the aircraft could fly with yaw and out of balance, confirmed by the ball out to one side (slip indicator), without any particular rudder input to cause it and no sense of imbalance. Perhaps that was why no rudder trim was thought necessary on the Bf.109. So, in close formation, when staring at the turn-and-slip indicator is not to be recommended, it was sometimes awkward staying in position and looking tidy from the ground when the aircraft was flying askew to the leader but, again, this effect diminished as you got to know this highly intriguing aircraft.

There were many sequences that we flew to capture distinctive footage that never made it into the film as far as we could see, noting that cutting, splicing and editing sequences could easily make them unrecognisable. Connie Edwards and I were tasked with flying a shot where a Spitfire pursued a Messerschmitt across the airfield at low level as it carried out a strafing attack. It was effectively a tail chase at a hundred feet with tight turns and reversals all within the airfield boundary. It was exhilarating to fly, calling for care to avoid the Messerschmitt's slipstream which, in any tail-chase manoeuvre, can throw the chasing aircraft around quite violently if it flies through vortices from the wings or prop wash of the aircraft in front. It did not, as far as I could see, appear in the film.

As July became August, steady continuous rain bounced off the wings of parked Spitfires, Hurricanes, Messerschmitts, Heinkels and a lone B–25, that comprised the thirty-fifth largest air force in the world. The summer of 1940 was unusually dry and sunny in southern England. The summer of 1968 was not, as leaden skies delivered astonishing amounts of rain day after day. The RAF pilots, familiar with the vagaries of British weather, were pragmatic, relaxed, even a little bored at times. The Spanish pilots became wistful, homesick for the blue skies of Spain where their families ate paella without them. More intriguing were the worried looks of the film people as they tried to reassure nervous investors. With no flying, what had clearly been an over-optimistic schedule continued to slip. The production portion of the $14 million budget was coming under strain and lavish seafood and champagne lunches in

The low-level tail-chase was great fun but never made the movie.

grandiose marquees and splendid sunshine gave way to sandwiches and mugs of tea under umbrellas.

An army of generously paid film people with those intriguing job titles – dolly grip, gaffer, best boy, wrangler etc. – played cards and did what film people do when not on set, which was predominantly to search for unconventional ways of having fun. Drinks flowed, work slowed, romances blossomed even more than usual in the party atmosphere. We pilots were not unaccustomed to daytime drinking, especially when the clouds might suddenly part and throw a narrow ray of sunshine on the scene to catch the attention of cash conscious executives. Film people were accustomed to springing into action at short notice and would urge us to take advantage of the gap in the clouds. We were, however, more in touch with false clearances and unimpressed with 'sucker holes' between clouds that dispensed heavy rain. We were cleared to operate under VFR (Visual Flight Rules), which meant being able to see the ground to recover, albeit through what might be a hole in the cloud. And we were strict about what conditions we felt were safe and practical for filming. This was not with any deference to budgets, directors' careers or the value of wonderful vintage aircraft but to maximise our chances of landing again and making the bar by opening time. Were we to have embarked on shooting scenes during which small holes became no holes, we would have had a tricky diversion or the prospect of an illegal descent using any radio or radar service that was available. Flying in cloud occasionally was unavoidable in the English climate but never intentional during the filming.

It was during this period of continuing bad weather that I had the tremendous privilege of showing His Royal Highness Prince Charles around a Spitfire when he made a private visit to RAF Duxford. The rain was falling in sheets as he arrived and it didn't stop, but he was determined to see everything. As he sat in the cockpit of a Mk 9 Spitfire asking searching, intelligent questions, I perched on the wing in my best blue uniform for formal occasions trying to ignore the rain soaking through the material and running down my back, legs and other places as I endeavoured to respond. It was a unique opportunity to have a conversation with a member of the Royal Family about something he was clearly interested in, having had flying lessons in an RAF Chipmunk earlier that year.

There was no let-up in the weather as pilots continued to reject any notion of climbing through several thousand feet of cloud to find the sun, relying on ageing instruments and in complete disregard of aviation law. This led to desperation amongst film crews as they wondered what pilots were for. 'Let's take the planes somewhere sunny,' said a bright young film person. 'How about Ireland?' suggested a fresh-faced executive. One of the RAF pilots diplomatically pointed out that English weather largely comes from the Atlantic across Ireland, whose weather was clearly worse than ours as we spoke, and we weren't bloody well going there. The plan was hurriedly dropped.

Showing HRH Prince Charles the Spitfire cockpit in damp conditions.

Another nameless RAF pilot suggested we find somewhere we would be happy to visit on holiday as much as fly for the film, and a flight plan for a transit to Montpellier in the south of France was duly filed.

It was with a deep sense of privilege that, on 10 August 1968, I sat in the cockpit of Spitfire Mk 2a G-AWIJ flying out over the white cliffs of Dover towards France. This was the Spitfire that had flown operationally in 1940, the year I was born. I tried to imagine the last time this aircraft was here piloted by some innocent, probably inexperienced young man courageously facing the prospect of killing or being killed.

The weather was overcast with a cloud base of 800 feet in drizzle as nine Spitfires and three Messerschmitts hung on to the tail of the Day-Glo green and orange B-25 as we coasted out heading for le Touquet and then on to Dinard for an overnight stop. The next day the weather had improved and we headed for Bordeaux as the next place to refuel, taking a cautious approach with such valuable aircraft and more valuable pilots. The Spitfire's Merlin overheated easily on the ground and, with a long distance to taxi into the Bordeaux International Airport terminal, we knew that brakes would protest which together meant a hot and smoky arrival. We shut down, unstrapped with some relief and strode nonchalantly to the terminal building, sporting authentic flying helmets and goggles and wearing camouflage green flying suits. We noticed a number of shortsighted, elderly Frenchmen, wearing berets and drinking their morning coffee and Pernod, staring open-mouthed at what seemed to be a ghostly reawakening of

Flying over France in the Mk 2 photographing the leader.

I took this from the Mk 2 in line abreast with another Spitfire in the formation.

hostilities thought to be long settled. Memories were soothed with smiles and more Pernod and we were given a 'bonne chance' for our safe passage to Montpellier over significant high ground to the north-west of the town. But the weather was now sunshine and blue skies to make the flight to our seaside destination a pleasure. Once the welcoming party of television cameras and journalists had dispersed, we settled into our hotel and contemplated with relish flying in clear weather with gastronomic adventures to come.

The daily filming routine resumed, interspersed with making the acquaintance of the good people of Montpellier to bring business to their cafés, bars, and restaurants, reliving our schoolboy encounters with the language. The film people were very familiar with these forays into foreign parts and knew how to maximise their enjoyment. They could announce 'The bill is paid by the film company' in many languages as they relaxed in luxury hotels and fraternised with the locals in bars, restaurants and other establishments, discussing anything but films. It seemed a well-practised style of living wildly at someone else's expense, dispensing largesse, bonhomie and rounds of drinks.

Airfield conditions were pretty basic and the aircraft acquired a convincing operational look as we kept up a busy flying routine of up to four sorties of over an hour each day. Each of us had our dedicated RAF ground crew who took proud ownership of the aircraft and pilots allocated to them. Perhaps they too appreciated

After operating at Montpellier the aircraft acquired an operational look.

I flew the Mk 2 (now 'P7' at BBMF) throughout the detachment to Montpellier, displaying here authentic flying helmet and goggles which I still have.

the sunshine of southern France, staying in hotels and exploring local culture, as they wrote letters home describing how long and hard the working day was. Level and upward-looking shots were fine but it was quickly discovered that shooting downwards took the Mediterranean coastal terrain into the shot which did not look a lot like Kent, especially in August, and this presented a challenge in the cutting room!

Above: I had a dedicated RAF groundcrew 'minder' for my battle-weary Mk 2 Spitfire.

Right: The South of France did not look a lot like Kent.

Year 1968		AIRCRAFT		Captain or 1st Pilot	Co-pilot 2nd Pilot Pupil or Crew	DUTY (Including number of day or night landings as 1st Pilot or Dual)	Day Flying			Night Flying			Flight Time	
Month	Date	Type and Mark	No.				1st Pilot (1)	2nd Pilot (2)	Dual (3)	1st Pilot (4)	2nd Pilot (5)	Dual (6)	Total Cols. 1-6 (7)	Captain (8)
—	—	—	—	—	—	— Totals brought forward	460·55		260·35	294·25		20·40	2028·35	1650·20
July	2	Spitfire 9	GASD	Self	Solo	Filming - Leading & Spit. Passes on Chopper	1·00						1·00	1·00
July	3	Spitfire 9	G-ASJV	Self	Solo	Low Level Pass Practice at Manston	1·30						1·30	1·30
July	3	Spitfire 9	G-ASOV	Self	Solo	Filming - Victory Rolls - Leading 3 Spits	·80						·80	·80
July	4	Spitfire 9	G-ASJV	Self	Solo	Filming - 4th of 4 Spits with Chopper	1·45						1·45	1·45
July	5	Spitfire 9	G-ASJV	Self	Solo	Filming 1051 Form Canadian One of Eden Bf 5	·40						·40	·40
July	5	Spitfire 9	G-ASOV	Self	Solo	Hawkinge - Duxford	·40						·40	·40
July	8	Spitfire 2	1J	Self	Solo	Filming - One Bf 11 Spits in Formation - Rates	1·30						1·30	1·30
July	9	Spitfire 2	1J	Self	Solo	Film ·6 - as above	1·25						1·25	1·25
July	12	Spitfire 2	1J	Self	Solo	Filming - 16 Spits in Victory Dog Fight Scene	1·30						1·30	1·30
July	16	Spitfire 2	1J	Self	Solo	Filming - Formation	1·30						1·30	1·30
July	18	Spitfire 2	1J	Self	Solo	Filming - Formation	1·30						1·30	1·30
July	18	ME 109		Self	Solo	Jet Formation	1·00						1·00	1·00
July	19	ME 109	205	Self	Solo	Aborted Film Sortie Left T. R.W.	·20						·20	·20
July	21	Spitfire 2	1J	Self	Solo	Filming - Peel off in Vics	1·35						1·35	1·35
July	22	Spitfire 2	DT	Self	Solo	Filming ·6 Pic in Vics - Passes on Chopper	1·25						1·25	1·25
July	24	Spitfire 2	1J	Self	Solo	Air Test T 4 WXO A/C	·25						·25	·25
July	26	Spitfire 2	1J	Self	Solo	Smoke Test	·15						·15	·15
July	30	Spitfire	N	Self	Solo	S.C.T. Formation + Hatos	·30						·30	·30
August	1	Gnat T1	XS101	Self	F/Lt Tait	·F Aeros Cts.	·40						·40	·40
August	10	Spitfire 2	GANIJ	Self	Solo	Duxford - Cambridge	·10						·10	·10
August	10	Spitfire 2	GANIJ	Self	Solo	Cambridge - Le Touquet	1·10						1·10	1·10
August	11	Spitfire 2	GANIJ	Self	Solo	Le Touquet - Dinard	1·20						1·20	1·20
August	12	Spitfire 2	GANIJ	Self	Solo	Dinard - Bordeaux	1·35						1·35	1·35
August	12	Spitfire	GANIJ	Self	Solo	Bordeaux - Montpellier	1·40						1·40	1·40
						Totals carried forward	487·10		260·35	294·25		20·40	2054·30	1655·53
							(1)	(2)	(3)	(4)	(5)	(6)	(7)	(8)

A page from my log-book shows the daily routine.

Overall some 5,000 flying hours were clocked up by the aircraft in the film, with 110 hours of shooting aerial sequences edited down to forty minutes required for the film. We saw the 'rushes' at the end of each day and were entranced by many wonderful shots, most of which did not appear in the film. Perhaps they are still sitting in an archive somewhere waiting to be uncovered … . The Mk 2a Spitfire that I flew throughout our time in France is now with the BBMF, sporting the RAF registration P7350 and affectionately known as 'P7'. I logged thirty-eight hours flying the aircraft out of seventy-six hours in all marks of Spitfire, including the Marks 2, 5, and 9, deducing that the two-seaters were both adapted Mark 9s.

By the end of August flying shots in the film were largely completed and, after some muted farewells, it was time to fly the aircraft back to Duxford. This was uneventful, retracing the route we had used previously but in good weather. More eventful was the news that five years of requests for an exchange flying tour with the United States Air Force had finally been granted and I was posted to the 4782nd Combat Crew Training Squadron at Perrin Air Force Base, Texas, to fly the Convair F-102 Delta Dagger interceptor, affectionately known as the Deuce.

Chapter 7

The Delta Dagger

The Braniff Airways flight broke clear of the high cloud layer to give us our first view of the state of Texas. Five times the landmass of England, it was absolutely flat for as far as the eye could see with a scattering of small towns dispersed widely over what looked like huge areas of sandy coloured emptiness as dusk approached. As we descended further, despite the failing light we could see more signs of life as car headlights trailed along the highways out of the urban sprawl of Dallas and Fort Worth where we landed minutes later at Love Field. Perrin AFB (Air Force Base) was about seventy-five miles north of Dallas on the border with Oklahoma close to Lake Texoma, a large reservoir, where the surrounding terrain was again devoid of significant features. The most common sight was the nodding donkeys or 'pump jacks' extracting oil as they had done for many years in Texas following the oil boom of the early twentieth century. It was to be my 'local area' for the next three years flying the F-102. With the Cold War

Fighter aircraft with a purpose American-style.

still raging, the aircraft was one of the 'Century Series' fighters that the Americans introduced during the intense arms race of the period.

Our journey from the UK had included a short stay in Washington DC for a briefing on how to deal with the differences we might encounter between the American and British ways of life that could surprise us. This was a little puzzling since the main reason we had wanted to go the USA was precisely because it would be different and we like surprises of the pleasant kind. The gentle warning was aimed at wives who might be a little disorientated as their husbands became absorbed in their new routine. They could feel isolated, even homesick, as they handled the culture change was the thought. Perhaps my wife Anne would be swept off her feet by the onslaught of American friendliness and enthusiasm for having a good time. In fact we were both welcomed, entertained and befriended with such generosity we not only negotiated the lifestyle but emulated it with gusto.

The purpose of the exchange scheme was greater mutual understanding with a free exchange of ideas on military operations between close allies and to act as an ambassador for the UK. A careful balance was needed to show that we Brits can work, play and party as well as anyone else but with taste, decorum and charm. Honourable thoughts but I'm sure you can imagine how that balance could go adrift when subjected to the legendary American hospitality and an unending search for fun, especially to break the ice with any toffee-nosed Brits! My wife seemed to find us a balance which meant entertaining and being entertained, on and off the base, in a whirlwind of parties, boat trips, dinner parties, barbecues, and balls in the 'O' Club (Officers' Club). We were the only Brits on the base, and probably for miles around, so we had to find our own way to co-exist with the foreigners. We did find them to be more foreign than we expected, but socially they were some of the nicest, kindest and most entertaining people we have met. We established close friendships that lasted forty years, with visits and shared holidays in the USA and Europe.

My predecessor and his wife had developed their own style of handling any over-exuberance at parties they threw, which included a less than subtle way of announcing that it was time to go home. They played the National Anthem, the British one, complete with massed bands, at conversation-stopping volume – quirky but it worked. Our technique was to outlast our guests. One guest couple wasted no time in spreading the word about Lloyd-style entertaining. This was after a curry evening when assembled friends saw a reflected glow from the tiny kitchen flickering on the tiny dining-room walls as the Bombay Duck (dried fish) in the oven caught fire. We feigned lack of concern after extinguishing the blaze, and topped up the wine before sitting down to chicken curry with well-cooked Bombay Duck. We did become close friends and shared much common ground with two successive Australian exchange officers and their families who changed over during our three-year tour and were known for throwing parties that were also far from dull. We are still in close touch.

Recent holders of the post had flown the single-seat Lightning with the pilot operating the on-board radar for the final stages of an intercept after initial direction from a ground controller. My own background did offer some useful experience. Instructing on the Gnat developed the ability to think quickly to avoid being written off by over-eager students and it was suitably demanding to fly. But it had no radar. The Javelin was delta-winged and did have radar but the extra seat carried a navigator who enjoyed twiddling the radar knobs and levers and working out intercept geometry. It might have been a reflection on the limitations of pilots who should be left to steer and squeeze the trigger when told to. Or it might have been a continuance of crewing habits developed during the Second World War for aircraft used in the night-fighter role. The F-102 was a single-seat interceptor. So it was back to being a student for six months to learn to fly the aircraft, do the radar thing and become an instructor pilot or 'IP' in USAF terminology to teach all that to American pilots.

I went through two conversion courses in quick succession with some overlap. One was with eight pilots just out of training or re-streaming from other types, for the standard F-102 OCU course. The first task was to learn enough about the aircraft systems to start flying it before getting deep into radar theory and intercept geometry over the rest of the course. The other programme was a conversion to the Lockheed T-33 trainer aircraft which was used as target for intercept training and which, in common with all other IPs, I was to fly regularly. It meant two ground schools, two sets of operating procedures, two very different handling techniques at pretty much the same time – my first of many new experiences.

The T-33 was an early jet but very capable and widely used.

The ubiquitous T-33 or 'T-Bird' has seen service with many air forces, mainly as an advanced trainer, with over 6,000 built following its introduction in 1948. Powered by an Allison J33-A-35 single jet engine with a centrifugal compressor delivering 5,400lb of thrust it had a maximum sea-level speed of 478 knots and a service ceiling of 48,000 feet which, with tip tanks and extra equipment, we could never quite reach. At Perrin its role was to represent Soviet bombers in any attack on the USA or its bases overseas. Its radar return was of course much fainter than a large bomber but that would equate to detecting the larger targets at greater range. It carried an underwing electronic counter-measures pod and dispensers for chaff – strips of tinfoil as used in the Second World War to confuse radars and radar-guided missiles. It was straightforward to handle but with heavy controls, especially as speed increased, only the ailerons having hydraulic power boost. But I had come from flying the Gnat, which had very responsive controls. Landings I found interesting as I switched between types.

As any pilot knows the first thing to get sorted when converting to a new type is to find out where the wheels are in the flare and embed that in the brain as a perspective of height above the ground, supported by horizon and peripheral cues. Then it is getting used to the rate of speed loss as power is reduced, adjusting pitch for a soft touch. This is not usually a problem but the T-33's elevator was particularly sensitive at the 115 knots recommended threshold speeds, and very easy to overuse until you learned to adjust the speed slightly for the fuel weight and stroke the elevator soothingly. It's a bit like climbing into another car and getting used to accelerator and brake-pedal pressures to drive smoothly. The T-33 was one of the early straight-winged jets like the Vampire that came over the end of the runway carrying only modest drag at landing speeds, even with undercarriage and flaps down, and it floated on and on as you caressed the elevator to get the kiss of a smooth touch-down long associated with pilot competence, an idea now largely defunct when an on-speed *thump*, especially in wet or crosswind conditions, is safer. Tell that to the airline passenger as he arrives home a touch suddenly on the Gatwick runway and he might think otherwise, but 'greasers' are for dry windless days in the sun on long runways with light traffic. I rapidly got used to the T-33's idiosyncrasies and charms. It was fully aerobatic but a bit cumbersome after the agile Gnat sports car of an aircraft.

Navigation equipment included VHF Omni-directional Range (VOR) with Course Deviation Indicator (CDI), Automatic Direction Finder (ADF) and DME. These were all based on ground radio beacons which preceded inertial systems and the more recent GPS from which the SATNAV in your car was developed. In 1968 it meant that the T-33 could fly in the same regulated airspace as any airliner and hence take advantage of a comprehensive air traffic control system that provided separation and

T-33 cockpit with flight instruments of the era. Note markings at top of artificial horizon above turn and slip. (*Courtesy Bentwaters Cold War Museum*)

controlled approaches into airfields. With its 5,447lb of fuel, curiously displayed in gallons (813), the T-33 could fly 1,000 miles non-stop, a feature that was to provide very special opportunities for travel over the coming months.

Differences in instrumentation from RAF aircraft got my attention on the first night conversion sortie. My gung ho IP, complete with big cigar (during the briefing that is), thought it would be clever to mix night familiarisation with instrument training on the range of navigation aids. So I spent most of the sortie head down on instruments, trying to use the 'geometry on the instrument' USAF techniques to decide how to interpret the VOR/CDI and turn the right way. Many of you who are pilots will know the problem and I later taught a different technique emphasising situational awareness. As I focused on the all-black AH with white markings at the top, not the bottom as per RAF instruments at the time, a loud American voice told me to close my eyes while he (illegally) rolled the aircraft several times. He then handed back control to regain level flight whereupon I happily stabilised wings level upside down with the evenly spread lit-up settlements across a flat Texan landscape looking identical to the starry night sky. My momentary disorientation and colourful expletives from the IP, who knew the T-33 engine stops after thirty seconds inverted for lack of fuel, confirmed my suspicion that things were not right and to his relief I quickly rolled upright. Despite these interesting episodes I quickly got used to this robust if dated aircraft.

The Deuce was supersonic after area-ruling modifications.

The Deuce, the USAF's first delta-wing fighter, was easy to fly after 700 hours flying the Javelin. The delta design brought structural strength, good manoeuvrability and strong vortices at higher angles of attack producing extra lift accompanied by high drag. With no tail plane that would normally include elevators it had 'elevons' at the wing trailing edges to provide both aileron and elevator control in response to normal stick movements, which solved the Javelin's problem of elevator function when the delta wing blanked off airflow over the tail at high angles of attack. Other innovations were speed brakes just above the jet efflux that stored a brake parachute for reduced landing roll, which was deployed on every landing. It was powered by one Pratt & Whitney J-57 engine delivering 11,700lb of thrust, increasing to 17,200lb in afterburner, which gave a rate of climb of 13,000 feet per minute. It was supersonic, achieving Mach 1.2 at 40,000 feet but only after a major redesign, to become the first aircraft to employ 'area ruling', adopting a coke-bottle-shaped fuselage to solve aerodynamic drag problems at transonic speeds. It could operate to 53,000 feet, with a range of 1,173 nautical miles.

The pilot sat in a roomy 'office' of a cockpit, typical of American fighters, which has since been widely adopted in fighter aircraft. It had a logical layout with standard instrument panel, TACAN and HSI. This combined a VOR system showing bearing to a beacon plus course deviation with an embedded ILS display. Other system displays and controls were well laid out to provide the usual array of dials and switches that appear to the uninitiated to be rather busy but mostly required only momentary attention from pilots, depending on the phase of flight. Mounted on top of the control column were two short 'sticks', one of which stayed locked to operate the flying controls, the other unlatching for interception work to operate the radar scanner and lock on controls. It was re-latched for recovery. A radar-scope took up a central position and became a key element of instrument scanning during intercepts which were mainly practised clear of cloud for safety reasons but obviously in any weather for real.

Conversion flying, after systems training in the (static) simulator, was in the two-seater TF-102, affectionately known as 'The Tub'. Instructional technique was essentially *you fly, I'll watch*, which suited me fine. I soloed after four sorties and happily worked my way through the OCU course with lots of simulator time, dual sorties for anything new, but mostly single-seat flying, using a Nadar radar-scope recorder for debriefs. Although operating the radar was something new, interception techniques and geometry were pretty much common to any air defence operation and were familiar to me.

The RAF was easy to spot during F-102 conversion. I later used USAF kit.

The cockpit was a roomy office with good visibility.

… and we took our own back-pack parachute to the ejection seat.

On completion of the course I had a few sorties to check I had the standard to teach students what I'd just learned and to practise landing from the right seat, where stick and throttle hands were reversed with throttle on the right console. Landing and close formation flying were an amusing dexterity challenge for a right hander. My instructional credentials were already established and off I went to take up my primary job of training mainly first tourists, which I was used to, and I settled quickly into the job.

The F-102 was a stable platform for instrument and radar work, interceptions following well-established profiles related to target height, speed, tactics, defences and the height and weapons available to the interceptor. Radar-guided missiles were carried for head-on attacks supplemented by heat-seeking missiles for attacks from the rear. If a frontal attack failed, a tactic called 'front-stern re-attack' was used to position close behind the target for another attempt. Unguided rockets were housed in the missile-bay doors under the fuselage, usually delivered in a 90-degree broadside attack as sailors might describe it.

The rocket attack was reminiscent of the Red Arrows synchro-pair displays as they hurtled towards each other and missed their partners by feet. A 90-degree collision course was set up on the radar keeping a target dot in the middle of a circle generated on the screen. If you were successful in tracking the dot the target aircraft would appear in your line of sight growing rapidly in size as the range closed. Firing was at rather close range, which it would have to be with unguided rockets, but it felt just a tad short of collision point. After a simulated last-minute firing, the escape manoeuvre was to break hard behind the target. These attacks were not practised at night.

When intercepting a highflying target, it was common to resort to a maximum rate climb in full afterburner climbing at 400 knots until reaching and maintaining Mach 0.9. If the target was still well above, the technique was to level out and accelerate for a 'snap-up' climb to provide semi-active missile guidance with on-board radar, or secure infra-red homing for a heat-seeking missile, escaping after weapons release, with falling speed, by rolling inverted and using gravity and elevator to dive away.

Alerts and scrambles were practised from a hangar or 'barn' similar to the RAF's hardened shelter where I could revert to the RAF practice of completing pre-take-off checks from memory instead of the standard USAF 'read the checklist' procedure. I was always quickest, although it seemed to make little impression on pilots trained to do things 'by the book'.

The F-102 was straightforward in the circuit with the high-lift/high-drag characteristics of all deltas. There were no flaps, the drag at 170 knots approach speed with gear down being considerable. Approach angle and speed were easily controlled with power to about 160 knots over the threshold and a nose-high touchdown at a bit less. The air trapped under the delta wing provided a natural cushion, requiring little flare, and the aircraft virtually landed itself if you held the attitude and closed

The two-seat 'Tub' positioned in the alert hangar or 'barn'.

Imposing to look at, the F-102 was a capable interceptor and straightforward to handle.

the throttle. Young USAF IPs wishing to express their manhood, or perhaps their frustration at being an IP rather than that front-line jock throwing weapons around, used blips of afterburner to maintain 170 knots around the final turn to display how tight they could keep the circuit, rolling wings level just before the runway threshold. It was a testosterone-driven 'don't try this at home' technique, not to be emulated by course students or those with less to prove.

Instructional techniques were not widely discussed as this was not a flying training unit as much as an operational conversion squadron and once airborne it was more about 'here's how we do it' then 'now have a go' than anything more complex. All IPs were qualified to operate the simulator and ran through each sortie with their students providing as much commentary and repeated exercises as needed before trying it for real in the air. One technique, however, was new to me. After the initial conversion trips in the two-seater Tub the student was launched off in the single-seat aircraft for his first solo. But he was not alone. His instructor would take off alongside and 'chase' him in loose formation for the entire exercise, offering advice and re-assurance should he need it. For the landing pattern (circuit in the RAF of 1970), the task was to fly in close enough formation to check his speeds and approach path, correcting him over the radio as necessary all the way to his 'low approach', with the instructor then peeling off to watch the overshoot and pick up with him again. The RAF instructor would simply brief him on the ground and say 'off you go', possibly sitting in the control tower with a cup of coffee, hoping to see him return. The USAF shepherding approach was more of a challenge to the IP than the student coping with a first solo but it was fun to fly.

I found the USAF to be comprehensively regulated with a manual and a procedure for pretty much everything, whether it was for flying, engineering, administering or just walking along. It was therefore a surprise one day to be part of a Squadron Open Day for families and others on the base when the usual tight control of flying gave way to having a bit of fun, specifically for pilots' wives. I reflected on family days at fighter bases in the UK where wives and children would see operational aircraft from a safe distance as I helped my wife, complete with helmet and flying suit, strap into the left-hand seat of the TF–102. I strapped into the right seat, closed the canopy, checked she was comfortable, more or less, and started the engine. After-start checks and taxiing to the take-off point were normal. On clearance from ATC, I lined up on the runway centreline, ran up the engine to take-off power, released the brakes, engaged full afterburner and with a roar and a push in the back we shot forward to a tense silence from the left seat. At near lift off I cut the power, slowed for the next exit and taxied back for photographs and refreshments. That was the 'inclusivity for wives' event, another new experience – certainly for my wife – and I guess it was not practised on squadrons at home due to fears of 'Scandal! Waste of fuel! Why not me? 'reports by diligent journalists, or tightlipped comments from conscientious Health and Safety persons just doing their job … .

I took my wife for a ride in the TF-102 on Wives Day Out.

It was astonishing to discover IPs could take a T-33 away at weekends to anywhere in the USA (apart from Hawaii – more's the pity!). It was euphemistically called 'navigation training', perhaps loosely to do with the USAF's need to be ready to deploy anywhere on the planet, negotiating air traffic control and navigation challenges in difficult weather and possibly alone. This took on a special meaning for me with no experience of flying under anything but military control. I could fly in the same airspace as commercial traffic, talking to the same ATC centres, along the same routes – something of a departure for an RAF fighter pilot for whom, at that time, controlled airspace was enemy territory and an 'airways crossing' akin to flying through the Heathrow circuit. So every six weeks or so, with clearance from an understanding wife, I accepted requests from students to fly them home in exchange for fly fishing, golf, sightseeing or just that warm American family hospitality, seeing life in the States from an 'insider' perspective. This meant flying long distances with two or even three flights to reach the northern border or either coast from Texas, allowing for ultra-safe fuel margins and a whim to land at as many bases as was reasonable. To illustrate, from Dallas to Seattle is some 1,400 miles direct, New York similar, San Diego 1,000 miles, Palm Beach Florida similar. Of expeditions by air to many parts of the USA, three stand out in my memory.

I landed the T-33 at as many bases as I could justify, for the experience.

A young student, well, younger than my 30 years, approached me for a ride in the back seat to anywhere I happened to fancy. He had been re-streamed from a course flying the F-105 Thunderchief after a mid-air collision with an eagle that came through his windscreen, taking him off the course for repairs to his face. That, anyway, was his story which I had no reason to disbelieve and he did have convincing scars. His surname of 'Basher' did make me think, but he was a great character with what I quickly came to realise was an impressive if mischievous sense of adventure. I picked a route with his help to take in a colourful mix of Western States. We landed and refuelled at Cannon AFB, New Mexico; Luke AFB, Phoenix, Arizona; Navy North Island, San Diego, California; Nellis AFB, Nevada and Holloman AFB, New Mexico. After a pleasant if rather liquid stop at Phoenix overnight, we delayed our departure to San Diego the next morning for our heads to clear. With a typically sunny forecast over the desert terrain in eastern California, we got airborne, cancelled our flight plan to enable free visual flying and descended to 1,000 feet or less to fly by dead reckoning to the Navy base at North Island where, avoiding the bar, we visited the wonderful local zoo. The next day we filed a flight plan to Nellis AFB which is close to Las Vegas. As we approached the breathtaking Grand Canyon, my GIB (Go In the Back) suggested lightly that we should again cancel our flight plan and take a closer look at the Canyon before landing. I innocently complied and dropped into the canyon to take in the fascinating panorama of erosion and geology. It was so visually impressive that, on spotting the Colorado River at the bottom of a narrow gorge 400 feet deep, I flew lower, dropping briefly into the gorge at 300 knots for a blurry photo and then, exhilarated, climbed out to land shortly after at Nellis. It was only later that I learned that this escapade was virtually a court martial offence (or the equivalent) in the USAF, due to inattentive pilots in past years having flown into one of the many cables stretched across the Canyon. Strict exclusion rules were widely known across the USAF which my young friend had conveniently forgotten – if he ever knew them.

That evening I was treated to the 'All Night Gambling with Free Drinks' experience which those of you who have been to the Las Vegas 'Strip' will know about. Not being a gambler, I watched Ned play Crap Dice, blearily pondering whether his encounters with eagles and canyons were recklessness or bad luck as he lost game after game. But he was excellent company. The next day we flew back via Holloman AFB into Perrin with a 300-foot cloud base and half-mile visibility, landing from a PAR approach after another experience clocked up.

The opportunity to explore the USA by personal jet was a unique perk of the job and might trigger fond memories in older ex-RAF readers of a 'Station Flight' at many RAF stations of the 1950s and 1960s where a spare aircraft or two would be available for 'communications' flying. In my time it was typically a Meteor and easier to get your hands on if you were of senior rank or in favour with someone of senior rank.

Descending into the Grand Canyon.

The Colorado River at the bottom of the gorge taken at 300 knots.

The T-33 at Perrin was available to all instructor pilots any weekend and there were plenty of aircraft. It was the chance to get a glimpse of the American way of life in the company of ordinary Americans who happened to be in the air force, with families all over the continent. I flew down to New Orleans in formation with a fellow IP to visit his family, enjoying Cajun food and a very warm welcome. My neighbour, a logistics officer, wanted to visit his previous air force base at Eglin AFB, Florida, and introduce me to some of his friends. Redwood forests and trout fishing on the McKenzie river were the highlights of a weekend taking another IP friend to see his family in Eugene, Oregon. This trip was also memorable.

The route we chose to Portland, Oregon, about a hundred miles north of Eugene, involved refuelling stops at Buckley AFB, Colorado, and Mountain Home AFB, Idaho, flying over a wide variety of wild and mountainous terrain that illustrated vividly the beauty of North America. It has just about every physical feature and climate of the populated world and it was easy to understand why large numbers of Americans did not see the need for a passport. The trip to Portland and drive to Eugene were pleasant, the hospitality typically warm and the fishing idyllic. We duly drove back to Portland and filed a flight plan for the return to Perrin along the same route and it was my turn to fly in the front seat. Routine study of the weather forecast showed a small risk of thunderstorms over the Rocky Mountains of Colorado. On arrival at Buckley, the weather forecast for the final leg to Perrin was fine overall but still with a risk of isolated

Having my picture taken en route to New Orleans.

thundery showers over the hills, which we could if necessary fly around, although with no radar we would be relying on air traffic control warnings and our eyes to spot them. We took off in bright sunshine with puffy white clouds in the distance which, naïve that I was, looked like fulfilling the innocuous forecast. As we flew on and the clouds darkened my colleague in the back got a little fidgety saying we could always turn back and think about it. I didn't actually say 'Wimp, I'm used to bad weather' but thought as much, and pressed on as the cumulus clouds grew at an alarming rate and the escape route behind us closed. It was a freak weather occurrence that caused all commercial airliners on nearby routes to divert and our VOR and ADF needles to dance around to the magnetic tunes of the thunderstorm cells, rendering them useless. Oh yes, and the radio was becoming intermittent. At flight level 330 the clouds were well above us and all around. Basically, we were lost up the proverbial creek without a paddle and my colleague in the back was genuinely frightened. I controlled my self-reproach at getting into this situation, albeit unwittingly, and repeatedly asked ATC for a diversion to the nearest available airfield – when I could contact them. I must have lived a life to please the gods because the controller, also under pressure, finally responded in a clipped voice with 'Cannon Air Force Base, two o'clock forty miles, steer 160 degrees, cleared for immediate descent' as a gap in the clouds opened and I launched into the descending spiral taught in early flying lessons, but much more vigorously, with throttles closed, speed brakes out – might have even lowered the gear – and down we plunged. The rest was fine and we landed at Cannon under darkening skies, breathing a little hard, but feigning nonchalance for the ground crew. As we climbed out the airfield was overwhelmed by a 'Roll Cloud', something I'd never seen and haven't seen since. It was the leading edge of a vigorous thunderstorm cell, the updrafts picking up the West Texas dust, reducing visibility to zero in its wake. The flight back to Perrin the next day was relaxing.

In exchange for the perk of free jet travel to anywhere, IPs were on a weekend standby roster to cover operational or compassionate needs of base personnel to get somewhere quickly, but nobody expected to get called out on their watch. Sure enough, on one rainy, cold, blustery Saturday in February, I got the call to fly a young airman first class to Selfridge AFB, Michigan, for compassionate reasons. The weather was solid cloud to 38,000 feet. At cruising level in the narrow T-33 cockpit, with no auto-pilot, en route charts stretched across the cockpit covering the instruments, I became busy with navigation, radio calls and snatched glances at the instruments behind the chart to stay upright and on heading, so that conversation with the AFC in the back was limited. Needless to say, we did get there to land on an icy runway in snow flurries and approaching dusk. I decided to go south again due to the worsening forecast which could mean explaining to my wife why I was spending the winter 1,000 miles north of her, and filed for Columbus AFB, Mississippi, for an overnight stay to calm my nerves with a glass or two and a night's sleep in the Bachelor Officers' Quarters. It was all

The Roll Cloud races over Cannon Air Force Base.

The refuelling crew seem unconcerned as the storm arrives.

part of the stimulation and drama of new flying experiences that many of you will have known in one way or another.

Flying in the USA was certainly adventurous at times for an RAF pilot used to moderate UK weather with its fronts, depressions, winds and occasional thunderstorms topping out at the tropopause, typically 35,000 feet. Perrin was in 'Tornado Alley', where Pacific fronts meet the warm moist air from the Gulf of Mexico with all those thunderstorm triggers we learned about in meteorology exams to produce big weather. I was occasionally nominated to fly west of the base to track incoming violent weather, looking for rain, hail, tornadoes and the like. Perhaps exchange officers were dispensable. When the sky turned a curious green I flew back and advised a cease-flying decision, whereupon the aircraft were lashed to the ground and we headed for the bar. On one occasion I diverted to the base met office to see on the radar a nearby thunderstorm that showed its top to be at 75,000 feet. Size matters with thunderstorms.

There were other flying encounters. I had one sortie in the back of the Deuce's successor, the F-106, for an air combat mission. Very smooth and impressive, with an eerie silence punctuated by short radio exchanges and heavy breathing as long-range battles with some very capable missiles were fought with little or no visual sightings of the opposition.

En route to Lake Michigan I could only snatch a glance at the Airman First Class in the back.

In a visit to Connie Edwards on his ranch in West Texas, I drooled over his hoard of Mustangs, T-6s, Bf.109s and a Spitfire which I'd flown only a few months earlier in the filming of *The Battle of Britain*. After a couple of beers he got me airborne in his Super Cub and, to my surprise, pulled out the rear stick, got out and said 'take it for a spin'. That was the first and only time I've ever flown immediately after drinking – but it was a sunny day, a private strip, at just few hundred feet in a remote part of west Texas, so I easily swallowed my flight safety conscience for twenty minutes. He also owned a Cessna 310 which we flew with wives to go to the races at Ruidoso, New Mexico – so easy when you don't worry about money.

A passenger flight in the famous C-47 Skytrain, colloquially known as the Gooney Bird, also known as a Dakota or DC-3, was a more sombre occasion. Two weeks before I had been flying a T-33 as target for students to practise interceptions at medium level. One of them, on completion of the exercise, flew to his home town in Oklahoma just across the nearby border and carried out an unauthorised low-level aerobatics display, with his parents watching, when he lost control and crashed. The trip in the C-47 was to take a group from Perrin to attend his funeral. It brought back vivid memories of another funeral in my first year at Cranwell when a student about to graduate was killed in a crash after take off when his engine failed and he didn't manage to eject. We had urgent lessons in the rarely used ceremonial drill for military funerals, and I slow marched through Cranwell village with reversed arms to the cemetery where, in a 'firing party', we fired the traditional three-volley salute over the coffin. The short flight to Oklahoma was a similarly sombre tribute to a lost comrade, although as we flew along in the venerable C-47 there were private thoughts about flying escapades you should avoid.

Socially the tour with the USAF merits adjectives from both languages. Very enjoyable and stimulating might be the reserved English characterisation. In American it might be 'It was a blast!' We certainly found the Americans on the base to be warm and friendly, and met many civilians in the local towns – Sherman and Denison – who seemed to have a lifestyle dominated by parties. An RAF colleague flew into Perrin in an unmarked T-33 wearing an unmarked flying suit and answering no questions except 'would you like to come with us to a Luau this evening' to which he said 'Yes', imagining, accurately, that there were parties like this all the time at Perrin. The entrance route to the party was across small rafts in the large open-air swimming pool that also cooled bottles of champagne lowered to the bottom, with hostesses in Hawaiian dress serving drinks. We shared thoughts of introducing similarly themed parties back in the UK, but felt that we could not guarantee the balmy Texas temperatures or the singularly American style and hospitality. The next day the base commander was obliged to refer to the serious business of risk of death by broken champagne bottles after many partygoers hurled themselves into the pool as the party got more exuberant. This was not written into Base Safety Procedures but no doubt would be.

At work the USAF pilots appeared to take rules and regulations seriously but privately expressed humorous scepticism regarding their efficacy since their quality seemed to be judged by their length not their content. It left little doubt as to what was required of you and how to stay on the right side of the authorities but could be regarded by lackadaisical Brits as a bit rigid. It would prove a shock to some USAF exchange officers flying with the RAF or RN in the UK during the Cold War period when they were left to make their own decisions in an operational environment that relied on self-sufficiency more than guidance. To evade Soviet radars attacks had to be flown at very low levels, navigating by map and stopwatch, perhaps assisted by a navigator, without much help from the ground. This changed with the arrival of the advanced avionics and navigation aids which relieved some of the handling demands on pilots but required intelligent use of airborne systems, increasingly from two-man crews. In my time at Perrin I got to know several pilots who had just served in Vietnam, notably my neighbour who had flown F-105s in the air defence suppression of 'Wild Weasel' role with no shortage of self-sufficiency or independence.

The only international incident that comes to mind in operating the F-102 was flying in formation with the Australian exchange officer to Houston to pick up a Union Jack from the British Consulate for a Queen's Birthday celebration. On returning to Perrin the weather was, as forecast, thick cloud down to 500 feet in rain with good visibility at the airfield and we'd briefed to recover in formation, which we saw as routine. All was well as I formated on my Aussie mate, and we popped out of cloud and did our thing down to a normal formation touch-down. The ATC controller, in a reproachful voice, said he would have to report us for doing this below the regulation minimum of 600 feet cloud base for formation landings, taking no account of the professional execution. We didn't take this too seriously and, happily, nor did anyone else but it serves to illustrate rule-driven approaches that are a necessary discipline for some when others might use competent discretion more than rigid regulation. Perhaps USAF pilots would secretly agree.

The Union Jack was duly stashed away until the day of The Queen's birthday approached. And here comes the play on cultural differences of which our Monarchy is an iconic symbol. It seemed a good idea to visibly, but diplomatically, display our loyalty to the Her Majesty, our history, the Empire, whatever, in a country without a monarchy but with what we perceived as a private wish to have one. Less grandly, the Aussie couple and ourselves, having stoically batted off relentless, friendly, respectful but faintly mischievous jibes (especially after a few beers) at the elitist, stuck-up, unduly formal nature of the British aristocracy, of which we four were patently not part, saw a chance for a bit of fun.

I mounted the Union Jack outside our modest semi-detached base housing home a week or two before the official Queen's Birthday, which prompted many queries as to what it meant. In parallel, we sent out invitations from the Aussie couple and ourselves to a cocktail party in the Officers' Club. The Base Commander and his top team of colonels plus a few other 'wheels' and our squadron colleagues were all invited with their partners. The bar staff, who were used to slinging drinks along the bar in noisy happy hours taking no cheek from anyone whatever their rank, were tickled pink to be invited to walk around serving drinks and canapes on trays, dressed in their best uniforms at what was seen as a unique occasion, which indeed it was. Between us we provided delicate cocktail snacks and a variety of exotic drinks, taking advantage of a peculiar loophole in the Texas liquor laws.

Texas was a dry state at this time and when meeting with friends for dinner in a Dallas restaurant we had the doctor amongst us take his black bag full of booze to go with the mixers we bought, with waiters turning a blind eye. Foreign visitors working in the State could also legally import spirits. This meant driving into an underground access to the Liquor Control Board building in Dallas, knocking on a plain wooden door to be discreetly handed crates of inexpensive liquor we had ordered by phone and, with no one in sight, whisking it off back to Perrin. A larger than normal order provided for the Queen's Birthday adequately. The party was a great success – a first for the Americans – the only discomfort being to guess what to do if the British National Anthem was played. We did not put this to the test as protocols and formalities seemed to dissipate with each drink, amidst much handshaking and back-slapping – for the guys that is.

The RAF back home continued nursing its junior officers for the stardom that perhaps 5 per cent of them aspired to, and I did not escape the two-year correspondence course as an intermediate step along the yellow-brick road of promotion, development and the opportunity to prove that three years at RAF College Cranwell was an investment worth making. Meanwhile, my wife approached the end of nine months preparing to produce our second child – another daughter as it turned out. I was on the golf course playing the game of my life when the golf professional raced to the fifth green in a golf buggy with a message for me to go immediately to the hospital to join my wife who was completing the job. When I arrived things had stopped moving and after checking with the doc that all was well he and I sat on the end of the bed discussing golf until I was sent away to await news which came a couple of hours later with the birth of a second daughter, who enjoyed dual nationality.

I experienced not one serious emergency in over 900 hours flying F-102s and T-33s which is a credit to USAF standards of maintenance and dedication, procedures and all. It was also reassuring to have the aircraft checked over externally just before take off by a dedicated crew looking for leaks, unlatched panels, etc., known appropriately as 'Last Chance'. We did practice forced landings, but it was a bit tongue in cheek since you had to be over a hard long runway, higher than 10,000 feet at the start, gliding at a speed of 220 knots, with a rate of descent of 6,000 feet per minute, and the ram-air turbine deployed to produce hydraulic and electrical power to control the thing. Seventy-six per cent power against speed brakes simulated a failed engine.

This imitation of a brick-built commode would leave little time to think of anything except where the ejection seat handle was. But there was a procedure.

There was also a Federal Aviation Authority procedure for issuing an Airline Transport Licence to military pilots with the requisite flying hours on passing a multi-choice examination on aviation subjects and a flight test. I applied, took all the necessary tests and welcomed an intrigued FAA Flight Examiner dressed in his business suit to Perrin AFB to fly in the right-hand seat of a Delta Dagger – a first for him. After dressing him in appropriate attire, we went through the motions of a full flight test, including the almost aerobatic forced-landing spiral and some general handling when he got to handle the aircraft a bit. It was more exciting for him than were most working days and he duly handed me a certificate authorising me to fly passengers commercially in the USA or anywhere that operated under FAA rules or their equivalent. Flying passengers in a USAF jet trainer was an unlikely career prospect but it was a useful contingency for the future when I could simply add a type to the licence after a conversion course.

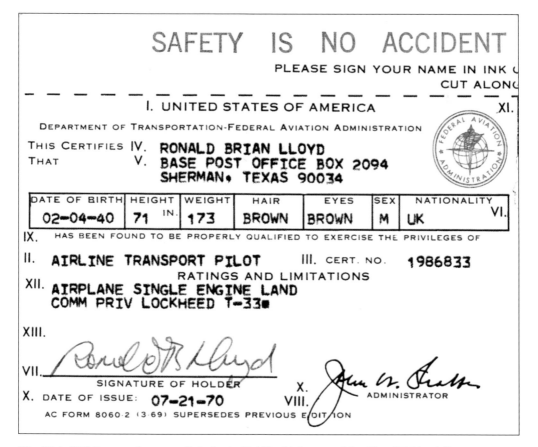

The FAA ATP licence after a test flight in the F-102 which covered Lockheed T-33 privileges.

Flying any aircraft type can produce experiences we remember for the exhilaration, the challenge, the satisfaction and, yes, the close shaves, even accidents. But if we live to tell the tale then it's nostalgia, privilege and memories of friends on whom, in the fighter world, you relied heavily and shared a beer with. Long may that continue! It was with wistful sadness that I delivered a TF-102 to Davis Monthan AFB in Arizona, known as 'The Boneyard', for 'storage' which meant it would probably never fly again. All aircraft have their day.

As my three-year point approached, I sat in the Perrin air traffic control tower in my Day-Glo red flying suit, feet up on the desk, doing the job of 'Senior Supe' – the duty instructor monitoring all flying to deal with student problems in the air, weather, changes of flying state and any other aspect of the flying operation. The phone rang. It was personal for me and a life-changing moment. It was the RAF co-ordinator at the British Embassy in Washington with my posting instructions, sending me to work at the Ministry of Defence in London after a three-month course on how to be a staff officer. It was the dreaded *Ground Tour,* which was inevitable for a supposed career officer, but it meant not flying for a while to follow the path to the top of the Air Force – something everyone was assumed to aim for. The job was to manage the Lightning and Phantom OCUs and operational training in general in the fast-jet force, covering policy, course scheduling, provision and financing of aircraft establishments.

Chapter 8

Flying the Desk

For the ambitious officer a posting to the MoD could be seen as the gateway to stardom. For those enjoying fast-jet flying it could also be seen as the end of the line. Take off the flying gear, wear a suit instead of a uniform, swop throttle and afterburner for a pencil, strap into a desk every day and join the tide of commuters coming in at eight and going out at six. It was a key part of the career plan – do some flying, go to Staff College, do some staff work, have a go at commanding something and wait for the promotion if things go well. I did not subscribe with any enthusiasm to the conventions of career development, a feeling reinforced by experiences to date. A tour and married life in Cyprus, working with a film company and three years living in the USA had already provided a diversity in our social and family life somewhat removed from the lifestyle at a typical RAF station. This disparity was to continue.

Despite the efforts of world leaders to slow the inordinately expensive arms race and agree on some restraint, the UK defence posture was still one of deterrence and high spending. But the economic strain became too much and many cuts were made, including the innovative TSR-2, the P-1154 and the F-111 procurement, to weaken our capabilities in the opinion of analysts. Less British development funding led ultimately to joint projects such as the Tornado and Eurofighter but, in the mid-1960s, the MoD had committed for economic reasons to buying the McDonnell Phantom from the USA for both the Royal Navy and the RAF. The Navy needed air defence of the Fleet for which the Phantom had been specifically designed while the RAF wanted a strike and ground attack replacement. The Navy had smaller carriers than the US Navy and needed a more powerful version and other carrier-related features. Single service competition for resources is very British and can lead to interesting compromises. The Government also needed jobs in the UK, so the Treasury and MoD decided to replace the Phantom's General Electric J-79 engine with the Rolls Royce Spey, which meant lots of work to change the rear end of the aircraft to accommodate it. The project ran into the sand with serious installation difficulties and delays. It was at this point that I sat down to fly my desk at MoD Lacon House in Holborn, central London.

As I began planning the next year's budget for aircraft needs and crew training programmes, the message came from on high, very high, that due to curtailed deliveries of Phantom FGR 2s, 'OCU operations will have to cease so that front-line squadrons can continue operations and fulfil their vital role.' With some trepidation I wrote a note to my Wing Commander boss saying 'not a good idea' and we should only half close the OCUs to sustain a limited flow of crews to squadrons as incumbent crews left, and to ensure less disruption to the career paths of valuable officers until the technical problems diminished. This was passed up the chain of command and, to my enormous surprise, came back down with the message from the top 'OK then, good idea, go and put that to 38 Group.' This was the Command responsible for the operational squadrons. It was my chance to exert the power of the policy maker, all of three weeks in the job. The audience would be a roomful of senior officers fearing unwelcome delays in new aircraft deliveries as they were diverted to the OCU. I donned my best uniform and with the file under my arm set off for RAF Upavon to brief them on my plan. Happily the presentation went well as did the interrogation at the end. I had left them guessing as to how far up the MoD hierarchy the endorsement had come from and did not have to play that card. The episode gave me the confidence to say what I thought for the rest of the tour which I thoroughly enjoyed.

Flushed with the euphoria of success, I wrote a paper about a strategy for the air defence of the UK in the event of a Soviet attack capitalising on 'front-line' experience. It reflected my doubts about fighter aircraft of the day being able to intercept incoming bombers in time as Soviet aircraft performance and the increasing threat from missiles grew. I marked it with an appropriate security classification and submitted it to my boss as a concept paper more than a factual report. He passed it up to the Director, an Air Commodore, who liked it and passed it up the chain of command where it disappeared, I was told, into the office of Vice Chief of Air Staff, above which it is hard to go. It was then classified at a level to which I had no access and I never saw it again. But my boss was pleased for some reason and the learning about how large organisations work was to come in useful in civilian life. Deterrence did rely more on submarine-launched weapons but air defence fighters continued to protect bases and ships from conventional attack.

Flying hours were hard to come by but the role of staff officer negotiating aircraft establishments and course scheduling did come with privileges and I had several rides in the Lightning T.5 and a Royal Navy Phantom FG.1 to keep in touch. In the two years as 'our Man at the Ministry', I spent many weekends at No. 6 Air AEF based at White Waltham, flying Air Training Corps (ATC) cadets in the Chipmunk with which I was, of course, familiar. The cadets varied in age and certainly in build and maturity, such that the smallest boys were barely visible looking over my shoulder into the rear seat even though they sat on a parachute. There was clearly an initiation test for new cadets which meant asking the pilot to fly aerobatics whether they wanted to or not. On the cadet's second flight it was OK to respond to any invitation to fly aeros with a 'no thank you sir', having now passed initiation and being qualified to talk authoritatively about every manoeuvre – once on the ground. Others could not get enough gyratory experience. Most were keen to at least hold the controls for some basic flying but there was no compulsion. The benefits for me were to reconnect with the airborne environment in which all the antennae of awareness, concentration, readiness for problems were out, but it was mainly to indulge in the sheer joy of flying however slow and low-powered the aircraft. Thinking ahead, I acquired my Commercial Pilot's Licence (CPL) under a CAA scheme specifically for current RAF-trained pilots, specifying just the vintage de Havilland Chipmunk as the initial type. Fortunately, the boss of 6 AEF where I flew with cadets happened to be an authorised CAA flight examiner. It was hardly the type to offer at an airline job interview but it formalised 5,000 hours of experience and all the requisite skills for a civil flying career were I to go down that route.

The presumed career path to the top continued with the news that I was to attend Staff College which was normally a year's course at the Bracknell location. It was now 1973 and it so happened that we had bought our first house at Bracknell, some 400 yards from the College Building. What could be more convenient? But that sense of adventure and avoiding convention came into play when I heard of other exchange opportunities, this time at staff colleges in India and Australia. At about this time I was becoming uncertain whether the RAF was the only life for me. One of the features of a Permanent Commission was an option to retire early after sixteen years of service or at the age of thirty-eight, whichever came first. To keep my options open, I enthused about Staff College and, working almost weekly with colleagues in the Air Member

The Lightning was a showstopper when it came into service. These are Mks 2 and 3. (*BAE SYSTEMS*)

The Mk 6 Lightning delivered more range and operated in new roles. (*BAE SYSTEMS*)

for Personnel (AMP) department, I was discreetly asked which one I would like to go to. India would mean relocating to the Nilgiri Hills in the south, Australia would be Canberra, the capital. In India the first act on arrival was to draw a horse from stores followed by meeting the servants who would look after the house, cooking etc. My wife and I discussed this only briefly, taking into account the children's education – they were nine and three – and our friendships with Australians. The decision was Canberra and the Australian Air Force (RAAF) Staff College at RAAF Fairbairn.

The course consisted mainly of visits to every part of Australia to examine industries and companies from mining to sugar production to vineyards to largescale irrigation projects, discussing management techniques that might apply to running an air force. The visit to a mine, where we descended some 3,000 feet to look at working in the heat seemed, however, at odds with a pilot's natural environment of 40,000 feet in the other direction at minus 50 degrees. But any doubts about how well the RAAF was run were quickly dissolved by the efficiency with which these 'jollies' were planned and executed. Our host in each location appeared to have been heavily prebriefed to provide the best food, wine and entertainment possible and, especially, I was told, during the visit to the wine growing regions north of Adelaide, a trip I sadly missed due to 'flu. We studied military history, problem solving, analytical skills, concise paper and reports writing, strategy and planning. The military history focused on the war in the Pacific during the Second World War which was fascinating.

Life with little flying continued. I did get airborne in a Mirage fighter for some enjoyable formation practice to counter the brain pain of academic study in amongst the liquid lunches and obligatory parties. But the airborne experience that made the greatest impression was sitting on a hard seat in a troop-carrier A-model Hercules transport. It was the noisiest aircraft I had ever flown in. Australia is a continent of 3-million square miles in old money (7.6-million square kilometres) and we travelled in ear-splitting discomfort but good spirits to every corner at 280 knots, which translates into many noisy hours, only compensated by the warm welcome and hospitality of our hosts on arrival.

The demographic scene had been set on our first trip, which was to Perth, to be received by Sir Charles Court, the Governor of Western Australia. His opening words were, 'The population of Western Australia, which covers a million square miles, is one million people. Seven hundred and fifty thousand of them live in Perth. So we have

Staff College had its more exciting moments flying the RAAF Mirage which was conventional to handle. (*Courtesy Air Commodore D. Bowden RAAF*)

plenty of room for new people and new development.' We visited the vast Ord River Irrigation Scheme designed to attract people from the populated eastern parts of the country which did not appear to fulfil expectations. What it said about managing an air force did not take up much of my end of visit report. But the lobster was delicious.

My next posting was to fly Phantoms at RAF Leuchars in Scotland. After ground tours, the established pattern was to do some intensive refresher flying related to the operational role. I had some three months before the courses started and, after a short leave, to recuperate we settled back into the house in Bracknell after letting it for a year and sorted out some domestics. Then I checked into No. 6 AEF again at RAF White Waltham to fly cadets as I had before. My wife, with our daughters of five and ten, needed the small car we had bought, so I acquired an ageing Renault 4 with the gear lever that moved in and out of the dash and a floor that had already been welded for corrosion, the weld showing similar tendencies. But I enjoyed driving that car for all of 250 miles to RAF Leeming on several weekends where, for three weeks and thirty flying hours, I flew JP 4s and the pressurised Mk 5. The course covered all types of handling, including formation, instrument flying and low-level navigation, all of which came back as if there had been no pause, which was gratifying. And it was great to be back in the cockpit.

The next refresher phase was at RAF Brawdy in Pembrokeshire to once again fly the famous Hawker Hunter, this time the Mk 6 and Mk 9, so it was back to the dream pilot's aircraft. Here, too, the handling was straightforward after the same intensive emergencies and procedures in the static simulator that I had originally experienced. It was a joy to get back into a fast jet, albeit by now a graceful 'old lady', as more advanced types had taken the top slots. Everything was going well, assessments fine, flying as stimulating and challenging as ever in company with like-minded pilots at the top of their game. The prospect of flying the mighty Phantom jet over my old stomping ground – well, stomping North Sea if you prefer – where I had flown the Javelin many years before was enough to distract me from thoughts about life outside the RAF, but not for long.

A health glitch and the need for some treatment brought me up short as I came off the course to recover, hoping for another chance to fly something interesting. It was intensely disappointing not to fly the Phantom but it was to prove a fateful stroke of providence. Any unexpected change of course in life, brought about by choice or circumstances, is a time to reflect and reassess. I had joined the RAF to fly and, if called upon, to fight and kill in defence of what this country stands for in common with every serviceman or woman. I had enjoyed unconventional and adventurous flying with a diverse social life for nearly twenty years. Another twenty years, however, was not going to work for me. As I talked about my future over a beer one evening with a very competent personnel officer, that thought was at the back of my mind (and perhaps his) when the offer of an unorthodox flying job caught my interest.

'How would you like to command one of the largest university air squadrons, liaising with five universities in Yorkshire?'

The trick with any unexpected life change is to shrug your shoulders and turn it into opportunity. So it was that the 'Yellow Brick Road' to stardom with the Wizards at the top of the RAF was to turn into the A1 to Doncaster to command Yorkshire Universities Air Squadron (YUAS) at RAF Finningley. I was to leave the RAF three years later, only to be asked the following year if I would consider rejoining, with a promotion, an offer I chose not to take up. Flying instruction at the primary stage was to prove the perfect entrée into club flying. For now though, since I had a few months to kill before joining YUAS, it was back to catching the early train to Waterloo for more staff work.

I worked in MoD Air Defence Operations in Whitehall alongside a group with the grand name of UKADGE – the UK Air Defence Ground Environment. These were the radar controllers who had directed the intercepts I flew in the Javelin who were curious to work with one of the pilots they had barely seen. They were responsible for a comprehensive system of ground-based radars and communications that monitored air activity in UK airspace and maintained readiness to direct aircraft and missile responses to attack from the air. Most of my time was spent travelling with the Group Captain Head of Department to Brussels where he chaired one of a myriad of working groups within NATO, this one about deployments of missiles and the infrastructure to support them. Week-long meetings were to be a revelation of how international diplomacy works – or doesn't.

The fifteen member states of NATO all sent representatives to what I quickly realised was, for some, an opportunity to look for joint policies to favour the home nation. For others it was a pleasant break from working in the depths of their respective defence ministries to enjoy the delights of Brussels in good company. Since I was just the staff officer, I could observe behaviours in and outside the meetings, which threw into sharp relief the national characteristics I had thought to be a subject of lighthearted humour but found that they had curious validity. The handsome young Italian officer mentioned on arrival that he had 'meetings' elsewhere in Brussels and he would next show up on Thursday, looking a little tired, to put the Italian position without the need for discussion in confident style and an enigmatic smile, possibly related to the other meetings. The French and Belgian officers came with highly individual positions that readily diverged from the consensus, delivering these with fervour, passion, flamboyance and style as the mood took them, to reflect their strong commitment to NATO. The Dutch and the Danish were Anglophiles in line with our MoD thinking. The Germans always had two officers attend and were in daily touch with Bonn before agreeing anything new, one presenting their position succinctly with minimum fuss and in precise language, while the colleague checked his watch, looking at the day's schedule. A dishevelled British Army major, nearing retirement, lay back in his chair enjoying his pipe and delivering opinions he appeared to have just arrived at as authoritative and routine for someone used to making snap judgements under fire. The Americans sent a full colonel, who outranked everyone but my Group Captain boss, armed with a brief to direct the committee along sensible American lines, with the benefit of comprehensive research conducted back at the Pentagon. It was a strong set of strategic arguments that received a curiously muted response from the Europeans. The decisions seldom went his way, despite the logic and potential rewards of resources if they had. So, at each meeting a new full colonel arrived with a different personality to try to get some sense out the Europeans who were in some cases making decidedly modest contributions to the NATO budget. The undeniable logic of the adage 'He who pays the piper calls the tune' has finally emerged in modern-day American thinking on NATO and on their disproportionate budget payments. Unsurprisingly, it was the Dutch and Danes with whom I shared some very pleasant evening suppers. The other officers were not unfriendly, on the contrary, but they had other things to do in the evenings, especially our Italian colleague.

It was now time to take on 120 University students from Leeds, Sheffield, Bradford, York and Hull, together with lectures in a campaign to recruit officers for a service I was about to leave. That might sound like a contradiction but it wasn't. Then and now I would thoroughly recommend a life in the RAF as one of the most adventurous, purposeful and exciting ways of spending early adult years. With undeniable bias, I would advocate RAF life with even more enthusiasm for those motivated and fortunate enough to fly fast jets. This is with due deference to the enormous satisfaction of controlling larger aircraft with their own demands for crew management and specialist skills.

Chapter 9

The Bulldog

The move to flying light aircraft with students selected purely for their interest rather than suitability or capability to become RAF pilots was for me a distinct change of direction towards general aviation. GA flying covers everything that is not airlines or military and ranges from commercial operations to private flying, to sport flying and research. This diverse environment was to present different perspectives on being airborne, not at the rarified heights of fast-jet flying, but with a large community of people sharing a curiosity that can become a passion, especially at flying clubs. A UAS is a military operation but while most students take on an RAF Volunteer Reserve status they were in the same position as any young man or woman joining a flying club in terms of their flying abilities.

The Bulldog was a perfect aircraft for *ab initio* training. Powered by a 200hp Lycoming with a variable pitch propeller and a maximum weight of 2,350lb, it meant a fairly lively performance with a cruise of 120 knots, 600 miles range, and it was fully aerobatic. Its large canopy provided superb visibility to the pilots sitting side by side in a cockpit that had a proper stick, not one of those 'yokes' or 'spectacles', a curse of the popular training aircraft so often seen at flying clubs. With a natural

The Bulldog was a capable trainer, conventional to fly and with good performance. (*BAE SYSTEMS*)

bias from RAF experience, I have always found the rotational controls yoke that disappears into the instrument panel like a car makes the controls feel spongy and indirect compared with a stick straight out of the floor. Aircraft with such controls are very good at flying in a straight line but landing in a gusty crosswind where fast response to control movements is required presents an unnecessary challenge for the inexperienced. The cockpit was well laid out, with military-style levers and buttons that were clearly marked. The instrument displays were simple but no navaids were installed, so navigation relied on geographic awareness, good planning and the single radio to obtain bearings, QGH let-downs through cloud or a radar service when it was available. It had a fixed tricycle undercarriage and conventional flaps, with an approach speed with full flap of about 70 knots and a threshold speed, depending on weight and any turbulence, of 65 knots. The landing itself was conventional and highly controllable with responsive controls and a powerful engine. Remarkably, the crosswind component limit for a safe landing was 30 knots with the crab technique working best providing the speed was right.

Basic aerobatics in the Bulldog were a delightful way to enjoy a sunny afternoon if you were feeling energetic and liked gyrating. While it was displayed at public airshows it did not match aircraft such as the Pitts Special with +6, -3 'g' limits and Extras

Bulldog in slow flight. (*BAE SYSTEMS*)

at +10/-10, whose airframes were designed specifically for vigorous controllable manoeuvres, including spins and flick manoeuvres that look good especially if they have coloured smoke to show the gyratory flight path. But for all the basic five, plus a few others, the Bulldog was exhilarating and the best aircraft for teaching simple aerobatics that I have flown. There was a tradition at each UAS to run a students' regional aerobatic competition, competing between squadrons and students at low level where 1,000 feet was the minimum height appropriate for young students. Since it was my job to check out any aspiring participants just before these competitions, I had to withstand many efforts to overstress both aircraft and me before offering rather firm advice on restraining enthusiasm and sticking to the rules to ensure their survival before authorising flights.

As part of established practice in RAF training, before allowing a student to fly solo aerobatics we demonstrated spin entries and recoveries and allowed them to practise. However, the follow-up investigation of an unrecoverable spin, from which my predecessor and his student had baled out, was a close look at spinning characteristics by a test pilot at the Empire Test Pilots' School at RAF Boscombe Down. The conclusion was that the Bulldog was safe for dual spinning but that instructors needed more familiarity with partial-control spins for their own good and to guide students.

The Bulldog was an excellent classroom for basic aerobatics. (*Courtesy YUAS*)

Side-by-side seating and excellent cockpit visibility made the Bulldog ideal for pilot training. (*BAE SYSTEMS*)

It has taken many years for aerodynamicists to understand aircraft behaviour in spins. The centre of gravity has a significant effect on recovery characteristics, and each aircraft type needs a specific clearance for spinning in its certification. The light aircraft I flew all responded to the conventional recovery procedure but this was invariably after a premeditated entry from a wings level stall. Unexpected entries from a vigorous manoeuvre can surprise inexperienced, even experienced, pilots and induce errors in the recovery drill. An incipient spin can occur unexpectedly during manoeuvres using aileron with opposite rudder or in the initial phase of an intentional spin demonstration when the aircraft suddenly 'departs' from controlled flight. Neutralising the controls promptly and holding them firmly – they may jerk around without pilot input – will usually avoid entering a fully-developed spin in either situation, and it is useful for a student to practise this. The departure can also take the form of a 'flick' when elevator and rudder inputs are vigorous and the aircraft enters this incipient stage with a rapid rolling motion either intentionally for display purposes or as a result of mishandling. This might well be with 'crossed controls' applying significant rudder opposite to aileron deflection, when wings are near their stalling angle of attack, usually at low airspeed. With inattention during early solo circuits this can happen during the finals turn or climbing turn after take off with distressing results. The risk is minimised by student awareness.

A variation of these encounters with autorotation is the partial control spin. Here, a spin is entered with pro-spin control movements but short of full deflections, and power may well be at moderate or high settings. The spin that develops can be different from a standard spin for the type. In the Bulldog this spin is flatter, that is pointing less at the ground than the horizon which seems to be going round faster as a consequence. The recovery procedure is the same as for a fully-developed spin, but it can take longer before the spin stops, with the rate of rotation sometimes speeding up before it does so. This delay and speeding up can persuade a pilot under pressure at a high rate of descent to think that it is not going to recover and he moves the controls to other positions which then prevent recovery.

So, after taking a look with a CFS instructor at these rather special spins, it was my job to take my six flying instructors up to practise partial control spin entries and recoveries. For some reason I was glad when these flights were complete. I had always had a healthy respect for spins in any aircraft having flown Javelins, Gnats and F-102s which were not cleared for spins. It was a good reason for teaching accurate flying and careful speed monitoring when flying in the circuit to land. Awareness of pro-spin conditions was the key to avoiding unpleasant surprises.

Conversion to the BAe Bulldog and QFI refresher at CFS RAF Leeming naturally concentrated on primary pilot training. During the early part of my original QFI course I had practised instruction at this level on the Jet Provost, using the exact same sequence of lessons I had received at Cranwell, so the principles were familiar. But the change of approach from instructing on the Gnat and F-102 was intriguing. Not only were the students I would fly with mostly learning from scratch but only a few cadets, already selected to join the RAF, had undergone officer selection and pilot aptitude tests. The rest were undergraduates whose interest in flying and the RAF had arisen as a natural curiosity reinforced by pro-active recruiting campaigns mounted by all UASs during Freshers' Week at the beginning of the first study year. The rationale was to recruit graduates who might be best equipped to work in ever more complex operating environments in the air or on the ground. Why would they join a UAS? For a start it was free flying in RAF aircraft with RAF instructors and the prospect of a PPL that would cost a fortune at a flying club. Add in officer status with use of Officers' Messes (clubs in effect), adventurous pursuits such as skiing and orienteering and the fun and camaraderie of fellow students away from the academic environment and it became attractive. Some students saw success in their studies as the most important thing and challenge enough. Or they were not of a mind to subject themselves to the pressures of flying at weekends, preferring perhaps something they knew they were good at – cricket, rugby or more romantic pursuits. We would uncover those priorities during recruiting interviews which were similar to any officer selection process. Neither we nor they knew how they would take to the airborne environment, or whether they had any of the required aptitudes. But the UAS system had proved historically to be a reliable source of successful officers and pilots who made up a significant proportion of those who flew in the Second World War, including the Battle of Britain. They operate to this day.

YUAS had eight Bulldogs and six QFIs plus dedicated ground crew. Cadet flying was at weekends with staff continuation flying during the week. There were no limits on flying hours and only weather kept us from flying at every opportunity to include night flying and low-level cross-country navigation, sometimes in loose formation. I trained the QFIs to arrive back at the airfield in a 'Box 4' formation from which we did a dramatic 'card break to land' from 500 feet in both directions, which was as close as I could get to emulating the Red Arrows' 'Bomb Burst' manoeuvre for pilots who had come from flying Hercules transport aircraft. But Finningley was a navigator training base, with only YUAS training pilots, so this break to land routine was something of an assertion of piloting skills for all to see, albeit in a small, slow aircraft that sounded like an angry bee.

Summer Camps, where the Squadron would be allocated a little used airfield for six weeks of continuous flying training during University vacations, were intensive and tiring. This was mainly due to efforts to keep up with enthusiastic, energetic, boisterous, testosterone-fuelled undergraduates keen to fly, but keener to drink, party and explore friendly relations with local females who could put up with them – of which there were many. Quite apart from separation from families we QFIs endeavoured to take part in the fun while keeping some degree of order – a difficult balance after a few beers. It proved especially difficult at the end of camp formal dinners when, in keeping with RAF tradition, vigorous 'mess games' were played after a large meal and unhealthy amounts of alcohol. An example is 'Carriers', where tables were lined up to represent an aircraft carrier deck towards which you ran at full speed and hurled yourself into the air to land face-down with arms extended to represent wings and could not be used to cushion the 'landing'. The winner was he who slithered farthest on the polished table without dropping off the end into the 'sea'. If you did, you bought a round of drinks for the other crazies in the competition.

One of our summer camps was based at RAF Fairford with a runway so long that the end was not normally in sight in British weather. The airfield was constructed in 1944 as a base for American and British troop carriers and gliders to mount the D Day invasion of Normandy. Since then, due to its strategic location, it has been developed as a base for a succession of heavy USAF bombers, including the B–36, B–47, B–52 and for the KC-135 tanker aircraft. It had even been used as one of the bases ready to recover the space shuttle in the event of an abort minutes after lift off from the USA. Perhaps that was because the runway length had grown to 3,046 metres, more than enough to take off and land several times in a Bulldog. Memories of converting to the Gnat eleven years earlier with this giant airfield all to ourselves were vivid. It was designated as a Concorde test and training airfield at the time of our camp, which is when I enjoyed another out of the ordinary experience.

I took a telephone call about a visit by Concorde to provide a British Airways captains' conversion course. This meant circuits and bumps with touch-down and rollers at the field. Newspaper headlines reporting a collision between a majestic and pricey Concorde and a Bulldog flown by a novice undergraduate out for some summer fun, all due to RAF carelessness, haunted top RAF people and I was asked to arrange for Bulldogs not to cut up a Concorde on final approach to land. In gratitude for an effective procedure, which kept the two types a serious distance apart when the Concorde was on the approach, I was invited to observe a training flight from the flight-deck. So it was that I stood immediately behind the two pilots in a Concorde empty of passengers and with a light fuel load, powered by its four Rolls Royce/Snecma Olympus 5 engines, each producing 38,000lb of thrust in reheat. You can imagine the performance which felt like a jet fighter and it handled like one. I was in the company of a training first officer, meaning he trained them. He positioned himself alongside me but we had to stagger a bit due to the narrow entrance to the cockpit so he was just in front of me looking back to commentate on what the pilots were doing during each landing. The Concorde, with its long and graceful delta-wing form, landed at very high angles of attack requiring the nose cone and windscreen visor to be lowered to provide the pilot a view of the runway.

The first approach and landing was a demonstration by the training captain. I was able to look forward and see the whole fascinating procedure. We landed firmly and it was very noticeable how far the nose had to travel, under pilot control, to lower the nose wheel to the runway before opening up the power again to lift off and climb hard with an immediate steep turn downwind that no passenger would ever see for the 'learner' to have a go. So far, so intriguing. As we turned again onto finals after a wide circuit, the trainee pilot set up a smooth and stable approach for his landing. The first officer continued to describe everything that was happening, looking forward then back at me to calmly and comprehensively explain everything. We had passed through about 500 feet on the approach, as I could see on the altimeter, with the approach going so well that neither of the pilots had reason to say anything. But my friendly first officer seemed to have missed the height. The landing was so smooth that it was difficult to detect the touch-down and the pilot began lowering the nose all the way to the runway when, to my astonishment, the first officer, on looking forward at this moment and seeing the nose going down quickly, threw himself to the cockpit floor and covered his head with his hands in the crash position. He had reverted to instinct in thinking that we had not yet landed, that the speed was too low, the height still well above the ground and it was an emergency stall recovery he was seeing which, in such a heavy delta-wing aircraft just above the ground, was not going to work. As we rolled and took off again he rose to his feet sheepishly and I was too embarrassed for him to say anything, so nothing was said then or subsequently. Perhaps the Concorde really was a pioneering project of its day. It was certainly very impressive and a privilege to fly in, even if, unsurprisingly, we did not go supersonic.

The job of recruiting from universities was a niche role in the RAF. It was clearly not a front-line operational task, but working with university lecturers called for the sort of diplomacy I had routinely employed during exchange tours and was intriguing. Among university professors at that time there was a diversity of views on the morality of using military force to solve problems with the attendant violence and loss of life. Those who had empathy with some sort of defence posture, other than 'pretend it isn't happening', and had a passing interest in flying were highly supportive of YUAS and happily accepted the annual invitation to fly in the Bulldog. They were also intrigued to see me arrive in my Austin Princess staff car, complete with driver, when invited to various dinner events including the rather grand University Defence Studies Dining Club occasions where my RAF-blue mess kit looked dull alongside the many colourful regimental rigs of ex-army officers in their reds, greens and golds.

Yorkshire UAS served five universities – Leeds, Sheffield, York, Bradford and Hull. There were some 125 students flying at weekends, comprising a handful with RAF cadetships and a reserved place in the RAF and a majority who, whilst selected for mild indications of suitability for RAF aircrew training, were in reality most unlikely to think about joining the military and were there for the free flying and the fun. One cadet did respond very positively, evidenced by his eventual promotion to Chief of The Defence Staff, and he reminisced with fond memories at a YUAS reunion a few years ago in the rank of Air Vice Marshal.

By now I had accumulated some 5,000 flying hours, each flight no longer than two hours, which meant a lot of busy flights with little cruising at altitude. While Bulldog flying was not exactly fast and furious it offered plenty of interest and challenge. More than that, flying at low altitude with time to look at coast lines, hills and church steeples eerily suspended above white cotton wool fog in winter was a truly uplifting experience available to all pilots and their passengers who can fly in such aircraft. It perhaps offers a better flying experience than the crowded airliner with tiny windows and little to see – unless of course you are the pilot.

I continued to contemplate life after the RAF. Many pilots follow a natural route into civil aviation for a job they know they can do for a reasonable income and with continued flying. I had many airline pilot friends to ask about this life and, while I did not know if that was for me, I felt I should acquire the requisite qualifications. In the UK that was at least a CPL and IR, preferably with a transport type rating. The CPL is quite a hill to climb for aspiring civil pilots but is more than covered by RAF pilot training from which the standards and skills derive. Two aircraft at Finningley were to help me fulfil the other requirements.

The scenery from low altitude was breathtaking as in any light aircraft. (*BAE SYSTEMS*)

The Dominie was the military version of the HS-125 executive jet transport aircraft and was used in the RAF for navigator training. Some quiet persuasion and a few beers got a couple of rides in the pilot's seat and this convinced my instructor/ examiner friend that I could meet the requirements of a multi-engine rating to put on my CPL which had just the humble Chipmunk entered after the perfunctory check ride at No. 6 AEF. I completed the daytime requirements for the HS-125 type rating without difficulty. It also meant flying the Dominie at night and, after some slightly firmer persuading and more beers, I eventually slotted into a night-training sortie and slid into the seat for the requisite approaches and landings, including single-engine handling. It was a very easy aircraft to fly with no asymmetric problem on one engine. I now had a passenger transport aircraft rating on my UK licence.

The Scottish Aviation Jetstream was based at Finningley for multi-engine pilot training and was, happily, backed by a full motion flight simulator. This was fitted with the flight instruments and navigation displays installed in airliners of the day. When it was not occupied by students, I was able to grind away on my own in 'the box' to get more familiar with the IFR (Instrument Flight Rules) regime which is central to professional flying in the civil world.

The RAF Dominie at Finningley was the route to a multi-engine-type rating on the HS-125, shown here. (*Crown copyright Chief Photographer Defence Imagery MoD*)

In the RAF the qualification for flying in cloud and bad weather was a graduated system of ratings allowing limitations of cloud base and visibility to reflect experience and competence, demonstrated and regularly checked in an Instrument Rating Test flight. This test had specified levels of accuracy and handling. For fast-jet pilots of the earlier years it did not generally include flying in controlled airspace where civil IFR traffic flew, only receiving clearance to transit through such airspace with strict radar monitoring.

IFR as opposed to VFR, which is basically flying in good weather, good visibility and not in cloud, is a set of rules and procedures a pilot must observe when he cannot legally fly under VFR and when the airspace he is flying in specifically requires IFR. To do this legally the pilot must hold an Instrument Rating added to his pilot's licence. Airspace where IFR is mandatory includes that above major airports (Control Zones), the airspace around them (Control Areas), and air routes (airways) reserved for airline traffic. These airspace 'reservations' are designated on air navigation charts with horizontal and vertical dimensions as part of 'Controlled Airspace', which itself is defined as airspace in which Air Traffic Control Services are provided. There are exceptions made for pilots flying under VFR to enter or transit through controlled airspace with clearance and under strict air traffic control if the weather meets certain criteria and safe clearance from other traffic is maintained. The whole system is geared to the safety of aircraft carrying passengers commercially, i.e. they paid for the flight and expect in return to get to their destination without incident in virtually all weathers. In addition, all flights are expected to conform to what were known until 2015 as 'Rules of The Air' to keep aircraft separated in flight, an example being to fly at different heights on magnetic headings in each quadrant of the compass – quadrantal heights – while cruising. These rules have now been overtaken by conformance with Standardised European Rules of The Air (SERA) bringing few changes but replacing UK quadrantals with a 'semi-circular' system where IFR flights heading eastbound use whole thousands of feet beginning with odd numbers (1,000, 3,000, 5,000 etc.) and with even numbers flying westbound (2,000, 4,000, 6,000 etc.). VFR flights fly at heights 500 feet above or below these levels so flying eastbound 3,500, 5,500 etc. and westbound at 4,500, 6,500 etc. – plus ça change

It will be apparent that this system of civil aviation is very different from military flying where the objectives and priorities are defence of the nation, not flying us to holiday destinations or business meetings. Many of the procedures are common and, in peacetime, civil and military aircraft share the same airspace and conform broadly to the same rules. Military airfields have their own jurisdictions and any special procedures specific to their role. A transition from military to civil flying requires a change of mindset. In this new world of flying the pilot is part of a global profession working under a regime of very strictly monitored rules, regulations and procedures. Pilots collectively conform to this code of practice to ensure the safety of passengers, avoid colliding with each other and to deal with the vagaries of weather that can threaten safety if the rules are ignored. It is a comprehensive system with many interlocking components and it takes time and experience to learn how to use it efficiently. The professional pilot, the air traffic controller, systems and equipment engineers, meteorologists, and those managing airfield equipment are key elements. International flights are governed by the International Civil Aviation Organisation (ICAO), an agency of the United Nations based in Montreal, but there are variances within a country's national airspace where internal flights are regulated by authorities of that country – CAA, FAA etc. There are some very thick manuals describing the details of airspace management which pilots must be familiar with, especially for periodic competency checks.

To find employment in commercial aviation the pilot must have at least a CPL with an IR and the aircraft he is flying must have specified equipment which is working OK. It's a simple enough definition but, as I said earlier, flying under IFR represents for most pilots the key difference between flying for pleasure and flying as a profession. In the world of general aviation, some private pilots add an IR to their licence and fly under IFR but it is not common and most who hold an IR will also have a CPL.

So there I was in the Jetstream cockpit contemplating my future, which might mean many hours sitting in a cockpit anticipating an arrival at the next airport. Then there were the passengers to think of as they put their trust (with little choice) in the guys at the front who they hope are having a good day. Gone were thoughts of aerobatics since Jetstreams and Jumbo Jets don't do good slow rolls and passengers would spill their G & Ts. More seriously, it was a mindset of conformance to the required procedures and standards of accuracy, with the overriding factor of safety – of passengers, of other flights and of you and your crew.

As I sat in the simulator it felt like learning to use a computer by intuition. There was no instructor and I had not learned about the Jetstream as an aircraft. I just knew how to fly on instruments and needed to learn about the IFR environment – how to fly along airways with the appropriate reports, clearances to carry out the next portion of the flight, holding patterns near airports, let-downs to same, airfield approach patterns and final approach techniques, all as depicted in en route charts and on let-down or approach plates. These are booklets containing diagrammatic representations of the approach, departure, IFR let-down and runway approaches to each runway. They depict magnetic tracks, heights, holding patterns, fixes and precision approach details in plan and elevation. Topographical maps of the surrounding terrain would be carried for any deviation from the published tracks or you just felt like flying VFR and showing your passengers the scenery.

Most of the IFR procedures were familiar to me, having used them in the States but that was seven years previously and I was out of currency. I had mostly used TACAN, VOR and radar services for en route navigation and descents through cloud, and PAR for

Scottish Aviation Jetstream. The simulator was my classroom. (*BAE SYSTEMS*)

runway approaches more than the ILS used widely today. Interaction with controllers was a matter of following instructions on heights to fly for separation, clearances to proceed through each stage of the let-down, adherence to position reporting procedures and any other safety-related instructions. But I would now have to demonstrate 'non-precision' holding patterns and terminal approaches to a point on finals from which a landing could be made, referring throughout to transmissions from an NDB (Non-Directional-Beacon) located at or near the destination airfield, with bearings to that beacon shown on the ADF instrument in the cockpit. Today, NDB approach procedures are rare, largely replaced by GPS. But this was 1980 and NDB procedures were alive and well.

Details of this procedure, if you are not a pilot or aspiring pilot, can be a bit of a yawn so just a verbal sketch to illustrate why this particular procedure was regarded as a demanding and potentially sweaty exercise during the IR flight test of 1980. There is always wind blowing in the atmosphere, with different wind speeds and directions at different heights at a given time, not always forecast accurately. Holding patterns and approach paths designated on approach plates are drawn in plan relative to the ground and designed to avoid hills and obstacles such as radio masts. Flying directly over an NDB causes the ADF needle to reverse through 180 degrees and provides a fix from which the patterns are flown. The holding pattern is shaped like a racetrack with specified times to complete the circuit, typically four minutes which, with no wind blowing, would mean one minute for the straight bits and one minute for each 180-degree turn, flown at a rate of 2 degrees a second known as 'rate 1', standard for most instrument procedures. But there is a wind blowing which can be quite significant for a light aircraft flying at, say, 90 knots and 4,000 feet, leaving behind any surface friction effects of lower heights. During the straight parts of the racetrack a mental calculation is required to take into account the *component* of the wind causing drift and accommodate this by adjusting the heading to stay on the published track over the ground. During the turns the rate of turn needs adjusting to accommodate the constantly varying wind effect on flight path over the ground by slackening or tightening. Head or tail wind component of the wind will increase or decrease ground speed. This requires less or more than a minute to fly the straight bits and stick to four minutes back at the beacon. It is all somewhat imprecise, relying throughout on a needle on a dial showing the bearing to the beacon, such that staying within the prescribed accuracy limits is a gamble or an art form depending how good you are. Much of the activity is mental dead reckoning, which is a superb test of a pilot as he works to fly on heading at the correct height and speed, make radio calls and carry out checks to the satisfaction of the examiner under his 'view limiting device'. There is more detail on these let-downs online if it interests you, but they are largely history. Only in the more remote parts of the world would pilots find a need for NDB let-down skills and they do not appear in today's IR flight test. The rest of the test covered IFR departure procedures, joining an airway and flying en route, approaches, holds and runway approaches using ADF and, separately, an ILS with missed approach procedure, plus staying in control within prescribed limits when an engine fails at climbing power. Recovery from unusual attitudes was thrown in for good measure.

Having never paid money to fly in any aircraft, expensive, sophisticated or vintage, I was loath to spend more than necessary on training for the IR but did not want to risk failing with a retake for reasons of pride as much as expense. The motivation to prepare intensively with free simulator time was therefore strong. After cramming in the practice and swotting up on a vast array of books for the ground school examinations, I booked in for a short course on the Grumman GA 7 Cougar at an hourly rate expensive enough to concentrate the mind. After four flights and five hours I flew to Stansted for the two-hour flight test which was the most demanding flight test I ever experienced, mainly for the threat of ignominy if I failed. Remarkably, I passed and scurried back to Elstree more than relieved.

The pressures on pilots in bad weather were greater before the arrival of ground radar which today is used for close monitoring of traffic in many phases of flight and for both VFR and IFR traffic. In the 1960s and 1970s there was heavy reliance on radar for area navigation and runway approach guidance. The evolution of radio navigation aids, inertial navigation systems, GPS and rapidly advancing avionics transformed the job of the professional pilot and, thankfully, technical failures in modern aircraft are rare. Nevertheless, the basic piloting skills still have to be there as Captain Sullenberger found when he skillfully ditched his Airbus 320-214 in the Hudson river with no loss of life. The cost of relying unduly on avionics and being unprepared for a reversion to basic instrument techniques was illustrated by the tragic loss of the Air France Flight 447, an Airbus 330, in 2009 killing 228 passengers and crew. The cause was attributed to the probability of ice crystals distorting airspeed measurements which disconnected the autopilot, leaving the crew to recognise a stall situation which they handled incorrectly. Whether the evolution of aircraft design will eventually eliminate the role of a pilot remains to be seen. Certainly autopilots are broadly safer and more accurate than the average human after many years of use and refinement. However, in 2019 the loss of life in accidents involving automated stall-avoidance systems installed in the Boeing 737 Max 8 has reaffirmed the necessity for a pilot to be able to take over when something goes wrong. We are familiar with the increasing use of unmanned flying vehicles and driverless cars. The test question is 'would you be happy boarding a jet to fly to Florida with no pilot on board?' Maybe, one day.

In the world of general aviation there are still thousands of aircraft and flights that have no requirement to meet the levels of sophistication or scope of regulations described above. At pretty much any flying club in the UK there are to be found basic aircraft with basic systems that continue to fly after many decades of use, alongside many historic types. Having flown the Spitfire, I was not surprised to come across more types that few had heard of as I explored the civil flying world. I was to find that club flying can revisit the adventure and thrill that I had experienced in my early piloting days when simply being airborne was a pleasure.

I unceremoniously departed the Royal Air Force in September 1979, having set up my first job working on the introduction of the Tornado aircraft into the RAF with a GEC company in Camberley. A careful family plan had anticipated the new lifestyle and

Leading a farewell 4-ship formation. Picture was framed and presented to me by YUAS groundcrew.

location some time previously. One daughter, who had been boarding at a school near Oxford, where we planned to live, became a day girl. The other continued at a local state school and both went on to university. We sold the house in Bracknell and bought a small Georgian farmhouse where we were to live for more than twenty-five years. As soon as I could, I left the defence company to work for the first importer of modems (modulator/demodulator) converting digital signals into analogue for transmission then back to digital, as the digital data networks and, ultimately, the internet age got under way.

I decided that a career as an airline pilot was not for me, although I added a Full Flying Instructor Rating to my CPL and renewed this, the CPL and the IR regularly for some years as a contingency. There were several reasons for this decision. First, after the type of flying I had experienced I could not contemplate sitting in a cockpit on long-haul flights doing very little except wait for something to go wrong. This, of course, is to diminish the job of the airline pilot outrageously and it can be very rewarding, even exciting, as any pilot who had flown the runway 13 approach into Hong Kong's Kai Tak in the 1990s would bear witness. Typically, aircraft as large as a Boeing 747 would descend on final approach under modified ILS guidance to 650 feet and two miles from touch-down, lining up on a checkerboard mounted on a hill straight ahead. They would then commence a visual turn through 47 degrees to roll out at 140 feet, dealing with any cross wind, to land on a runway of 10,930 feet that seemed shorter for heavy aircraft that used most of it, turning off just short of the sea – very occasionally in the sea. The approach was world famous, known variously as the Checkerboard Turn, or by passengers seeing it for the first time as the Kai Tak Heart Attack as they looked out of the 30-degree bank turn at people on the roofs of buildings a few feet below. Equally exciting for me as a passenger, even for the pilot, was an arrival at Moscow with Aeroflot at dusk in snow as we landed in what looked less than minima and the airport immediately closed. Perhaps there are extra pressures on pilots in Russia. While such excitement arises for pilots or passengers on rare occasions, most flights are uneventful. When I asked a close ex-RAF friend flying with Cathay Pacific, based in Hong Kong, what was the most challenging aspect of the job of a training captain he replied 'staying awake'.

Long haul also meant extended periods away from home with implications for family life that suited some very well and others not so well. There is the short-haul job of course, but it still didn't match the stimulation and excitement of fast-jet flying although it did mean visiting a lot of places, mainly to sleep in hotel rooms. Then there was the prospect of flying as a first officer with a wait before becoming a captain at the age of 40 with a retirement at 55 or so. I thought all this through, discussed it with my wife and chose only to keep the option open. Meanwhile, I set about building a new career as a business executive, initially in the UK but then with considerable travel to the USA, Asia, the Middle East and the Soviet Union as it became the Russian Federation. It meant lots of airborne time as a passenger but I could not stop looking for the chance to fly in something smaller with me at the controls.

Chapter 10

The Clubs

With a salary to support family and social life sorted out, I set about finding weekend work as a flying instructor at clubs around London. My qualifications made this straightforward and at various times I taught PPL students at Denham, Booker, White Waltham, Enstone, Oxford Kidlington and Blackbushe. At these clubs the aircraft ranged from Cessna 150/152 /172 to Piper Tomahawk, Cherokee, Warrior/Archer, Slingsby Firefly T-67, Zlin and anything else I could get my hands on. They were all designed as much for training as for going places and were quite suitable for both – forgiving, docile, vice-free.

So after RAF flying what was different about flying clubs? There was no one answer. For me the abiding memories are of the sheer variety of students, instructors, and clubhouses. Students were of all ages and motivations. Instructors ranged from novice to highly experienced, either of which could be effective or otherwise according to their understanding of instruction and of people, measured by results and popularity. The clubs are regulated by the CAA with powers increasingly being transferred to EASA as I write in 2019 and before any possible effects of a UK departure from the European Union. The emphasis throughout is safety via airworthiness, pilot licensing and adherence to regulations and procedures to ensure this for all airspace users. That said, I found the ethos of the well-managed clubs to be predominantly a fascination for flying and a burning desire on the part of most members to be good at it for self-satisfaction, achievement, status with friends, to fulfil a dream or to explore the possibility that they, too, could join the professional pilot ranks in the immaculate dark suit, the white shirt, the cap and the silver braid. But who can afford the high cost of flying? Either those with plenty of money or those who make enormous sacrifices to pursue the dream of at least trying to fly a plane. It seemed so macho, so distinctive, so romantic to take to the skies and get away from that mundane job, that desk, that repetitive lifestyle and try true adventure that so many longed to experience. Those are the feelings I sensed in many students I flew with, sometimes seeing apprehension, sometimes pride at a success, sometimes despair at not being able to perform. They were not selected after rigorous testing for aptitude, suitability, determination, leadership or anything else apart from their ability to pay. I particularly admired those who spent hard-earned cash on flying, denying themselves other pursuits because they were fascinated by the freedom, elegance, romance of strapping yourself into a machine and taking to the skies like a bird. They flew when they could afford it with gaps between sorties that could slow progress for lack of continuity but still fulfilled a dream I knew so well. Most of the students I flew with were men but today women have taken up the profession in ever-increasing numbers and can be seen in every role historically reserved for men, from airline captain to front-line fighter pilot to flying instructor.

Some 'students' were flying for the first time in a small aircraft, having been bought a 'trial lesson' by family or friends, often without being asked whether they would like that. They could be excited, apprehensive, curious, intrigued or near terrified, but not wishing to show it and I enjoyed putting them at ease. I had seen many putting on a brave face as they approached a small, single-engine aeroplane for the first time and my instructional experience with RAF *ab initio* trainees then came into play with reassuring briefings and gentle handling. Memories of my own surprisingly gyratory first flight in a Chipmunk had its effects. After following me through on the controls they were encouraged to briefly hold them and fly gentle manoeuvres enabling them to say, truthfully, that they had actually flown the aircraft.

Whilst instructing at Blackbushe Flying Club I was approached one day by the part owner of Rollason Condor D62B, one of a group with shares in the aircraft. Would I care to become the group's flying instructor at an agreed rate? I took a look at this quaint and rare machine and, after a couple of flights to check its handling and listen to the engine, I agreed to give lessons for £5 an hour expenses. I was keen to offset a business career with a sustained weekend flying routine, rather than sporadic club work, in anything that could get me airborne, especially without paying for it.

You may not have heard of a D62B Rollason Condor – nor had I. It is based on the French-designed single-seat Druine Turbulent and was built in Britain by Rollason at Croydon as one of just forty-nine, with thirty-six still flying in 2006. It is a side-by-side trainer with a tail wheel, a fabric-covered wooden structure, and a 100hp Continental engine. Its charm, simplicity and ruggedness, very distinct from the Cessnas, Pipers and other mass market workhorses, made it intriguing to fly. But it was the absolute 'minimum aeroplane'. I did not flirt with the microlights that offer such economic ways of taking to the air, and although I did experience the glider's sensitive, responsive and intimate relationship with the atmosphere we live in, with its moody updrafts and downdrafts, I lacked the skills and patience to coax it into performing and the true glider had no throttle. The Condor's cockpit was cosy, the two seats close together, with very basic instrumentation and control columns that grew out of the floor, not the instrument panel. The fuel state was indicated by a cork float in the fuel tank forward of the cockpit attached to a thin wire rod projecting vertically out of the tank. With full fuel the rod projected several inches out the tank with a 'bobble' on its top to make it more visible and prevent it from disappearing down the hole into the tank as the fuel level dropped. When the bobble ceased to bounce and rested on the tank you were fresh out of fuel. More experienced Condor pilots were remarkably relaxed

The Condor was basic but rugged with a charm of its own. This is the specific aircraft in which I flew over 200 hours training private pilots. (*Courtesy Steve Homewood*)

Instruments were minimal but adequate in a decidedly snug cockpit. (*Courtesy Gary Coleman*)

as the bobble sank lower and wobbled rather than bounced, quite contrary to my RAF training for a healthy reserve to be carried in case the intended destination airfield is unavailable due to thunderstorm, low cloud, fog or other Act of God. But it was a terrific primary trainer with light, sensitive controls, predictable stalling and spinning characteristics and would land gracefully on three points, providing you got the speed and attitude right – a challenge and great learning exercise for beginners. It cruised at around 80 knots, approached at 70 or so, with hedge speed of 55 to 60 knots, so very similar to most light trainers of this vintage. It was great fun if not of jaw-dropping performance.

After instructing for a year or so at Blackbushe the word got around about the hotshot ex-RAF guy instructing on the yellow Condor out of that shabby hangar (shed really) at a remote spot on the field. I was duly approached one day in the café by a tall redheaded young man who said plaintively 'I keep ground looping my plane, can you help?' A ground loop is when the misuse of rudder or brakes when landing a 'tail-dragger', or an unfriendly wind, causes the aircraft to veer away from the chosen direction – down the runway for instance – and rotate horizontally, putting

The simple venturi tube generating suction for the gyroscopic instruments can be seen under the fuselage. You might also just spot the fuel level wire rod protruding from the filler cap on top of the engine cowling.

strain on the undercarriage which could collapse, and more strain on the pilot facing embarrassment from chortling observers who were probably flying simpler aircraft. He owned a Fokker S-11 Instructor built for the Royal Netherlands Air Force around 1947, just a little before the Percival Provost on which I trained. The S-11 was an imposing aircraft, meaning rather big for a primary trainer, with what at first sight was an ungainly fixed undercarriage with legs that bent backwards halfway down as if it were half kneeling, perhaps to act as a shock absorber were it to be landed too firmly. Powered by a 190hp Avco Lycoming engine, it cruised at around 110 knots and was fully aerobatic. With a roomy cockpit and a tall stick rising from a deep floor space, it felt agricultural to fly but, with some heaving, was responsive in all the basic aerobatics. Landing was conventional for a tail-wheel aircraft and, with a few words and demonstrations of keeping straight, the owner overcame his penchant for involuntary 180-degree turns on the runway. In the course of the refresher flying to refine his techniques, we covered forced landings. This was just as well because within six months he had an engine failure after take off at Denham with a successful landing and minimal damage. Then, with small son on board, the propeller came off making another unplanned landing in a field necessary.

The owner of the Fokker S-11 was a keen aviator.

The most notable experience in the aircraft was accepting an invitation to join an S-11 rally at Lelystad in the Netherlands where we flew in a formation of twelve S-11s for a local display. The radio of our particular aircraft was not quite as reliable as the rest which made formation changes interesting, but the whole expedition via Biggin Hill, across the Channel, landing at Oostende then on to Lelystad and the company of a crowd of jolly Dutchmen, many of whom were ex-air force, was intriguing. In the process I became familiar with the challenges of adequately maintaining a privately-owned and -operated vintage aircraft on a tight budget.

I instructed at clubs for twenty years, renewing the IR a few times, after realising that the airlines were not for me, nor was working at the Oxford-based commercial pilot training academy, who did show interest. I retained a flying instructor rating until 2001 which required a flight check and a grilling on procedures, aircraft systems, ATC, meteorology and anything else the examiner thought he could legitimately ask, conducted in a context of instructor/student teaching and briefings. With only irregular weekend flying I used these renewal sessions to update my currency. Conveniently, a CAA-employed flight examiner, whose day job was checking 757 crews for competence as part of their licence requirements, had an interest in light aircraft and was intrigued to fly in the unusual types I elected to take the test in. This varied from Condor to T-67 Firefly, Fokker S-11, and Zlin 242. He grilled me mercilessly on each renewal, which was exactly what I needed to keep up with the latest changes.

It was the unusual aircraft he was photographing more than me as we enjoyed good weather at Lelystad.

Twenty years of working life after leaving the RAF was almost as varied as the twenty years that preceded it. After two years working with RACAL in the modem market I moved to become Operations Manager in a company at the forefront of digital colour-printing technology that included programming newspaper printing presses. From there I worked for International Aeradio (IAL), running a marketing team in the business of airport developments and air traffic control services. IAL was the company set up in 1947 by BEA and BOAC to provide ATC services to ultimately thirty-one airlines worldwide in more than fifty countries, so it had a track record and a long-term heavily discounted air travel concession. This translated into a generous travel budget which I was to take advantage of, travelling across Asia, Indonesia, Australia, New Zealand and the Pacific islands pursuing business opportunities. IAL's owner was British Telecom, now just BT, to which I moved to do the same in telecoms.

I led a Joint Venture project to provide a satellite link connecting Russian internal networks to BT for international access to more countries, which meant many trips to Moscow and St Petersburg, sometimes flying between the two. On one occasion the Moscow-based agent for the company gained access (I never knew how) to a private company aircraft to fly me and a colleague from Moscow to St Petersburg where the satellite earth station was to be located. We were duly driven to an almost deserted airfield on the outskirts of Moscow and dropped off next to an elderly looking Antonov AN28, where two unlikely looking pilots with no English gestured for us to climb aboard and sit in the small and empty passenger cabin. The departure from a busy Moscow control zone was interesting in that we stayed very low for several minutes, presumably on some sort of VFR clearance below the airline traffic, before climbing into the overcast to level above the cloud for the cruise. Never to miss an opportunity for a new experience I unstrapped and approached the flight-deck to indicate I would like to sit in the right-hand seat using one word signals such as 'pilot', pointing to my chest, and 'fly', pointing to the seat which did prompt a reaction. The captain looked intrigued and gestured to his jeans and T-shirt-clad partner acting (perhaps literally) as co-pilot who vacated his seat and courteously assisted me into it. This startled my colleague who, whilst vaguely aware of my military background, did not see me as anything other than a business analyst and contract negotiator and certainly not a pilot to entrust with his life. But the captain, a jolly man with a broad smile that I hoped had not been put there by vodka, immediately handed over control, merely pointing at various instruments for a heading, height or power change. He decided quickly that I knew what I was doing despite my lack of currency and ignorance of the Antonov. Intrigued by now and with further pointing and smiling, he watched as I flew the descent through thick cloud into St Petersburg. It was extraordinary that he found it amusing to continue to let me fly the approach to the field, the ILS runway approach and even the landing with no English spoken, only the pointing and smiling. After taxiing into the parking spot and climbing down the steps, with my BT colleague faintly admiring, if relieved to be on terra firma, the captain, still beaming, indicated his friendship as someone of the piloting fraternity by hugging me and placing his pilot's hat on my head as we posed for photos. My office colleagues back in London thought it was 'a likely story' or in today's jargon 'fake news'.

With a busy and, by now, well-paid job, I did less instructional flying and simply hired aircraft once or twice a month to get myself airborne, fly aerobatics and spinning just as a nostalgic challenge. The Slingsby T-67 was ideal for this. The club based at what bravely calls itself London Oxford Airport operated two of these aircraft, one of which was the much sought after (by me anyway) 200hp version which had been used by the Hong Kong Police. This is a delightful aircraft to fly with superb cockpit visibility, a powerful engine with variable pitch propeller and, of course, a stick. Its light composite construction and powerful engine produced a high power-to-weight ratio ideal for a lively aerobatic performance which is why I hired it.

The commercial pilot training school at Oxford then bought two Zlin 242 aircraft to expose budding airline pilots to spinning and aerobatics; these were for hire to make their operation more economic. After a checkout, in which I found the aircraft to be more than suitable for aerobatics, I transferred from the Slingsby for my monthly fix. I usually flew solo but, after pledging a free flight in a fundraising auction for a choral society, I took the winner, a local lady landowner and farmer, over her farm for a

Having confronted the Soviets during the Cold War it was ironic to fly the Antonov.

The captain (right in picture) promoted me with his cap on landing.

The Zlin 242 was a sturdy aerobatic machine with lively handling and easy to fly. (*Macedonian Air Force via Zlin aviation*)

display of aerobatics which she had no hesitation in requesting, having arranged for an audience of family and friends. Her whoops and squeals were sufficient assurance that she was enjoying the experience as we viewed her house from upside down.

As the millennium came and went, licensing arrangements were changing, as were the medical standards to align with EU rules. I was also changing – in age and in activities – attempting to play golf, choral singing, travel, walking, writing, teaching business English, even DIY beyond changing light bulbs. When my instructor rating expired in 2001 I decided not to renew it. By now I was operating on a limited flying licence that still allowed me to fly aerobatics occasionally. The Zlin was no longer available and, since income was tailing off and retirement approaching, I became only an occasional flyer, always for the handling, the aerobatics, the spinning, sometimes in a CAP-10, sometimes in the T-67.

Chapter 11

So What? A Conclusion

My story is a snapshot of flying at a point in history when pilots were kept rather busy handling the aircraft and working out how to do the job it was designed for. Much of what they did has been taken over by computers and that might suggest that something has been lost. I do not believe it has, and what we see in professional flying are changes in the methods and activities of the pilot, but not in the way he or she responds to being airborne in the same atmosphere with the same challenges and enjoyment. In general aviation, too, there is just as much fun and satisfaction as there ever was with some new flourishes.

I have focused on flying experiences using a biographical chronology only as a convenient framework because it is the enormous fun and stimulation of being airborne that I wanted to share more than anything else. Those with a sense of history will appreciate the value of recording one particular phase of military flying, recognising the risks and adventures of earlier manned flight and the impressive advances that came after. Drones, pilotless airliners, driverless cars, computer-controlled spacecraft, surgery with no surgeon may all come about. But the adaptability, imagination and resourcefulness of the human will find new ways to provide the stimulation we need, taking full advantage of artificial intelligence. For the aspiring pilot there will be much to do and much to enjoy for many years to come.

My last flight as I write was in June 2014 enjoying, as ever, aerobatics, proving that I could do all the other stuff including a landing.

After aerobatics in the T-67 out of Staverton closely watched by Tizzy, Tiger Airways instructor.

XH 903 in the log book. I flew it a number of times.

Reunited with Javelin FAW Mk9 XH 903 at Staverton which I flew with 33 Sqn in 1961.

MAY	31	JAVELIN 9	XH907	SELF		SOLO		FORMATION
MAY	31	JAVELIN 9	XH756	SELF		SOLO		FORMATION
								JAVELIN T MK3
								JAVELIN F.A.W. MK 9
JUNE	2	JAVELIN 9	XH903	SELF		F/O McCRACKEN		P/'s CINE
JUNE	2	JAVELIN 9	XH903	SELF		F/L BRUNSKILL		CLOSE FORMATION
JUNE	5	JAVELIN 9	XH903	SELF		F/O McCRACKEN		P/'s
JUNE	5	JAVELIN T3	XH437	SELF		CPT BAILEY		NIGHT CHECK
JUNE	5	JAVELIN 9	XH758	SELF		F/O McCRACKEN		P/'s
JUNE	6	JAVELIN 9	XH905	SELF		F/O McCRACKEN		P/'s
JUNE	6	JAVELIN 9	XH756	SELF		F/O McCRACKEN		P/'s

GRAND TOTAL [Cols. (1) to (10)]   Totals Carried Forward
40f   Hrs.   20   Mins.
421   40

XH 903 in the log-book. I flew it a number of times.

Many ex-military people, regiments, ships' companies and squadrons have reunions, associations, preservation societies and that is a fine thing. I have not felt inclined to be pro-active here but have enjoyed gatherings of 77 Entry from RAF Cranwell days and one YUAS Dinner by invitation. I do succumb occasionally to nostalgia and it was for this reason that I linked up recently with RAF Coningsby for photos with the Mk 2 Spitfire, now known as P7, that I flew with its original registration G-AWIJ in 1968 during the filming of *The Battle of Britain*. No. 29 Squadron, with whom I flew the Javelin in the 1960s, is also based at Coningsby and more opportunistic nostalgia took the form of another photo with their current equipment, the Typhoon fighter.

Reunited with the Mk 2 Spitfire I flew in the film as it is prepared for flight in the hangar at RAF Coningsby where the BBMF is based.

The presentation of the aircraft by the BBMF is immaculate, compared with its well–worn look in 1968.

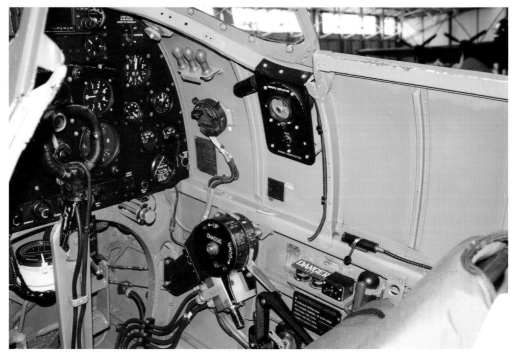

Cockpit of the Spitfire Mk 2, now known as 'P7', in immaculate condition.

No. 29 Squadron, now equipped with Typhoons, is based at RAF Coningsby.

The Typhoon presents a purposeful profile.

A very different cockpit from the Javelin with computers to do most things and expensive technology. The Head-up Display (HUD) is protected by its red cover.

Despite budget restraints the Royal Air Force continues to flourish with some superb equipment and a new generation of committed air and ground crews to operate it.

For some years I have taught children in my daughter's primary school classes about science in general and flying in particular. Their curiosity and attraction to adventurous pursuits is always good to see and I enjoy the whole day, using slides, videos and models they can build and fly. The next day they have a lesson on writing 'thank you' letters, thirty of which arrive by post in a large envelope a few days later. One letter from a charming, innocent, 7-year-old boy sticks in my memory. He wrote:

'Dear Ron, thank you for telling us about planes. I now know enough about planes to last me the rest of my life … .'

Glossary

AAIB   Air Accident Investigation Board

ACR-7   Airfield Control Radar, an equipment supplied to the RAF in the 1950s as a runway approach aid to assist pilots to land in bad weather.

ADF   Automatic Direction Finder, an aid to air navigation comprising an airborne receiver of signals from an omni-directional radio beacon, such as an NDB or radio station, that provides bearing to the transmitter with a cockpit display showing relative bearing on a fixed compass card aligned with the nose of the aircraft. Much less used today, it has proved a valuable aid for en route navigation and approaches to land at airports for many years. Its development originated from radio direction- finding experiments dating back to the nineteenth century, including work by Heinrich Hertz.

AEF   Air Experience Flight, an RAF training unit whose main purpose is to provide flying experience to cadets from the Air Training Corps and the Combined Cadet Force.

AFCS   Automatic Flight Control System. Flying controls are moved according to settings input by the pilot without him or her physically moving them with a control column. In various designs autopilot signals which operate the controls are integrated with inputs from other avionics equipment such as a Flight Director that calculates and displays to the pilot the attitudes required to achieve a specified trajectory, pattern or task.

AH   Artificial Horizon. This instrument displays the attitude of an aircraft with respect to the horizon in pitching and rolling planes.

AI   Attitude indicator. This instrument is a development of the Artificial Horizon, providing the same basic information on pitch and roll attitude with respect to the horizon but can use data not only from mechanisms within the instrument (as does the AH) but from external sources. The earlier AH gyro could topple during extreme attitudes – perhaps in aerobatics – as its gimbals came up against mechanical stops and erratic attitude information had to be ignored by the pilot. It routinely had to be 'caged' or held rigid during vigorous manoeuvres then erected manually for subsequent use. The AI avoided this problem with an automatic self-righting mechanism.

Aileron   The control surface on each wing that operates in response to the pilot moving the stick left or right to produce roll. To roll left the right aileron moves down, producing more lift from that wing while the left aileron moves up, producing less, hence the roll that results.

Airbrake   RAF term for what is now generally called 'speedbrake' derived from USAF usage. It is a device or surface that extends into the airflow in flight, when selected by pilot, to create extra drag that reduces aircraft speed.

Angle of Attack   The angle between the oncoming airflow and the wing chord line, generally designated as the line from wing leading edge to trailing edge. High angles of attack develop more lift and more drag.

ASI   Air Speed Indicator. This instrument displays indicated airspeed which is measured using ambient static and dynamic atmospheric pressures so that with increasing height, actual speed through the air (TAS), and relative to the ground were there to be no winds blowing, is increasingly higher than that indicated on the ASI. But it is Indicated airspeed that determines the way the aircraft handles and performs, including the speed at which a stall will occur. Dynamic or ram air pressure is what comes into the front of a pitot tube exposed to the free airstream. Static pressure is detected by static ports either on the pitot tube or elsewhere. The difference, measured by a mechanism within the instrument, is the resultant dynamic pressure due to speed through the air and indicated on the ASI dial. In modern fighters an angle of attack indicator is used in conjunction with airspeed to achieve optimum performance in particular flight manoeuvres including approach to land.

Asymmetric   Flying the aircraft with one or more engines having failed or throttled back to simulate failure.

ATC   Air Traffic Control.

ATP   Air Transport Pilot, the American term on a certificate issued by the FAA authorising a pilot to fly as captain in civil aircraft carrying passengers for hire or reward, most commonly for an airline. It is equivalent in its privileges to the British CAA ATPL (Airline Transport Pilot Licence).

Attitude   The orientation of an aircraft with respect to the horizon.

Base leg   The leg of an aircraft's visual landing pattern, or circuit, flown about 90 degrees to the direction of landing, usually in a descent, prior to turning onto final approach to land.

Boundary Layer   A thin layer of air that flows close to the wing surface in flight such that where the layer is in contact with the wing it is almost brought to a stop due to friction, but at points further from the wing surface accelerates rapidly to match the local speed of the airflow. The aerodynamics of the wing, including boundary layer characteristics, is a fundamental of aircraft behaviour and performance. A turbulent boundary sticks to the wing longer than laminar, delaying airflow breakaway with the accompanying stall and in some designs sustaining flow over the ailerons. Vortex generators can induce boundary layer turbulence but add to overall drag.

Break   Entering the landing pattern or circuit by flying at high speed over the landing point (or just to the side opposite to the active circuit direction for safety) then making a hard turn to reduce speed to below limits for lowering undercarriage and flap as the turn continues onto a final approach to land. Speed will be reduced faster by approaching the airfield below normal circuit height and climbing in the break. It originated from the need to reduce vulnerability to attacks by hostile aircraft when at low speeds preparing to land.

CAA   Civil Aviation Authority, the UK's independent aviation regulator.

CDI	Course Deviation Indicator, which shows an aircraft's lateral position in relation to a specific course (bearing) to or from a radio navigation beacon, typically a VOR. A position left of the course will show as a needle indicating that course to the right for the pilot to follow as required.
CFS	Central Flying School, the unit of the RAF that trains Qualified Flying Instructors (QFIs).
Chopped	Failing the course (*slang*).
Closing Angle Technique	Calculating a heading correction, after drifting off an intended track, to reach the destination directly on a new heading rather than returning to planned track.
Cocked Hat	The shape described on a map when three bearings from known points or beacons are plotted, not normally accurate enough to be coincident and forming a 'cocked hat'. The smaller the hat the more accurately the centre of the hat will indicate actual position.
Controlled Airspace	Airspace where air traffic control needs to have positive control over aircraft flying in that airspace to maintain safe separation between them.
CPL	Commercial Pilot Licence.
Crosswind	That component of the surface wind acting at right angles to the direction of landing.
DME	Distance Measuring Equipment, a radio navigation aid that measures slant range from a ground beacon and displays this to the pilot.
Double Track Error	A pilot navigation technique that, having discovered the aircraft is off track from a known point, perhaps by identifying a ground feature, calculates the angle between intended and actual track which is termed track error. A heading correction to the value of track error would parallel planned track, but the correction is doubled to take the aircraft back to planned track flying for the same time that has elapsed since leaving the known point. Heading is then changed by single track error value to maintain planned track. It works when less than half the leg to the next turning point has been flown.

Downwind   A position in the pattern/circuit to land, flying parallel and opposite to the landing direction prior to turning onto base leg. A radio call 'Downwind' is made at the beginning of the downwind leg after turning from the crosswind leg of a standard circuit.

Drift   The difference between aircraft heading and track across the ground due to the effect of wind.

EASA   European Union Aviation Safety Agency

ECM   Electronic countermeasures – such as jamming - designed to deceive the enemy by blocking, distorting or disrupting their electronic or electrical means of attack or defence.

Elevator   The flight control surface attached to and hinging at the tailplane (also called horizontal stabilizer) to produce pitch attitude changes by varying the downward force applied by the tailplane. Elevator up, pulling back on the control column, increases the force so the tail goes down and the nose goes up.

Finals   Last leg of the landing circuit/pattern when established on a descending approach to the active runway now straight ahead.

Flap   A device attached normally to the trailing edge of the wing to increase lift by changing its aerodynamic profile, bringing extra drag that helps slow the aircraft prior to landing. It creates the need for more engine power which, in jet aircraft, provides more precise control of speed. Similar high lift devices are also seen on the leading edges of the wings of some aircraft to modify the aerofoil shape of the wing and enhance lift during take-off and on approach to land. These are commonly called slats on modern airliners.

Flare   A reduction in rate of descent just before touchdown to achieve a soft landing. This can be more comfortable for passengers, can save wear on light aircraft undercarriage structures (fixed or retractable) and, if the speed is right, can reduce the chance of a bounce, with attendant risks in a crosswind. In heavier aircraft it can be better technique to land firmly, on speed, with less flare to ensure good contact with the runway and better steering and braking control in adverse conditions of wind, turbulence and rain that pools on the runway. For Naval carrier landings there is no flare.

Flick   A departure from stable flight by pulling the stick back suddenly and applying a large amount of rudder which creates rapid autorotation in a horizontal plane usually in an aerobatic display. It can be induced in any attitude and can occur unexpectedly during aerobatics. The entry to an intentional spin produces this characteristic, and is described as the incipient stage.

Flight Level   The designation of levels to be used by aircraft flying at high altitude to achieve height separation, agreed by national and international aviation authorities. Aircraft climb to a level determined locally, according to terrain, at which a standard pressure of 1013 millibars is set on the altimeter sub-scale by all aircraft for the subsequent cruise.

'g'   A term used in aviation to describe the force on aircrew due to manoeuvre. It is expressed as a multiple of the force of gravity or 'g', where 2 'g' means the body feels twice as heavy. Blood pools where the 'g' force drives it so for positive 'g', when pulling the control column back, it drains from the head, brain, eyes and upper body inducing 'blackout'. When pushing the control column forward (usually upside down) in opposition to gravity, it pools in the head and blood vessels in the eyes to cause 'red-out'. When flying straight and level, the 'g' force on the pilot's body is one which we refer to as his weight. In fighters a g-suit is worn to counteract these effects, automatically exerting pressure on the pilot's body as 'g' increases.

Gear   see undercarriage.

**General
Aviation**   Aviation operations which are not airline flying or aerial work. So it does not involve carrying passengers or freight for hire or reward, rather it is flying for business or leisure pursuits. It therefore covers a wide range from professional business travel to club PPL training and private flying.

GPS   Global Positioning System, set up by the United States as a satellite navigation aid.

Groundspeed   Speed across the ground resulting from the True Air Speed of an aircraft in flight, adjusted for local wind speed and direction.

Heading   The compass direction in which the aircraft is pointing. Magnetic heading is in relation to magnetic north, while true heading relates to true north. The difference being 'variation', which differs according to location on the earth's surface and changes over time.

Heading Indicator   The flight instrument that indicates heading to the pilot. The instrument has evolved from a simple magnetic compass to a DI (gyro stabilised direction indicator). In modern aircraft it is an electronic presentation on digitally generated displays integrated with other flight data.

High Key   Reference point designated by position and height in a pre-planned pattern for landing without engine power. For example, flying a Gnat or Hunter, High Key might be 5,000 feet above the ground over touchdown point and Low Key around 3,000 feet before turning onto a base leg – all depending on conditions at the time, notably the wind.

HSI   Horizontal Situation Indicator, replacing the conventional heading indicator, to present heading, VOR and ILS information in one display. A CDI and heading bug on the instrument can provide data to autopilot or flight director systems to fly a selected course or to couple to the ILS.

ICAO   International Civil Aviation Organisation (ICAO), an agency of the United Nations based in Montreal.

ICBM   Intercontinental Ballistic Missile.

IFF   Identification Friend of Foe. IFF is a radar based system essential in military operations to avoid attacking or being attacked by friendly forces. A transponder picks up interrogation signals and responds with identity and position information. The technique is used in military and civil operations for both safety and security.

IFR   Instrument Flight Rules that govern flight in controlled airspace and in specified weather conditions. To fly in controlled airspace, pilots must have an Instrument Rating and the aircraft they are flying must have specified navigation equipment that is working. The aim is to keep airline passengers and aircrews safe by requiring pilots to adhere to a comprehensive system of operational rules, to regularly demonstrate their competence to fly to prescribed standards and to have the requisite knowledge to do so as set out in national and international airspace management regulations and procedures. There are exceptions made in some UK types of airspace (for example around designated airports) where pilots without an instrument rating can transit under an IFR clearance where the weather allows the pilot to fly visually, under the direction of ATC and with specified weather minima determined locally.

Pilots with an intermediate (UK only) IMC rating, allowing them to fly in IMC, can transit VFR with lower visibility minima.

ILS Instrument Landing System, a radio based system where an instrument in the cockpit presents to the pilot the aircraft's position relative to a prescribed approach path to land. One needle shows deviation in azimuth responding to a Localiser signal transmitted in a horizontal pattern from equipment close to the runway. A second needle shows deviation from an ideal glide path responding to another transmitter located near the active runway, with signals orientated in a vertical pattern.

IMC Instrument Meteorological Conditions, weather conditions that require pilots to fly primarily by reference to instruments, and therefore under instrument flight rules (IFR), rather than by outside visual references under Visual Flight Rules (VFR).

IMC Rating A UK rating that allows pilots to fly in IMC with specified weather minima and after completing a specified training course. It requires less experience and skill to pass the rating test than the Instrument Rating and excludes flight in the airspace close to airports without a Special VFR clearance to do so in good weather under strict ATC supervision.

Incidence The angle between the chord line joining leading edge to trailing edge of the wing and the fuselage longitudinal axis, a line running from nose to tail.

Incipient spin The behaviour of an aircraft in response to pro-spin controls just after the stall and before entering the fully developed spin. The aircraft pitches and rolls suddenly before entering autorotation. This will typically be when demonstrating a spin, or as an introduction to spinning. If recognised, neutralising flight controls will often prevent full development.

Indicated Airspeed *see* ASI.

Instrument Rating The rating a pilot must have to fly legally under IFR.

IP	Instructor Pilot in the USAF. It equates to Qualified Flying Instructor (QFI) in the RAF.
IR	Instrument Rating. See *Instrument Rating* above.
Kts	Abbreviation for knots.
Leans	A contradiction between the attitude shown on the flight instruments and the messages conveyed to the brain by the vestibular system which can induce a pilot to attempt to compensate by leaning in the direction he feels will regain wings level, when the instruments show he is already wings level. It is more generally a reference to any form of conflict between instrument indications and what the pilot feels, requiring awareness, training and currency to deal with it by ignoring feelings and believing the instruments. Today while an experience of the leans is possible, the problem is of less concern in sophisticated aircraft that have better flight instruments, autopilots linked to flight directors and with more than one pilot. In military aircraft the leans can still be experienced by a pilot flying solo but AFCS can alleviate the problem if it occurs. Professional pilots may rarely, if ever, experience the leans in today's aircraft but awareness of the phenomenon remains important.
Low Key	Second reference point designated by position and height in a pre-planned pattern for landing without engine power. For the early jets this was typically a point in the descending spiral which would equate to a close-in base leg turn with height and speed targets known to provide margins for a safe landing, depending on wind direction and strength.
Mach	Mach is derived from Mach number, which is the ratio of velocity through the air (TAS) to the speed of sound in local atmospheric conditions, notably the ambient temperature. A ratio of one is widely known as the speed of sound. Transition through this speed creates significant changes to airflows over aircraft wings and fuselage with shock waves forming to create the 'sonic bang'.
MADDLS	Mirror Assisted Dummy Deck Landing, a naval pilot training technique that used deck markings painted on a land-based runway. It involved landing on speed with no flare to ensure firm and permanent contact with the deck, maximising the chances of engaging the arrestor wire.

Magnetic Heading   Direction that the aircraft is pointing in relation to Magnetic North. Changes in the position of the North Magnetic Pole relative to the Geographic North Pole are applied as a *variation* correction to true heading. Compass *deviation*, a range of very small errors arising due to the way the compass system is installed in the aircraft, is also corrected to arrive at the reading on the compass which the pilot steers.

MoD   Ministry of Defence.

Nacelle   A housing on an aircraft which can contain engines, fuel or equipment. It can be integral to the structure or mounted external to the fuselage. Engines mounted under the wings of modern airliners are contained in nacelles. This provides a measure of safety in the event of engine damage when any debris is contained within the nacelle.

NATO   North Atlantic Treaty Organisation.

NDB   Non-Directional Beacon, a ground-based, low frequency radio transmitter used for air navigation and as an instrument approach aid at airports. The NDB transmits an omni-directional signal that is received by the ADF (Automatic Direction Finder) in the cockpit. The NDB/ADF system of air navigation still exists but is being superseded by new technologies such as GPS.

OCU   Operational Conversion Unit, where pilots/crews convert to a new aircraft type and develop the skills for a specific role.

Officer Qualities   These are the characteristics thought to qualify a person to be a military officer and, in the case of aircrew, to have the ability, capacity, intellect and academic qualifications to operate military aircraft to their maximum effectiveness. Leadership, integrity, mental agility and self-confidence would be generic characteristics seen more widely to characterise a military officer.

PAI   Pilot Armament Instructor. These instructors developed the skills of pilots in gunnery and weapons delivery. They are more commonly called Weapons Instructors today since some fighter/bomber aircraft crew are not pilots but weapons system and avionics specialists.

PAR Precision Approach Radar is a radar guidance system providing lateral and vertical guidance to assist pilots to land in adverse weather conditions. It is controlled from the ground by air traffic controllers who transmit to the pilot deviations and corrections to regain or maintain a prescribed approach path for a safe landing.

Patter The language used by flying instructors to commentate on handling techniques as they demonstrate some aspect of aircraft control. It needs to be accurately co-ordinated with control movements, clear, concise and understandable to the student.

Pilot's notes The earlier title of the more modern Aircraft Flight Manual designed to provide guidance to crews on flying a specific aircraft type safely and effectively.

Pitch Aircraft rotation around the horizontal axis running wing tip to wing tip through the centre of gravity.

PPL Private Pilot Licence.

Precession A physical property of flight instrument gyros whereby the axis of rotation, which tends to retain its position in space, moves in response to forces applied to the spinning gyro. In the air these will be both friction in the gyro's gimbals and forces from manoeuvring, both corrected within the instrument. The property is exhibited by any spinning body, including an aircraft propeller. If high power is used for take-off in a tail-wheel aircraft, raising the tail quickly will exert a rotational couple on the spinning propeller disc which, due to precession, is applied 90 degrees in the direction of rotation to produce yaw. Calculations in precession use vectors whose size and direction represent the speed of rotation and orientation of the axis of spin. The topic for further research is Rigid Body Mechanics.

Q-code The Q-code is a standardized collection of three-letter codes all of which start with the letter "Q". It is an operating signal initially developed for commercial radiotelegraph communication and later adopted by other radio services. It is still in use.

QDM Q-code for Magnetic bearing *to* a station.

QFE	Q-code for atmospheric pressure at a specified datum such as airfield. When set the altimeter reads the height above this datum, usually calculated at the centre of the airfield which will be close to the height of all runway thresholds.
QFI	Qualified Flying Instructor in RAF terminology.
QGH	Q-code for Controlled Descent through Cloud in RAF terminology.
QNH	Q-code for atmospheric pressure at mean sea level (may be either a locally measured pressure or a regional forecast pressure (RPS)). When set on the altimeter subscale the instrument reads height above that datum, referred to as altitude and is the setting used for flying near the ground to ensure height clearance above high points. The pressure at sea level will vary with the passage of weather systems. Global extremes of around 925 and 1025 millibars have been recorded but the standard atmospheric pressure at sea level for the purposes of aviation is 1013.2 millibars and used to designate flight levels for aircraft flying at cruising height.. The hectopascal (hPa), inches of mercury inHG) and millimetres of mercury (mmHg) are also used as units of measurement for atmospheric pressure.
QTE	Q-code for true bearing/track *from* a station.
Quick Reaction Alert	A state of ground-based readiness in air defence operations ensuring the ability to take off rapidly and engage with hostile or potentially hostile aircraft to neutralise the threat.
Roll	Rotation about the horizontal axis running from nose to tail.
Rudder	Flight control surface hinging on the vertical stabiliser or tail fin mounted at the rear of the fuselage. It provides balance for aerodynamic efficiency and manoeuvring capability in the yawing plane.
Schoolies	Informal language (or *slang*) for trainee schoolteachers.
SERA	Standardised European Rules of the Air. These are the rules of the European Union Aviation Safety Agency which have superseded or modified national rules set out by agencies such as the CAA.

They broadly align with ICAO rules applied world-wide. The impact on UK aviation of leaving the EU has not yet been made clear but since the UK has taken a leading role in formulating the international approach to air safety future changes might be expected to align with ICAO's strategic thrust.

Slats

Part of the wing leading edge structure on some aircraft that moves away from the wing on extension struts or rollers to form a separate aerofoil - shaped panel extending over part of the wing leading edge to modify the wing profile. It also forms a gap or slot between the panel and the wing to accelerate airflow over the wing and modify pressure patterns. The combined effects, generally, are to increase lift, delay the stall and enhance handling characteristics during landing and manoeuvring.

Speedbrake

see Airbrake.

Spin

A stalled condition resulting in autorotation about a vertical axis. It can be entered intentionally or unintentionally when inputs of rudder are excessive for the aircraft type at or near the stall of a wing.

Stall

The point at which airflow over the wing breaks down with a sudden loss of lift due to angles of attack higher than those at which the particular wing can sustain normal airflow. It can occur at any airspeed but the highest risks for inexperienced pilots occur at low speeds close to those used on approach to land or just after take-off. Certain types of ice can accumulate over the wing to add weight and induce an earlier stall.

Swing

Involuntary, unintended yaw during take-off or landing.

TACAN

Tactical Air Navigation System, providing range and bearing to a ground station displayed graphically to the pilot. Operating in the frequency range 960 to 1215 MHz it equates to a more accurate version of the VOR/DME system that has been widely used in civil flying. In some aircraft an offset facility is provided to home to a point designated by the pilots, not dissimilar in concept to waypoints in modern Satnav equipment.

TAS   True Airspeed. This is the speed at which an aircraft is travelling relative to the mass of air through which it is flying. Measurement of TAS has evolved from early analogue devices incorporating density, temperature and compressibility corrections to indicated airspeed (IAS). Whereas IAS is close to TAS at sea level, as the aircraft climbs falling air density and temperature means that for a given IAS the actual speed through less dense air is greater. Increases in speed and altitude introduce the effects of compressibility such that speed is then measured as Mach Number.

Torque   Force that causes something to twist or rotate around an axis. The effect of torque is described as twisting moment.

Track   In aviation track is the path an aircraft describes over the ground. Its measurement is in degrees with respect to either magnetic or true north.

True track   Track using true north as the reference. Maps and charts are orientated to true north.

Turn and   Flight instrument with a needle or aircraft symbol to indicate rate
slip indicator of turn and a ball to show yaw. It shows a zero rate of turn when the aircraft is flying wings level, in balance, with no yaw; and with rate one to indicate turning at three degrees per second. This is a standard rate for instrument procedures, notably holding patterns, when awaiting clearance to commence an approach procedure. It is now used mostly as a back up to more sophisticated flight instrument and avionic systems. A black ball in a tube of fluid is sensitive to yaw with the ball centralised when in balance (no yaw) and displaced according to the rate of yaw. Neither this instrument nor a modified design, combining turn rate and yaw in a Turn Co-ordinator, provides pitch information.

UKADGE   United Kingdom Air Defence Ground Environment. This was the generic term for a system of radars, computers, control centres and their operators to counter the Soviet threat of the 1960s and 1970s. It was modernised during the 1980s under the label 'IMPROVED' UKADGE or IUKADGE. Its modern equivalent is known as The United Kingdom Air Surveillance and Control System (ASACS).

Undercarriage The retractable wheels used for landing and taxiing. In many light aircraft the wheels stay fixed down and do not retract.

UP Unusual Position, a manoeuvre, or sequence of manoeuvres, carried out by a flying instructor or examiner to simulate losing track of the aircraft's flight attitude or flight condition and, on handing over control, prompt a pilot to execute a drill to regain controlled flight. Losing track of flight attitude can lead to complete disorientation and loss of control when the horizon is not visible to the pilot.

USAF United States Air Force

Variation The difference between true north and magnetic north at a particular location on the earth's surface which varies (slowly) with time as the Earth's magnetic field shifts. It is applied as a correction to calculations of true track to determine a heading to steer on a magnetic compass

V-bomber The collective name for the Vickers Valiant, Avro Vulcan and Handley Page Victor bombers. Three distinct designs carried extra cost but provided flexibility the RAF needed in the 1950s.

VFR A set of rules established by aviation authorities on flying when in Visual Meteorological Conditions which means, in simple terms, when the pilot can see where he/she is going. They prescribe minima of in-flight visibility, clearance distance from cloud, and the height and amounts of cloud above the ground (known variously as cloud base or ceiling) for take-off and landing. In addition, whatever the weather conditions, types of airspace specifying IFR (Instrument Flight Rules) will not be accessible to pilots without the requisite qualifications specified by those rules. The aim here is to ensure separation between flights and safe operation at all times in airspace around airports where passenger-carrying aircraft take off and land.

VHF Very High Frequency.

VOR Very High-Frequency (VHF) is an Omni-directional Range system used for air navigation. The system comprises a network of fixed, short range, ground-based beacons providing range and bearing to and from the beacon, which is displayed in the cockpit. Often combined with a co-located DME, it can provide position.

Alternatively, two bearings from different VOR beacons will also give position information. VOR/TACs have been used extensively for en route navigation.

VSI   Vertical Speed Indicator, sometimes known as an RCDI (Rate of Climb and Descent Indicator). It shows zero when level, and is graduated in thousands of feet per minute up or down. It operates by measuring local static air pressure as height changes and feeding that into a chamber on one side of a diaphragm then, via a controlled leak, bringing the pressure in a second chamber on the other side to the same value. Different rates of atmospheric pressure change cause the leakage air to flow faster or slower in response and the rate of diaphragm displacement is measured and fed to the flight instrument. Once the aircraft levels, the two chambers have equal pressure and the instrument shows zero again.

Wheels   Jargon for undercarriage.

Yaw   Rotation about a vertical axis through the centre of gravity which is perpendicular to both wings and fuselage.

Index